The Family Detective

The Family Detective

DISCOVER YOUR FAMILY HISTORY

AND BRING YOUR PAST TO LIFE

NICK BARRATT

IN ASSOCIATION WITH
The Daily Telegraph

EBURY
PRESS

1 3 5 7 9 10 8 6 4 2

Published in 2006 by Ebury Press, an imprint of Ebury Publishing

Ebury Publishing is a division of the Random House Group

The Random House Group Limited Reg. No. 954009

Addresses for companies within the Random House Group can be found at www.randomhouse.co.uk

A CIP catalogue record for this book is available from the British Library

The Random House Group Limited makes every effort to ensure that the papers used in our books are made from trees that have been legally sourced from well-managed and credibly certified forests. Our paper procurement policy can be found on www.randomhouse.co.uk

Printed and bound by Scotprint Ltd

ISBN 0091912202
ISBN (from Jan 2007) 9780091912208

Contents

Introduction

Whenever I start writing about family history, I can't help feeling a little bit of a fraud. My background and historical period was, and still is, medieval England - specifically medieval English state finance and fiscal history - and it was in this field that I obtained my PhD from King's College, London, in 1996. It was only upon entering the employ of the Public Record Office, now The National Archives, that I encountered family history for the first time in my role as reader advisor, helping researchers to navigate their way round the 9.5 million catalogued documents housed there. Up to that point, I had always been led to believe that family history was little more than a hobby, and wasn't 'real history'. Yet several things quickly became apparent - first, the amount of time that was required to trace a family tree properly. In the days before the Internet revolutionised access to name-based records, all searches were conducted by hand and would take weeks to hunt down that elusive ancestor on a census record. It could take years to carry out searches that today might only take hours. Second, the sophistication of some of the researchers often put seasoned academics to shame in terms of the scale and scope of material viewed. Because family history research often spans several centuries, by definition you encounter different periods of social history, which means a wide variety of sources are required to fully paint a picture of ancestral life. I've encountered self-taught family historians who have mastered medieval Latin shorthand so that they can interpret manorial court rolls in the sixteenth century, whilst training themselves to understand how various records inter-linked, so that they could pursue their research to even deeper levels. Finally, it was obvious that the researchers were thoroughly enjoying themselves, particularly when making a great discovery and often because of, rather than in spite of, the complexity of the archive in which they were working. There was a real sense that they considered themselves to be detectives, rather than historians, and the enthusiasm they brought to the subject was refreshing.

My own interest in family history started from a professional perspective, when I was asked to act as the genealogical research consultant for the first series of *Who Do You Think You Are?* Previously, I had undertaken research for the media across a wide range of programmes, from houses to ship wrecks via industrial heritage, and my specialist skills were more concerned with the ability to find things in archives, rather than an in-depth knowledge of genealogy. Yet even though I was not researching my own family history, there was still intense satisfaction to be gleaned from making key discoveries, working on the individual story lines and showcasing important aspects of British social history from the perspective of the people who lived through momentous historical events. Two further series down the line, and the programme is just as exciting to work on as it was in the beginning - though genealogy itself has changed beyond all recognition in the intervening period. The Internet has brought record series into our homes, and family history is probably the third most popular use of cyberspace.

However, working on other people's family trees is a full-time job and consequently I find little time to look into my own past; a typical phenomenon, I guess, in most industries. Yet what I do know about my family suggests that there are plenty of mysteries still to be uncovered; it only recently came to light that a paternal great-uncle was a spy for the Soviets in the 1920s and 1930s, who had been stealing cyphers from the Foreign Office, whilst my maternal grandmother has photographs of her as a little girl with 'Uncle Arthur', who is none other than Arthur Chase of the Chase Manhattan Bank, new York - quite what the connection is, we have yet to discover, though she refuses to talk about it. Perhaps one day I'll try to look into it, possibly when funds are tight…

I hope you enjoy reading this book, and find the advice practical as well as interesting. The case studies are drawn from my column in the Weekend section of the *Daily Telegraph*, and serve to illustrate that there is far more to family history that simply building a family tree. The whole point of the exercise is to discover not just who our ancestors were, but what sort of people they were and how they lived their lives. With the development of online collections, the tree-building becomes also a preliminary stage to the real business of research in archives, libraries and museums across the country and indeed worldwide. With this in mind, it is perhaps more useful to think of your research as personal heritage rather than family history, because this includes associated topics such as house history, local history, social history, community history and so on. That is one of the joys of the subject - there's always something else to find out, and your ancestors will soon become your tour guide on a fascinating journey into Britain's history.

NICK BARRATT

Right: Family portraits are likely to survive for happy occasions such as weddings. Ask older relatives to name as many people as possible.

1

Getting Started

Opposite: Scrap books and albums often contain snippets of information about your family.

So you've decided to look into your family history. The biggest question now is, 'What happens next?' No matter how experienced a researcher you might be, the hardest part of any new project is to work out exactly how and where to get started. The first section of this book will provide you with some realistic advice on approaching and structuring your initial research, so I shall be covering your very first steps, suggesting ways to:

- set realistic research goals
- track down sources
- search effectively on- and offline
- organise your data efficiently
- shape a research plan, based on the information gathered
- contact helpful resources, when you eventually come unstuck – and don't worry; everyone does at some point, often sooner rather than later.

Above: You may recognise objects in family photos as treasured heirlooms, like a particular item of clothing passed down from generation to generation.

But, perhaps most importantly of all, I shall also introduce you to the main sources of information that will enable you to start constructing and expanding your family tree. And then, to show you how the basic research unfolds in practice, we'll go behind the scenes of one of my *Telegraph* columns.

Chapter I

First Steps

As you have probably gathered by now, researching family history is a detective process and, as the chief investigator, you need to begin by working out exactly what you want to research. Therefore, your very first step is to ask yourself some important questions. And although the answers might not seem obvious initially, they will become more so as we progress.

❧ Setting your goals

Let us start with the first couple of questions, as setting your research goals and parameters will allow you to map out the initial stages of your work and so enable you to sketch a research plan, which in turn will help you assess what skills, kit and equipment you'll need. It is probably best to write down why you have decided to start investigating your past – call it your mission statement, if you like. Everyone will have a different reason. For example, some people aim to work backwards in a linear direction as far as they can, finding as many new family members as possible; others prefer to tackle one generation at a time, establishing where their ancestors lived, what lines of work they pursued, how many brothers and sisters they had – essentially trying to find as much information about each person as possible. Indeed, you might have a very specific story you want to get to the bottom of, a family myth that has never been challenged concerning just one ancestor; or perhaps you hope to find new

Above: Even if you don't know who is in the photo, the company name can be researched and can lead you to where your family were living.

FIRST QUESTIONS FIRST

- Why are you embarking on this project?
- What do you hope to achieve?
- How much time can you devote to the work?
- What costs are involved?

- Do you have the necessary skills and equipment to make the use of your time effective, and the whole process productive?

members of your family from branches of the family tree that have been long neglected.

The reason it is vital at the outset to establish your research goals, and where possible to stick to them, is because it is easy to lose track of which branch of the family you are investigating once you get started. Similarly, the question of why you are researching your ancestors needs answering at the outset as, if all goes well, you will be generating hundreds of ancestral names. Unless you keep a clear track of how they all fit into your plan, you will be in danger of becoming swamped with data; and information overload can be frustrating. For example, when starting out many people decide to restrict their searches to the male side of the family, as (in general) surnames remained unchanged when passed from father to son, generation after generation.

Therefore it is much easier to stay focused when you work backwards. In contrast, when researching the female line, new surnames constantly appear through marriage, and before too long you will have a large number of names that are initially unfamiliar. This is not to say that it is easier to research the male line than the female – the same techniques will apply – only that it is sometimes easier to focus on your family surname first. However, there are circumstances where you may choose to leave the male line at an early stage, particularly if you have a common surname such as Smith or Jones. As long as you keep clear in your mind the reason behind a particular line of research, you should be OK; and remember, you can always change your overall goals as you progress and become more confident in your work.

Right: Dating a photo can be tricky, but clothes and objects, such as this child's bike, offer important clues. This picture probably comes from the 1950s.

COPYRIGHT   IDEAL STUDIO
RE-ORDERS OBTAINED AT   109 HIGH Rᵈ
ENLARGEMENTS 2/6 5/6 & 7/6   CHISWICK

❧ START WITH YOUR FAMILY

Regardless of the route you decide to take, researching a family tree is all about proving links between one generation and the next, and using this information to work backwards in time. To this end you should start by compiling as much data as possible about your most recent ancestors, and what better place to start than with yourself and your immediate family.

Opposite: Our ancestors loved to wear formal clothes for group photos, many of which can be dated to a specific period in time.

THE FIRST FACTS TO GATHER FROM YOUR IMMEDIATE FAMILY

- Dates of births, weddings and deaths of your children, siblings, parents, uncles, aunts, grandparents and great-grandparents.
- Full names, including surnames, first names, pet names and nicknames.
- Addresses where your relations lived and worked.
- Family anecdotes, legends and any 'skeletons in the cupboard'.

As gathering these basic facts will be the first piece of actual research that you undertake, it is important to do things correctly. You will be interviewing relations and asking some personal questions, so the best person to practise on is yourself! Write down everything you know about your family, starting with what you are most confident about, such as the birthdays of your children, siblings, parents, uncles, aunts and grandparents; any wedding anniversaries that you know of; and any known dates of death for relatives from older generations. This can be quite a revealing process, so you will need to ensure you get down precise, correct information and you might be surprised at how little you actually know – maiden surnames of great aunts can be rather elusive when you haven't spoken to them for ages. Not only will you start to build up a core of data, but you will also highlight the areas that you'll need to ask your family about; and this will be the next stage of your research.

INTERVIEWING THE FAMILY

Interviewing members of your family will require tact and diplomacy, as not everyone is comfortable with discussing events that took place in the past, and elderly folk may be unwilling to talk about family secrets that they consider inappropriate, sensitive or simply do not want to relive. Therefore it is best to start by talking to your closest relatives, such as parents, uncles and aunts,

before moving back a generation to grandparents, great uncles and great aunts. There are two elements to the process, and your prime incentive is to obtain as many hard facts as possible about names, dates and events – every scrap of information will be important in your quest. Older relatives are particularly important to interview, as they should be able to recall their parents or grandparents, people you might never have met but possibly encountered in family photographs.

It is important to establish where your family originated. Geography will play a key role in tracking down your roots, so during the interview process it is advisable to note down where particular events took place or where people lived at various times. This information will become more important the further back you work, as

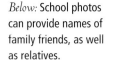

Below: School photos can provide names of family friends, as well as relatives.

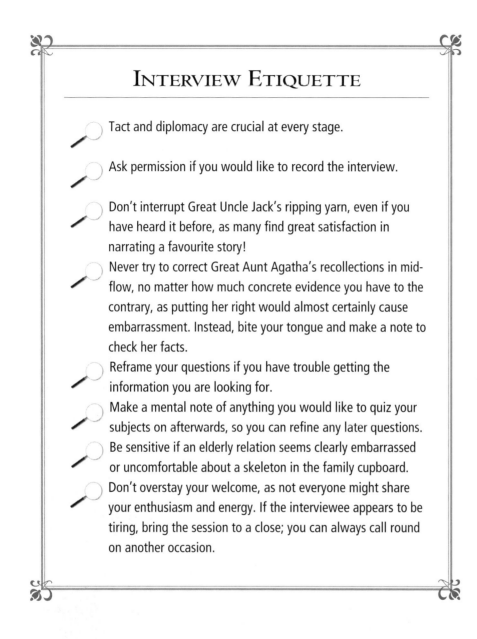

INTERVIEW ETIQUETTE

Tact and diplomacy are crucial at every stage.

Ask permission if you would like to record the interview.

Don't interrupt Great Uncle Jack's ripping yarn, even if you have heard it before, as many find great satisfaction in narrating a favourite story!

Never try to correct Great Aunt Agatha's recollections in mid-flow, no matter how much concrete evidence you have to the contrary, as putting her right would almost certainly cause embarrassment. Instead, bite your tongue and make a note to check her facts.

Reframe your questions if you have trouble getting the information you are looking for.

Make a mental note of anything you would like to quiz your subjects on afterwards, so you can refine any later questions.

Be sensitive if an elderly relation seems clearly embarrassed or uncomfortable about a skeleton in the family cupboard.

Don't overstay your welcome, as not everyone might share your enthusiasm and energy. If the interviewee appears to be tiring, bring the session to a close; you can always call round on another occasion.

people tended to stay closer to their historic origins within established communities before the onset of industrialisation and the growth of communication networks. You will soon appreciate the benefits of noting geographical clues when you start to look for more information about your relatives in the archives.

PET NAMES

A common problem with the interview process is that you cannot always rely on the information you receive. A particular issue is the use of pet names within the family; for example, Uncle Jack might actually have been born David John Williams, but preferred to have been called by a version of his middle name – so a search for Jack Williams may not actually reveal any relevant matches, which can be frustrating for you as a researcher, and even more so for Uncle Jack when you have to break the news that he did not exist in official records! Indeed, one person may be known by different first names depending on who you are talking to, so make sure you capture every version that you hear to ensure that you have the right person when you come to track them down in official records. However, a brief word of warning: the opposite is also true. Some document sources (particularly census returns) can record inaccurate names, ages and places of birth as well, so always try to cross-reference your information with as many types of source as possible – oral, written and official. Equally problematic is the fact that non-blood relatives can also earn the affectionate title 'uncle' or 'aunt' without actually being part of your family tree, so be prepared to do a bit of pruning. This is an important point, as the way we define family relationships is also somewhat fluid, and usually very subjective. When interviewing a relative, make sure you know their exact relationship to you so that you can keep track of who they have been talking about. There is nothing worse than trying to figure out exactly whom Aunt Rose was talking about when she referred to 'Cousin Elizabeth'. It's worth risking the wrath of an irascible aunt by asking who exactly were the parents of Cousin Elizabeth.

ANECDOTES

Gathering data, such as dates of birth, marriage and death, the places where people lived, and the names of distant relatives is only part of the initial interview process. A family history based only on raw data would be rather soulless, and you should always remember that you are dealing with real people who led interesting, eventful lives, though sometimes this is hard to appreciate

Right: Addresses on letters are a vital way of keeping track of where our ancestors used to live.

with the passage of time. And so the second thing to bear in mind when talking to people is that you'll need to gather together some of the family anecdotes that have been circulating over the years. This is often best done during one-to-one interviews, but you could always throw a family party or wait until the next large get-together, and even turn the research process into a game. For example, during a family gathering, you could ask every member to describe briefly some distant, but well-remembered, ancestor. You could then compare the varied recollections to obtain a more rounded view of the person remembered. If you have more than one branch of the family in the room at any one time, you could encourage everyone to reveal a childhood memory, or an important date or event generally remembered by the family. Don't forget, though, that some family members might be uncomfortable with this situation, so please respect their wishes to opt out! It is up to you to use your judgement as to the best way of proceeding.

Whatever method you use, you will quickly gather a large amount of anecdotal information about people, places, events and incidents that have shaped who your relatives are, and why you are where you are today. However, to get the most out of the process, you'll have to hone your interview techniques.

❧ INTERVIEW TECHNIQUES

Above: **This young couple has clearly made an effort for the photographer!**

The aim of the interview process is to obtain as much information as possible about former generations, but you should never forget that it is a two-way process. Here are some pointers to help you – and your subject – gain the most out of the process.

❧   Work out your questions in advance, and make them as clear as possible. It would be courteous to show your list to your subjects in advance to clarify what you are trying to achieve.

❧   Initially focus on basic biographical data, such as names, dates and places.

❧   Then home in on more personal questions about individual character and lifestyle, such as personal appearance, mannerisms, likes, dislikes and favourite places, as well as what they did for a living.

❧   Try to find out the part individuals played in major national events, such World Wars I and II.

Remember that, quite often, people will recall points of interest after you have departed, so be prepared to conduct several interviews with the same person before you can feel confident that you have gathered all the information possible. This is particularly relevant once you have started to track down documentary evidence, and you will be surprised how many people become interested in your progress and look forward to your updates.

❧ QUESTION EVERYTHING

A vital part of the investigative process, and the sign of a good historian, is to question everything you hear, rather than blindly accepting family legends or stories at face value. Memory can be fallible; and with the passing of time, dates, names and events can blur. It is your job, as investigator, to verify everything you have been told. A good way to do so is to compare different versions of one story for discrepancies; where names and dates match, you can be relatively certain that the information is reliable, or at least has a grain of truth in it. Nevertheless, family stories are just clues on the trail – circumstantial evidence that needs to be backed up with documentary proof. You may be surprised how little of what you have been told actually checks out against reality.

❧ ELECTRONIC AIDS

Capturing oral history is a vital part of your research, and today we are fortunate in having access to innovative technology that makes this process far easier. It might be worth investing in a tape recorder or even a video camera so that you can review your notes at a later date; and in any case, there are numerous software packages available that allow video footage to be incorporated into electronic family trees, providing permanent records of the people you have interrogated that can be passed down to future generations.

   If you are planning to record personal interviews with elderly relatives, make sure they are comfortable having their thoughts captured on tape for posterity. Also, there may be subjects that they are not comfortable talking about, and in these circumstances you should not push for more information, even if the topic is of great interest. Some family secrets are too painful for elderly relatives to talk about, even after the passage of time, as it may have directly affected them or their parents, and you should always respect someone's right to silence on the matter.

SEARCH THE FAMILY ARCHIVES

- Telling memorabilia
- Certificates and notices of birth, marriage, divorce, and death
- Obituaries and newspaper clippings
- Wills and title deeds
- Family bibles, sometimes annotated with family trees
- School reports and prize certificates
- Passports and other ID cards
- Employment contracts, wage slips and retirement gifts
- Invitation and memorial cards
- Ration books
- Wartime despatches
- Travel tickets
- Theatre, ballet and opera tickets and programmes

🙞 FAMILY HEIRLOOMS AND ARCHIVES

So you have exhausted your family's store of personal knowledge – but hopefully not their patience – and you're perhaps now wondering what is the next step on your quest. Well, I'm afraid it's back to the drawing board and time for another round of family visits, to unearth the wealth of family archives. You will be amazed at how much personal archive material is waiting for you to discover, tucked away in Granny's attic, hoarded in drawers or bureaux, or gathering dust in the basement. Here you will find documents that will get you so much closer to your distant ancestors, so it is time to start phoning around again to see what family heirlooms start to emerge.

In particular, you should keep an eye out for official documents such as birth, marriage and death certificates, as these often tend to remain tucked away in old envelopes long after someone has passed away, and then are handed down from generation to generation. These are the building blocks of family history – and I shall explain more about their importance later in the book, as they provide you with crucial data about family members, which you can use to build your family tree and start other searches. They often contain information about relatives you may never have heard of before. Another good reason for looking for certificates within the family is that it will save you a lot of time and money further down the research trail. In a similar vein, other official documents may surface from time to time – a will,

1942-43 CLOTHING BOOK

This book may not be used until the holder's name, full postal address and National Registration (Identity Card) Number have been plainly written below IN INK.

NAME _H. Margaret. Hunt_
(BLOCK LETTERS)

ADDRESS _86 Wodeland Avenue_
(BLOCK LETTERS)

(TOWN) _Guildford_   (COUNTY) _Surrey._

NATIONAL REGISTRATION (IDENTITY CARD) NUMBER

DMOE / 111 / 3.

Read the instructions within carefully, and take great care not to lose this book

Page 1

Right: Official documents, like this ration book, provide important data such as a name and address.

perhaps, that can be used to find out what goods or possessions a relative owned, or how much they were worth at the time of their death, as well as the names of their friends and family; or other documents such as employment records, ration books from World War II, legal papers, title deeds to houses, and school reports. All of these seemingly uninteresting and everyday artefacts can shed light on where your ancestors were at a given time, and what they were up to. Even old shopping lists can reveal what standard of living your ancestors enjoyed! However, there are potentially even more interesting items awaiting discovery.

THE FAMILY ALBUM

The most visual source of information will be old photographs, so start looking around to see how many family albums exist. Once again, ask elderly relatives first, as they might well have a stack of vintage photos, and they might also be able to name the people shown. There is nothing more frustrating than finding a photo

of someone, but without a clue as to who it is, or whether they are any sort of relation to you. It might be worth trying to scan old photos from various sources within the family, download them into your computer, and then print them out so that you can take them to show other members of your family, who might remember who that austere yet unidentified relative might be. Of course, always check on the back of the photos to see if a name or date has been written in; and it would be useful to start inscribing the back of any copies you have made so that you can make sure you know who it is you've located. Check for the location of

Opposite: An aspirational family portrait, showing how the family wanted the rest of the world to see them.

the photographer's studio if it is a formal shot, as this in its own right can be a useful clue to where the subjects were living, and when the photo was taken (as you can investigate the whereabouts of the studio through sources such as trade or commercial directories, often stored in local archives). You may have photos of relatives in military dress, in which case you can use clues in the uniform or background to establish the force in which they served, their rank, and even their regiment, ship or aeroplane.

Right: A date and a name is of great use in the hands of a family detective!

MARKET SQUARE
LISBURN.

McBride & Co

3.HIGH STREET
BELFAST.

Certified Copy of an Entry of Birth.

Pursuant to the Births and Deaths Registration Acts 1836 to 1874

Registration District of _Uckfield_   in the County of _Sussex_

Birth in the Sub-District of _Maresfield_

No.	When and Where Born.	Name (if any).	Sex	Name and Surname of Father.	Name and Maiden Surname of Mother.	Rank or Profession of Father.	Signature, Description, and Residence of Informant.	When Regist
Columns	1	2	3	4	5	6	7	8
67	Twenty Ninth November 1902 Perrymans Hill Dane Hill &c	Sydney William	Boy	Sydney John Stubbings	Mary Stubbings formerly North	Game Keeper	Sydney J. Stubbings Father Perrymans Hill Dane Hill	Twen Jan 19

1903

I, _John George Cruttenden_ _____ Superintendent Registrar for the District of _Uckfield_ in the Co

Do hereby Certify that this is a **True Copy** of the Entry No. _67_ in the Register Book of Births. No. _25_ for the said Sub-Distr

and that such Register Book is now legally in my custody.   **Witness my Hand** this ___Twelfth___ day of _J_

The Statutory Fees payable for an ordinary certified copy of an entry in a Register of Births,
Deaths or Marriages, if taken at time of registration, are 2s. 7d. (including 1d. for the Stamp),
but if taken at any time afterwards an additional fee of 1s. is chargeable for a search

Certificate of Marriage.

1901   Marriage Solemnized at _All Saints Church_ in the Parish of _Danehill_   in the County of _Sussex_

No.	When Married.	NAME AND SURNAME.	Age.	Condition.	Rank or Profession.	Residence at the Time of Marriage.	FATHER'S NAME AND SURNAME.	Rank or Profession of Father.
282	May 27 1901	Sidney John Stubbings	22	Bachelor	Gamekeeper	Danehill	Thomas Stubbings	Farmer
		Mary North	22	Spinster		Danehill	John North	Gardener

Married in the _Parish Church_ _____ according to the Rites and Ceremonies of the _Church of England_

(a) _____   By me, _Walter Summers Vicar_

This Marriage was solemnized between us, { _Sidney John Stubbings_ } In the presence of us, { _William Marchant_
{ _Mary North_ } { _Elizabeth Ann Streeter_

I certify that the above is a true Copy of the Marriage Register of the _Parish of Danehill_ aforesaid, the said Register being legally in my custody.

Extracted this _27th_ day of _May_ in the Year of our Lord

One Thousand _nine_ Hundred _and one_ _____ By me, _Walter Summers_
1901

Certified true Copy. Thomson?

(1) SOLDIER'S NAME and DESCRIPTION on ATTESTATION.

Army Number _T/230453_

Surname (in capitals) _STUBBINGS_

Christian Names (in full) _THOMAS JAMES_

Date of Birth _8-8-15_

Trade on Enlistment _MOTOR DRIVER_

Religious Denomination _C. of E._

Approved Society _Manchester Unity of Oddfellows_

Membership No. _1076_

Enlisted at _BULFORD_ On _7·11·40_

For the :- _D of W._

* Regular Army.   * Supplementary Reserve.
* Territorial Army.   * Army Reserve Section B.
      * Strike out those inapplicable.

For_____years with the Colours and_____years in the Reserve.

Signature of Soldier _____

Date _____

DESCRIPTION ON ENLISTMENT.

Height _5_ ft. _6_ ins. Weight _127_ lbs.
Maximum Chest _75_ ins. Complexion _RUDDY_
Eyes _GREY BLUE_   Hair _FAIR_
Distinctive Marks and Minor Defects
 SCAR BACK OF
 RIGHT CALF

 A & S GROUP 29
 PYTHON DATE (JULY 1941)

CONDITION ON TRANSFER TO RESERVE.

Found fit for_____

Defects or History of past illness which should be enquired into if called up for Service_____

Date_____19____
Initials of M.O. i/c. _____

9   10   Baptismal Name if added after Registration of Birth.

nature of Registrar.

Edward
Kenward

Registrar

of East Sussex
Maresfield

12/16. 1916
Wo Cullunder
Superintendent Registrar.

Above and Below: This collection of documents was found in an old envelope, and contained numerous birth, marriage and death certificates as well as army papers.

3547

CERTIFIED COPY of an
Pursuant to the Births and

ENTRY OF DEATH

Deaths Registration Act, 1953

certificate is 3s. 9d. y to find the entry, dition.

(Printed by authority of the Registrar Gener

D. C
R.B.

Registration District
ath in the Sub-district of   KINGSTON HILL.   SURREY NORTHERN   in the   COUNTY OF SURREY.

2	3	4	5	6	7	8	9
Name and surname	Sex	Age	Occupation	Cause of death	Signature, description, and residence of informant	When registered	Signature of registrar
Sydney John Stubbings	male	83 years	24 Keswick Avenue Kingston Vale. A Gamekeeper (retired)	1a. Advanced atheroma and cerebro-vascular accident. Certified by J.C. Marks LRCP.	Thos Pris. Daughter 24 Keswick Avenue Kingston Vale SW.15.	Twenty ninth June 1962	P.H.Ridgway, Registrar.

_____, Registrar of Births and Deaths for the Sub-district of KINGSTON HILL, ody.

WITNESS MY HAND this _24a_ day of _June_, 19 _62_.

y of the particulars on this certificate, knowing it to be false, is liable to

in the Register Book of Deaths for the Sub-district of KINGSTON HILL, , in the COUNTY OF SURREY, and that such Register

P.H.Ridgway

Registrar of Births and Deaths.

✿ FAMILY CORRESPONDENCE

Alongside photos, there are likely to be stacks of personal correspondence written amongst the family – rather a dying art these days, so there's even more reason to chronicle your relatives now before we stop writing to each other altogether and rely on instantly disposable means of communication, such as email, text or phone. Once again, you must be a diplomat and should not just barge into someone's house demanding to see their personal correspondence; there may be sensitive information contained inside love letters, for example. However, many people are happy to show you old correspondence provided you explain your mission, and if you are lucky enough to discover such a collection within the family, try to read the letters on two levels – with one eye on the sentiments and characteristics that emerge from the words, bringing you closer to the author and recipient, yet with the other eye peeled for historic detail such as names, dates, places or national events that can tie the correspondents down to a specific set of circumstances, which will make it easier to identify those concerned.

Below: Informal notes such as this postcard were an important way of keeping in touch with distant relatives.

POST CARD.

CORRESPONDENCE   ADDRESS ONLY

Photo & Pub. by R. Wilkinson & Co, Trowbridge.
Printed in Germany.

Dear. Brother & Sister
a line hoping all quite just
well. I recieved quite safe
many thanks for same.
I hee   ru are having a
rough   ime, never cheer up
make the best of life, tell
charlie morgan to come along
with the boys, Shinty (Y)
Remember me to all your love

Mrs. P. Morgan
200 St. Leonards. Rd.
Poplar
London E

Other artefacts will come to light during your research, such as heirlooms – a family bible, perhaps, inscribed with the name of the original recipient and even a list of subsequent owners – and other miscellanea, treasured possessions such as jewellery, uniforms, medals, retirement watches, newspaper clippings, sporting trophies and certificates, memorial cards, wedding invitations and goodness knows what else. You may even uncover a set of notes about your family, or find someone who has already done some research. This will save you a great deal of time – but it is a good idea always quietly to double-check that everything is correct and can be verified against original sources.

By now, you should have collected a mountain of information, some written, some oral, some physical. It is now time to gather it all together, and start sifting through the mass of material in order to prepare some research goals and draw up a plan of attack. The easiest way is to amass everything, and set it all down in a local fashion, so you can see at a glance how everyone is related to one another. It's time to draw up a family tree.

Below: Lengthy correspondence tells a great deal about family life.

copulation aueacques sa couisine ou couisin sans licence
de saint pere et pour ainse Si peult et doie scauoir par
ceste ticule que se aucun qui me seroit en second deter
auoit copulation aueacques une feme celle mesmes te-

CHAPTER 2

Organising your Data

With any project that involves generating large amounts of information, it is vital to keep track of your results, and researching your family history is no exception. One of the most widely recognised and practical ways of organising genealogical data is to construct a family tree, which is essentially a diagram showing how people in your family are related to one another, a visual map of your roots. You have probably seen at least one – the best example is that of the Royal Family, which is one of the longest unbroken trees in Britain and stretches back in time to William the Conqueror.

Opposite: A particularly elaborate family tree.

Whilst it is highly unlikely that you will emulate such an impressive lineage, the principles of constructing a family tree remain the same. Yet a diagram of your ancestors' names and biographical data is only the end product of your research; to research effectively you need to keep your notes clearly set out as you progress, otherwise you will not know what information to add, where you have researched and what you have looked at already.

Without organisation, your work is likely to run into problems at an early stage, so I shall give you some advice about how to keep your research notes in order.

Finally, before venturing into archives on your first real investigation outside the safety of the family unit, there will be a few words of warning about the dangers of rushing headlong into research without first establishing realistic expectations of what you will achieve in these early stages.

❧ CONSTRUCTING A BASIC FAMILY TREE

A family tree is a simple yet highly visual way of showing the relationships between members of the same family, using a universally recognised set of symbols. There are various ways of setting out a family tree, but simplicity is often the best policy at this stage, and I shall start by providing you with a step-by-step guide about how you can compile the first few lines and branches, based on what you have already gathered together from interviewing your family. As your work advances, you may wish to adopt other ways of keeping track of family relationships, and towards the end of this chapter I shall mention a few of the ways you can incorporate technology into your notes and organisational structure.

SO HOW DO YOU BEGIN A FAMILY TREE?

❧ Since this is your piece of research, why not start with yourself! Write down your name in the centre of a large, blank piece of paper. Thereafter, all other people on the tree will be described by their relationship to you. Write your date of birth underneath your name, prefixed by the symbol 'b' which stands for 'born'.

❧ Next, if you have any brothers and sisters, write their names alongside yours. These are your siblings. Always place the oldest on the left, and then work towards the right in descending chronological order. Make a note of their dates of birth below their names as well. Each line on the family tree is known as one generation, a group of siblings sharing common parents, and this is your generation.

❧ If you are married, write the name of your spouse alongside your own. Again, include their date of birth underneath, and, if a woman, the surname they used before marriage (also known as their maiden name). To signify the marriage, place a = sign between your names; alternatively you can use 'm'. Both are recognised genealogical symbols. Note the date of marriage underneath the '=' or 'm'. Usually the husband's name is written on the left-hand side of the pair.

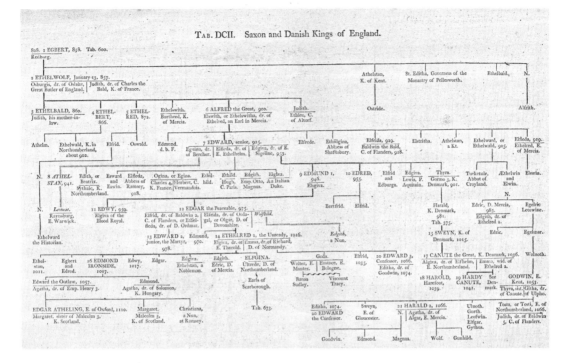

Above: Once you start to organise your data, your family tree will start to flourish.

⁂ Whether married or not, any children from the union should be listed below the names of you and your partner using the same convention (oldest on the left, youngest on the right); connect their names to yours via a single line running down from you and your partner, extending along and down to each in turn. The lines show that these children are your offspring, and collectively they represent the generation below yours. If you have grandchildren, they can be linked to your children in a similar way.

⁂ Now you have linked your immediate family to yourself, you can begin to work backwards – the main aim of your research. Leaving aside your partner's family for a moment, write the names of your parents above your own and your siblings, and connect yourself and your siblings to your parents with lines as you did your children to you. Remember to leave enough space to add the dates of your siblings' marriages, partners and details of their children at a later stage.

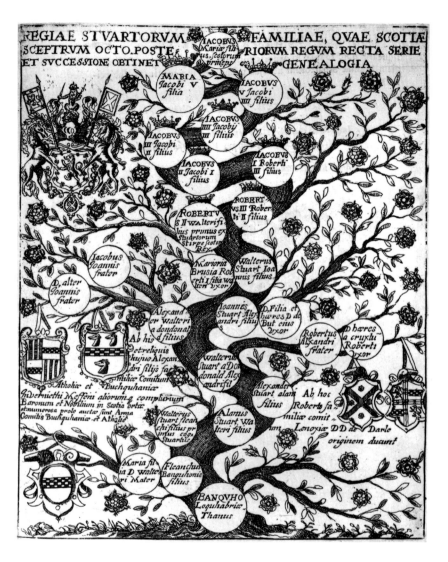

Right: Family history has always been popular, particularly during medieval times when elaborate trees were drawn up.

The next step is record the date of your parents' marriage and their dates of birth on the tree. At this stage you can include information about their brothers and sisters – your uncles and aunts – but to save your fledgling tree becoming too cluttered, it might be best to leave this until a later date. The real aim is to find out more about their parents, your grandparents. This may be where concrete information becomes increasingly scarce, so use a question mark to indicate dates or names of which you are not entirely certain and will need to verify through official sources.

In essence, the mechanics outlined above will permit you to continue to work backwards in time, adding new generations to your family tree every time you start another line. Once you have added all the data you know about your relatives, or were told during the interview process with members of your family, it is time to review your tree and start to formulate a research plan that will lead you to archives – more about that in the next chapter!

☙ TERMINOLOGY

The genealogical terminology shown below is important, as not only will it help you to organise your family tree as you make further discoveries, but also recognise how people are related to one another when you start to read through historic documents in archives. It is worth taking a few moments to familiarise yourself with some of the following phrases.

Blood relatives are people related to you through birth, rather than marriage. They are sometimes termed your biological family. Where applicable, the maximum number of each type of relative is provided, to give you an idea of how many people you should be looking for.

BLOOD RELATIVES

FATHER – male parent
MOTHER – female parent
You will only have one biological mother and father, and they represent the generation above you.

BROTHER – male sibling
SISTER – female sibling
These are your siblings, and represent the same generation as you.

SON – male offspring

DAUGHTER – female offspring

These are the generation below you on the family tree.

GRANDSON – son of your children

GRANDDAUGHTER – daughter of your children

GREAT-GRANDCHILDREN – for each successive generation, prefix with the word 'great'; thus the son of your grandchild is your great-grandson, and his son would be your great-great-grandson.

MATERNAL GRANDFATHER – your mother's father

MATERNAL GRANDMOTHER – your mother's mother

PATERNAL GRANDFATHER – your father's father

PATERNAL GRANDMOTHER – your father's mother

You therefore have a maximum of four biological grandparents.

GREAT-GRANDPARENTS – the parents of your grandparents

This generation is prefixed with 'great', and as you work backwards you should add another 'great' to every preceding generation. You have twice as many people to find each time you move back another generation. Therefore you have 8 great-grandparents, 16 great-great grandparents, 32 great-great-great grandparents, and so on.

UNCLE – the brother of one of your parents, and part of their generation

AUNT – the sister of one of your parents, and part of their generation

NEPHEW – the son of your sibling, and the same generation as your children

NIECE – the daughter of your sibling, and the same generation as your children

GRAND-NEPHEW – the son of your nephew, and the same generation as your grandchildren

GRAND-NIECE – the daughter of your niece, and the same generation as your grandchildren

FIRST COUSIN – the child of your uncle or aunt, and the same generation as yourself.

Above: **You can start to put names to faces once you've organised your data.**

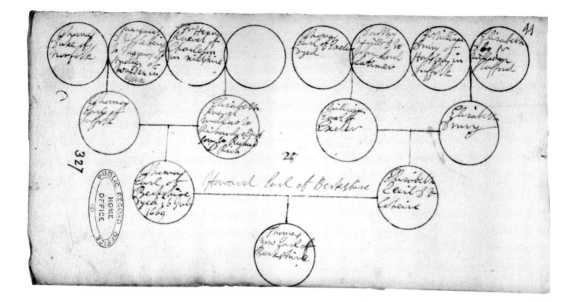

The following terms are used to describe more distant blood relatives:

FIRST COUSIN ONCE REMOVED – the son or daughter of your first cousin

FIRST COUSIN TWICE REMOVED – the grandson or granddaughter of your first cousin

FIRST COUSIN THREE TIMES REMOVED – the great-grandson or great-granddaughter of your first cousin

GREAT UNCLE OR AUNT – the brother or sister of your grandparents

FIRST COUSIN ONCE REMOVED – this term can also refer to the son or daughter of your great uncle or aunt, and the same generation as your parents

SECOND COUSIN – the grandson or granddaughter of your great uncle or aunt, and the same generation as yourself

SECOND COUSIN ONCE REMOVED – the great-grandson of your great uncle or aunt, and the same generation as your children

SECOND COUSIN TWICE REMOVED – the great-great grandson of your great uncle or aunt, and the same generation as your grandchildren.

Above: Family trees crop up in unexpected places. This one was used as evidence in a court case.

Left: This rather relaxed photo includes several generations of two families that have just been united at a wedding.

RELATIVES THROUGH MARRIAGE

There is a separate terminology to describe your relationship with your partner's family.

MOTHER-IN-LAW – the mother of your partner

FATHER-IN-LAW – the father of your partner

SISTER-IN-LAW – the sister of your partner; OR the name given to your brother's wife

BROTHER-IN-LAW – the brother of your partner; OR the name given to your sister's husband

Indeed, the addition of 'in-law' can be extended to cover all blood relatives listed above.

If either of your parents remarried, then you should use the following terms to describe their new family:

STEP-MOTHER – your biological father's new wife

STEP-FATHER – your biological mother's new husband

STEP-SISTER – the daughter of your parent's new partner from a previous marriage

STEP-BROTHER – the son of your parent's new partner from a previous marriage

HALF-BROTHER – a son from your parent's subsequent marriage

HALF-SISTER – a daughter from your parent's subsequent marriage.

Although all the terms listed above are clearly defined and used by genealogists in constructing family trees, you will probably encounter them in historic documents as well. However, their usage was not as strictly observed as today, and so you will often find 'cousin' used indiscriminately in documents to describe in-laws and second cousins, whilst brother or sister was often written instead of half-siblings and step-siblings.

Below: There has always been a great fascination with royal family trees, such as this one of Queen Victoria's family.

✣ OTHER TERMINOLOGY

You will probably encounter these commonly used terms during the course of your research:

SPINSTER – a woman before marriage

BACHELOR – a man before marriage

WIDOW – a woman after the death of her husband

WIDOWER – a man after the death of his wife

DISTAFF – the female side of the family

SPEAR – the male side of the family.

The following symbols are recognised by most researchers:

b.	born	m.	married
bapt.	baptised	mar.	married
bur.	buried	2.	second marriage
chr.	christened	=	married
d.	died	?	uncertain or unknown

✣ KEEPING TRACK OF YOUR NOTES

You have now completed your first family tree, which may well look a little sparse. That will soon change, as you use the information you have recorded on it to shape the next stage of your research. You should now be able to see instantly what you have gathered during your interview stage, plus snippets of data gleaned from the objects, artefacts and heirlooms scattered around the family. Just like a real tree, the lower part should be very sturdy, packed with full names, precise dates and relevant information, but as the branches start to spread out at the top, you are likely to have a lot of gaps, unknowns or question marks. Immediately, the value of your family tree becomes clear, as you can tell

Opposite: Four generations of the same family were captured in this photo.

at a glance what areas you need to research in the archives, and what documents you will need to acquire to fill in the blanks.

Whether you decide to use PC software or old-fashioned paper to keep track of your research, the underlying principle remains the same: it is vitally important to establish a settled method of note-taking at the beginning of your work, as once you start delving in archives you will quickly become swamped by the amount of information and documentation you have gathered. The system you decide upon has to be one that you are comfortable with, be it one that comes recommended or one that you devise yourself, but either way it is up to you to keep a record of what you have looked at, where you examined the sources, and when you did the research. Further advice is provided in the next chapter about how to take notes when working in archives, but the following general points will help you to keep your notes at home in order.

- Put a date on every note you make and try to record where you found that information, whether online, through an interview with a family member, or following research in an archive.
- Try to keep your notes in chronological order so you can work back and find something if need be.
- Many people organise their notes according to the person they are researching, whilst others arrange the data by generation, place or even the archive they visited, but regardless of the filing system you create, if it is in date order you can usually find something quite quickly.
- It is a good idea to keep information on different branches of the family in separate folders, particularly if surnames crop up in more than one side, otherwise it can get very confusing; and it may help to keep relevant sections of your family tree with each set of notes.
- Some people create a central filing system with names on card indexes, but these days computer packages can save you time and a vast amount of space, with instant data retrieval. The only caveat is to make sure you back up your work, and keep several copies to hand just in case your computer starts to feel unwell!

❧ Managing expectations

Before moving on to the next exciting phase of your work, it is important to prepare yourself mentally for the challenges ahead! One of the biggest obstacles you may face is that of unrealistic levels of expectation generated by your searches to date. (It has all been fairly easy so far!) Whilst everyone would like to take their research as far back as possible, in reality you will encounter problems as you make the transition from working within the family unit to casting the net wider, some of which may appear insurmountable. As you gain experience, and experiment with more document sources, ways around these obstacles may appear; but you should prepare yourself for initial disappointments and difficulties as you begin to find your feet.

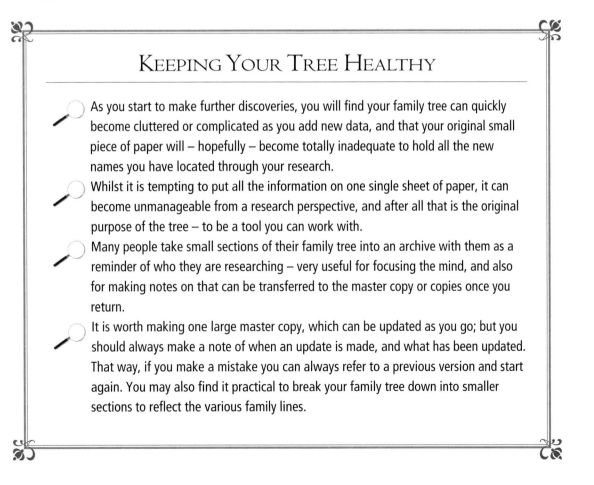

Keeping Your Tree Healthy

○ As you start to make further discoveries, you will find your family tree can quickly become cluttered or complicated as you add new data, and that your original small piece of paper will – hopefully – become totally inadequate to hold all the new names you have located through your research.

○ Whilst it is tempting to put all the information on one single sheet of paper, it can become unmanageable from a research perspective, and after all that is the original purpose of the tree – to be a tool you can work with.

○ Many people take small sections of their family tree into an archive with them as a reminder of who they are researching – very useful for focusing the mind, and also for making notes on that can be transferred to the master copy or copies once you return.

○ It is worth making one large master copy, which can be updated as you go; but you should always make a note of when an update is made, and what has been updated. That way, if you make a mistake you can always refer to a previous version and start again. You may also find it practical to break your family tree down into smaller sections to reflect the various family lines.

You will invariably come to an apparent dead end during your research. If this happens, DO NOT assume a link, or jump a generation because it appears to make sense, no matter how conclusive the evidence may seem. Always work back to the last verifiable fact, and then start out again on a different line until you find conclusive proof that your first supposition was correct – weeks of work could be wasted pursuing a different family altogether on the basis of an incorrect assumption. And where possible try to find at least one other source that corroborates the data you have uncovered. (This is one of the dangers of Internet research, a subject tackled in Chapter Five.) Having said that, there may not be any conclusive evidence available; it is then up to you to make a decision about how to proceed, and if you are convinced that you are still on the right track, based on the lack of contradictory evidence and sufficient circumstantial information, you can carry on, PROVIDED you flag up the fact that there is no supporting documentation, and that it may not be correct.

Another frequent problem is that of cost. During the course of your work you will probably have to part with your money on travel, copies of birth, marriage and death certificates and other documents, computer software, Internet access, books, publications and membership fees. Family history can be an expensive pastime, so if funds are limited this may affect your initial research objectives.

FOR THE TECHNOLOGICALLY MINDED

There is an increasing number of computer software packages that facilitate the collection and organisation of data, and enable you to construct sophisticated family trees that incorporate photographs, moving images and sound recordings that you made during your interview process. Some packages come with CD-Rom databases that contain millions of names – though when buying a package that promotes itself on the strength of the number of names it contains, bear in mind that the vast majority won't be of any use to you, and that in any case there are now many resources available online that contain similar if not more appropriate data.

There are also elements of physical discomfort involved in research. When you finally access an archive to follow up some of these leads, you may find that many documents are available on microfilm or microfiche. Whilst most people have no trouble viewing films or fiche, others find that the movement of the film can induce feelings of nausea. Similarly, if you are working at the Family Records Centre, where the original indexes to birth, marriage and death certificates are located, it can be physically tiring lifting the heavy volumes from the shelves, especially if you have a long span of years to check.

Finally, you never know what you will uncover about your family's past. You may be in for a shock, as our ancestors were prone to all sorts of dubious activities. It is this element of unpredictability that makes the research such fun, but whilst this information may be of interest to you, your findings may be distressing to older members of your family who were perhaps closer to events, or even remember the person in question. Always exercise caution when relaying your results to others.

Are you ready? If so, let's take the plunge and enter the world of archives, libraries and record offices.

Above: When ancestors 'disappear', a photo with an address can lead you to all corners of the planet.

CHAPTER 3

Establishing a Research Plan

Once you have exhausted your family's knowledge (hopefully as said earlier, without exhausting their patience into the bargain!) and organised the information they have provided into a basic family tree, it is time to seek documentary verification for some of the stories you have been told, and fill in the gaps at the top of your tree. This is when the research process becomes more daunting as, in order to draw upon wider resources outside the family, you will need to head into an archive or local study centre. For many, this will be the first visit to such an institution, and it can take a while to become acclimatised to unfamiliar practices and procedures. Having worked in an archive for many years, as both a member of staff and a researcher, I hope that the following suggestions and tips will help you to plan and execute your research more effectively, whilst you enjoy the thrill of working with the very stuff of history and discovering the secrets of your ancestors' past lives.

Opposite: The dress of these brothers gives a clue as to their professions, telling us they were of professional class status, with one almost certainly working as a banker.

Right: We can use this church to hazard a guess as to the location of the author of this cryptic note.

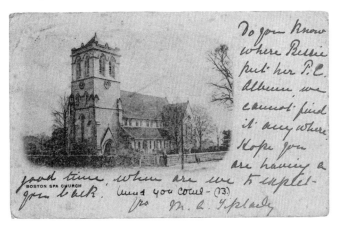

Addresses and other contact details of research sources mentioned here can be found at the back of this book.

❦

✌ LOCATING ARCHIVES

The most immediate problem is working out where you should go first of all, and so I shall describe for you how archives, libraries and other resources are structured, often referred to as the archival pyramid. Where possible, you should start your quest locally, and this means a trip to the nearest local studies centre, usually situated at your main library. Local study centres will have information about how to start your research, as well as resources such as photographs, newspaper clippings and possibly even ancestral files relevant to the area – so if you live away from where your relatives came from, you will need to find a local study centre in that area; this is why I have been stressing the importance of geography in your initial questions to your family!

However, the nature of information at the local study centre will probably be fairly limited, and so most people turn their attention to their nearest county record office or, in the case of a major town or city, municipal archive, which holds records that are relevant across a far wider geographical and chronological spread. County record offices are the repositories for local authority records and administrative papers for a particular county, along with deposited private manuscripts. Consequently they hold vast numbers of documents containing genealogical information. In addition, most county record offices provide microfilm or microfiche copies of material created by central government institutions, such as census returns for the county and indexes to birth, marriage and death certificates – which I shall be discussing shortly.

Families had a tendency to move around, especially during the twentieth century when the transport network became more advanced. Therefore you may exhaust the records in your own county record office as your research advances, particularly if your family's origins lay near the borders of two or more counties

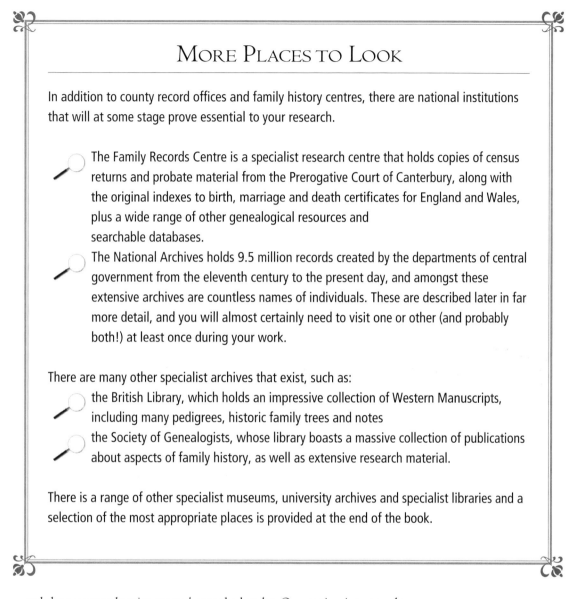

MORE PLACES TO LOOK

In addition to county record offices and family history centres, there are national institutions that will at some stage prove essential to your research.

The Family Records Centre is a specialist research centre that holds copies of census returns and probate material from the Prerogative Court of Canterbury, along with the original indexes to birth, marriage and death certificates for England and Wales, plus a wide range of other genealogical resources and searchable databases.

The National Archives holds 9.5 million records created by the departments of central government from the eleventh century to the present day, and amongst these extensive archives are countless names of individuals. These are described later in far more detail, and you will almost certainly need to visit one or other (and probably both!) at least once during your work.

There are many other specialist archives that exist, such as:

the British Library, which holds an impressive collection of Western Manuscripts, including many pedigrees, historic family trees and notes

the Society of Genealogists, whose library boasts a massive collection of publications about aspects of family history, as well as extensive research material.

There is a range of other specialist museums, university archives and specialist libraries and a selection of the most appropriate places is provided at the end of the book.

and they constantly criss-crossed over the border. One option is to travel to another appropriate county record office in person where relevant material is deposited; or alternatively you could visit your nearest family history centre, institutions run by the Church of the Latter Day Saints, where you can order up microfilms of national genealogical resources, thus saving travel expenses. The former option is probably the best, as it allows you to browse for clues whereas you need to let the family history centre know fairly precisely which sources you

Above: Assembling all the clues you've found, and making sense of them, will be a vital part of your work.

need to look at – and in many situations, an organic search of records can be far more productive!

There are various ways of locating your nearest and most relevant archive, but these days it is probably easier to go online. Perhaps the best website is that of The National Archives where you can access ARCHON, a directory of all British archives compiled and updated as part of the National Register of Archives. Links are provided where applicable to the websites of each individual organisation, where you can find information on opening times, locations and any entry restrictions or requirements. For those of you without access to the Internet, most libraries should have an up-to-date copy of Record Repositories in Great Britain, produced by the Royal Commission on Historical Manuscripts, whilst British Archives: A Guide to Archive Resources in the United Kingdom, J. Foster and J. Sheppard, provides an outline of each repository's holdings – though it is not updated as regularly.

℘ PRELIMINARY ORGANISATION

Having identified a likely place to start your research, be it at local, county or even national level, the next stage is to visit in person. This can be a daunting process for the uninitiated – there's a common misconception that they are dusty places full of dusty academics reading dusty old documents, but these days that could not be further from the truth. Even so, it can be difficult to get your bearings and there are some steps you can take to make the process a bit easier for both yourself and the people who will be helping you in the archive.

Where possible, always try to contact the archive in advance of your visit and let them know that you are coming. They can offer advice and guidance about some of the next steps you will need to take, and in many cases the archivists can suggest areas of research that are relevant to your quest – provided you ask short, focused questions rather than simply recounting what you know so far.

Before you can start looking at the records, most archives require you to register with them as a user. The requirements will vary from archive to archive, so make sure you know exactly what you have to bring with you, otherwise you might not be allowed in! Some will ask you for two forms of identification, one of which will need to have your address on it; others ask for passport photographs to complete the paperwork; and most will require you to show an official proof of identity such as a driving licence, passport or a British bank debit or credit card. However, at county level many record offices have signed up to the County Archive Research Network (CARN), and once registered with a participating archive your CARN ticket permits entry to all other record offices that are members of the scheme.

It is also worth checking the opening time of the archive, as there is rarely a standard opening pattern across the network – the days of Monday to Friday, 9 to 5 business hours are long gone and many archives offer extended opening one evening a week, and occasional Saturdays, in exchange for closing one day in the middle of the week. Furthermore, many archives close for up to a fortnight for 'stocktaking', which can be a movable feast that varies from institution to institution.

Archives can often be located in strange places, so make sure you know exactly how to find them, especially if you are coming by public transport. Most now provide maps and directions on their websites. If you are driving, you should also check there is sufficient parking, otherwise you could be in for a long walk! There are other practical issues to think about such as food and drink, as few have their own restaurants or cafés, though some provide hot drinks machines.

When you do make it through the door of the archive, you should spend some time orientating yourself, and then see if there is an archivist on hand at an enquiry desk to help get you started. This is where your organisational skills come into play once again! Make sure you have a list of short, sensible, focused questions – preferably only one or two at a time – which will help the archivist to help you.

Advance preparation is often possible; with so much information available online these days, many archives have provided literature about the searches you can undertake amongst their collections, usually in the form of information leaflets that explain how to search for your family and what the records are that you are going to use, and indicate any short cuts to the indexes and reference works that you will find on the shelves when you get there.

It will not just be leaflets that you'll find – many archives have prepared electronic versions of their catalogues that you can search by keyword either

Right: Clearly these correspondents share a private joke that, sadly, we might never uncover.

onsite or via the Internet. There will be some further advice about online resources a bit later in this book, but for now it is worth remembering that most electronic catalogues only cover document descriptions rather than full document content. Consequently, a keyword search will only reveal a fraction of relevant material available in the archive, and only if you are lucky enough for a document that contains the name you are looking for in its title. You should never assume a keyword search provides references to all relevant material, so you will need to check all available indexes in person when you get to an archive.

There is another good reason for searching manually – historical context. A keyword search can give you a few leads, or provide you with the references of documents that you may otherwise have missed, but it is still no substitute for knowing which sources you should access, and why – after all, if you want to know all about your ancestors, you will need to know about the documents in which their names were recorded, otherwise there is a danger that you will not fully understand the information they contain.

HOW TO WORK IN ARCHIVES

Rules and regulations within an archive are strict, and should be adhered to closely. Of paramount importance is correct document handling. If you are unsure about this, ask the archivist; but in general you should bear in mind the following points. The list might appear overly negative – lots of don'ts rather than dos – but at the end of the day, archives are responsible for their documents which are unique and irreplaceable, so for the sake of future generations we have to ensure they have the minimum amount of wear and tear.

- Never use ink, rollerball or ballpoint pens in an archive, always a pencil; ink will irreparably damage documents.
- Never use erasers, as left-over fragments could get caught up in the documents and cause just as much damage as ink.

- Pencil sharpeners are usually prohibited, as unscrupulous users have been known to unscrew the blades, cut out sections of documents and steal them.

- Some archives restrict what you can bring into the reading room to minimise the risk of document theft, and often insist that you carry your belongings in a transparent bag for security. This means you will have to think carefully about which notes are essential to your research.

- Minimise contact between yourself and the document – the oils in your skin can cause lasting damage to paper and parchment. If you need to keep your place when reading a document, use a piece of white paper and run your finger along this instead of across the actual text.

- Never lick your fingers when turning a page; apart from the dangers of picking up dirt and microbes from the document, your saliva will damage the paper.

- Do not eat or drink in the archive, or bring edible items into the reading room. This includes sweets, chewing gum and cough medicines.

- Always set up your document correctly. If it is a book, ensure that the spine is supported with foam wedges or cushions; rolled parchment documents should be laid out flat and held in place with weights; and maps should be placed under transparent protective sheets.

OTHER GENERAL RULES AND REGULATIONS

- Silence is important; you will appreciate this rule when you need to concentrate on your work!

- Laptop computers are increasingly permissible, but always check before bringing one; some archives have no power source, whilst others require certification that it meets safety standards.

- Make sure the volume on your laptop is turned down, and that your mobile phone is switched off.

- Some archives now allow you to bring digital cameras, as their own reprographic capabilities are sometimes limited. Once again, always obtain permission first.

- Always consider the needs of other users of the archives.

❧ TAKING NOTES IN ARCHIVES

You will quickly find that archives use their own reference system to identify all documents within their holdings, and the way in which the documents are assigned unique codes will vary from archive to archive. Every time you view an original document in an archive, you must make a note of its reference for your records, in order to keep track of the ground you have covered including what you might have discarded as irrelevant to your research. It pays to be thorough! For example, you should make a note of the exact page or folio from which you are extracting information so that you can find the entry at a later date; this information is usually written or printed clearly somewhere on the page.

Reading old documents can be problematic; handwritten sources can be notoriously hard to read, and many records before 1732 will be written in Latin, the official language of government. You may need to ask the archivists for assistance, or even consider obtaining outside help to get a clean transcription or translation of the item you're discovered. Advice on how to do this is provided in Section Two.

In general, when conducting research at an archive or elsewhere, you should consider the following points:

❧ One of the greatest challenges is keeping clear notes. It is easy to get confused if your notes are jumbled, so start a separate sheet every time you view a new document, or make another visit to the archive.

❧ Make sure you have a research plan for each visit, and try (where possible) to stick to that plan. However you should allow enough flexibility for unexpected yet important discoveries.

Below: It is tempting to use photos to try and spot a family resemblance passed down over the years.

The American Photographic.

- Ensure you keep research notes for each branch of the family separate, with a clear indication of the dates of your research trips so you are always working from the most recent set of notes.

- If you are using abbreviations in your notes, make sure they are consistent. Also ensure that you make a key to your abbreviations.

- Use draft or sections of your master family tree to record your findings and keep track of your current lines of research. When amending the master copy, ensure you record the date. Keep file copies of all older versions in case of loss or damage to the master copy.

- Try not to 'modernise' spelling in documents; surnames and places were often written phonetically, and thus will alter over time. Always make an accurate transcription of what you have viewed.

- Similarly, if you are searching for variant surname spelling, ensure you keep an accurate record of which names you have checked.

- If you are checking union name indexes, ensure you note which documents are covered by the index, and do not forget to record the date period you have checked.

- In general, it is easier to start with relatives nearer the present and then to work backwards in time.

ARCHIVE PROFILES

The two main national institutions that you will need to visit at least once during your research are the Family Records Centre and The National Archives; full addresses and contact details for these are given at the back of this book.

FAMILY RECORDS CENTRE

The Family Records Centre (FRC) was set up in 1997 to bring all the main biographical document collections to one central location – birth, marriage and death civil registration indexes, census returns and modern will indexes – but in the event, only the first two datasets were relocated to the FRC. The FRC is a

Government institution, and a joint venture between the Office of National Statistics and The National Archives.

The records are situated on the ground and first floors, with a basement area provided for lockers, a cloakroom, refreshments and space to eat lunch or discuss the day's findings.

FINDING YOUR WAY AROUND

The national indexes to English and Welsh birth, marriage and death indexes, plus adoption, overseas and military material, are located on the ground floor, which is run by the Office of National Statistics.

All other records – census, wills, death duty registers, divorce indexes and non-conformist indexes – can be found on the first floor, which is run by The National Archives. There is also an Internet area just outside the first floor reading room, which is primarily intended for readers who wish to pick up emails or browse online.

The first floor area also has a large array of computer terminals that provide access to online family history databases and search engines, such as the British Vital Records Index, the National Burial Index and trade directories. There are also maps, reference works and 'how to' guides to help you if you get stuck.

Unlike many archives, you do not need a reader's ticket to gain entry, nor do you need to book a seat in advance – simply turn up and start work! Your bags will be searched as you come in, and you are strongly advised to leave as much material as possible in lockers as space in the reading areas is limited. It is good practice to use pencils when taking notes, and you should also turn off your mobile phone whilst working in the searchrooms. Each floor has its own advice desk, where you can get help with your research. There is also a range of leaflets explaining how the FRC works, and the best ways to get the most out of the records. In addition, the FRC periodically runs educational seminars, talks and

WHEN YOU ARRIVE

workshops on all aspects of family history and many of these require advance booking. There is also a display and exhibition area on the first floor, featuring samples of the records held at the FRC.

LOCKERS, SHOPS AND REFRESHMENTS You will need some money for your visit. The lockers in the basement operate with a £1 coin, which is returned after you have finished using the lockers, and you will need sufficient money to pay for any duplicate certificates you order, plus the cost of photocopies made during your visit. There is also a shop on the first floor, where you can purchase books and magazines on family history and related subjects. Vending machines are situated in the basement, providing a range of hot and cold drinks and snacks. The FRC's popularity is reflected in the numbers of people who visit on a regular basis, and given the range of resources that it boasts, it should be the first place to visit on your 'to do' list!

THE NATIONAL ARCHIVES

The National Archives (TNA) was created when the Public Record Office (PRO) merged with the Royal Commission for Historical Manuscripts (HMC) in 2003. The collections are massive, with over 9.5 million original documents to choose from, order up and examine, as well as catalogues held by the National Register of Archives that you can browse for hundreds of other UK archives.

FINDING YOUR WAY AROUND TNA has three main floors: the ground floor is where you will find the lockers and cloakroom, as well as a shop, restaurant, Internet café and museum; the reference areas and reading rooms are located on the first and second floors, through security barriers that require you to swipe your reader's ticket to gain access.

So head to the first floor. There you will find an information desk where you should ask for initial advice and orientation. Depending on your enquiry, you will probably be shown to the main research enquiry desk, where members of staff are on hand to help you with your questions.

Also situated in this area are all the tools to help you get the most out of your visit, including the main set of printed catalogues, additional finding aids, leaflets, public search and ordering terminals and reference works on the shelves, as well as the holdings of the National Register of Archives.

On this floor, as well as various help points and photocopying facilities, you will find the document reading room, where (as the name suggests) you pick up your documents from numbered lockers and take them across to numbered desks on which to read them. Finally, a microfilm reading room and library are also to be found.

The second floor is reserved for large documents, maps and medieval and early modern material.

Because of the size of the collections, many people find TNA a little daunting, even off-putting – there's almost too much choice. It is best to start your research online by accessing their website (see contact details at the back of this book). There are sections where you can find out the basic steps, search their catalogues, read about some of the most popular searches and download specific information about documents and sources via research guides – many of which cover topics relevant to family history.

SOME PRELIMINARY RESEARCH

When you first arrive at the building, your bag will be checked at the security desk. You will then be asked to register as a reader to obtain a reader's ticket, which gives you access to the reading rooms and enables you to order documents. Simply enter your details on a computer, which takes no more than

GETTING YOUR READER'S TICKET

So Why do Most People Head to TNA?

The reason lies in the clues they have uncovered from basic sources such as census, certificates and wills — many of which you can also research, view or copy at TNA as well.

- Information about a military reference noted on a certificate can be followed up in a whole host of records at TNA. For example, a career in the army can be traced through pension and service records, pay lists and musters, medal entitlement and operation records, whilst similar material exists for the Royal Navy.
- The RAF was formed in 1918, and early service papers survive, as well as a host of operation record books for flights and missions flown in the Second World War.
- Britain's millions of merchant seaman can also be tracked through service papers, many of which provide photographic evidence of what our relatives looked like.

Of course, these personnel records represent only a small sample of the enormous range of documents you can uncover at TNA to further your knowledge of your ancestors; there are quite literally millions of other documents that might be of use, depending on the clues you pick up from the standard sources. For example, you may have found your ancestors living at an address in the 1901 census; you can see if they were still there in the early 1910s by checking the Valuation Office survey, as well as pinpointing the exact location where the house stood — or even still stands. An earlier land survey for predominantly rural areas, the tithe apportionments, can be used to locate families in the 1841 and 1851 census.

This is only the tip of the iceberg; there are apprenticeship records, legal papers from criminal trials, private court cases concerning property and inheritance disputes, older sources such as manorial records, naturalisation papers for immigrant ancestors, ships' passengers lists — there really is no aspect of our ancestors' lives that cannot be traced at TNA. Many of these sources are described in more detail in the second section of this book.

a couple of minutes, and then head to the registration desk where you will be asked for some identification — usually a passport, driving licence, bank or credit card. For overseas nationals a national identity card will suffice. You can register as a reader online in advance, but remember to bring the correct form of identification with you.

Once you have your reader's ticket, you can start your research. However, you will need to leave all your personal belongings in the lockers – this includes bags, overcoats, mobile phones, food, drink, pens, erasers, pencil sharpeners and other items which are prohibited in the reading room. In fact, all you should bring with you is some paper to take notes on – spiral-bound pads are acceptable, but no glued pads (this is for security purposes), a pencil, your reader's ticket, your locker key and some money for photocopies. These must be placed in a clear plastic bag, which TNA provides, for security purposes. If you have a laptop, this can be taken into the reading rooms as well, but should also be placed in one of the clear bags. Digital cameras are permitted, provided you register with the document copying section on the first floor.

THE READING ROOM'S RULES AND REGULATIONS

It is worth spending some time reading through the rules and regulations, especially if you have not worked with original documents before. You are given a list of 'Dos and Don'ts' when you register as a reader, including how to handle the documents. There are security guards patrolling who will help you set a document up properly if you are unsure of what you are doing.

The hardest part is finding your document reference, which is why it helps to do as much reading as possible before you visit, and make full use of the enquiry services. Once you have your reference, you need to order the document from the repository floors and you do this by making use of the ordering terminals, situated in every room. Select the document order option, swipe your reader's ticket through the barcode reader attached to the terminal, and follow the prompts to select somewhere to sit in the reading room. Then, enter the document reference and within 30 to 40 minutes it should be ready for you to collect in the main reading room – the locker number is the same as the seat you have selected, and the system is completely self-service – you help yourself, and return the documents to the main counter when you have finished examining them. You can examine three loose items on your desk at one time, but only one boxed item – this is to ensure that material does not get mixed up or lost.

YOUR DOCUMENT REFERENCE

READERS' GUIDES

To help get you started, and assist you with finding relevant resources in the archive, TNA has produced a range of readers' guides. These cover the most popular topics covered by the 9.5 million original records in TNA, and are designed to lead you straight to either the Catalogue, or other reference, works so you can locate relevant documents. They are available both online and onsite, and are divided into four principal categories – topics covering domestic affairs within England, Wales and the UK; legal matters; military themes; and overseas topics. They are the best way to understand fully a particular line, and will tell you about the records relating to that theme. This is an important part of your work, as you will have to think about why the document was created in order to interpret correctly what it was saying – don't forget, these are historic items, often hundreds of years old, and were not initially created with a twenty-first century family historian in mind!

TNA'S ONLINE CATALOGUE

TNA has also produced an electronic version of its catalogue, which can be searched online. You can submit keywords, and restrict the search to a specific date range, and any document descriptions that contain your keyword in their description will appear. However, many documents do not include in their official catalogue description all the personal names that they contain, so consequently many documents will not appear in your keyword search even though they may be relevant. It is therefore worth searching again by topic or place, and even then you should use onsite finding aids, indexes, guides, leaflets and the advice desk to make sure you do not miss any important items and that you get the most out of the collection.

So if you feel a little daunted on your first visit, it is worth coming back again and again until you become more familiar with the procedures. The time investment you make will be rewarded many times over as you discover the joy of researching in original material that sheds light on the lives of your distant relatives. This, after all, is the addictive nature of family history and why so many people find it Britain's most exciting pastime.

Opposite: This photographic portrait has started to fade, so it might be worth taking it to a restorer.

CHAPTER 4

The Basic Sources

So far, I have looked at the early stages of your research, focusing on how you can obtain raw data about your family from interviews with relatives, family legend, heirlooms and documents found within the immediate family. The organisation of this information into a structured family tree linked the names of your relatives with dates of notable events in your family's history; the real importance of the tree is that it visually highlights areas that require verification or further research. It is the task of the methodical family historian to seek concrete evidence to confirm the tree you have already constructed, and obtain new data that will permit searches further back in time to previous generations of your family.

It is now time to learn about the basic sources that all family historians use to research their ancestors in England and Wales – certification data, census returns, probate documentation and parish registers. These documents record a person's journey through life and beyond, and by careful manipulation of the sources, not only should you be able to add lines and branches to your family tree, but also begin to understand more about the lives of your ancestors.

The following sections are not intended to be exhaustive reference works; there is plenty written about the documents already, both in specialist books and online, so instead I want to provide you with sufficient data to understand why the sources are important, how they can be located, what information they contain and how you can use these data to widen your research to other sources.

Opposite: Digital imaging software might be able to preserve the beauty of this young girl for years to come.

However, a quick reminder before we start: when you are looking at any primary source material, it is important to remember to contextualise the data you obtain. None of the following types of document was specifically created for the benefit of twenty-first century family historians, so care must be taken when interpreting their contents to avoid making mistakes and getting frustrated if you can't find what you are looking for.

CIVIL REGISTRATION OF BIRTHS, MARRIAGES AND DEATHS

Today, every birth, marriage and death is officially registered and a certificate created to record details of the event. These certificates provide crucial evidence for the family historian, not just about the person concerned but also about relatives involved. Registration in England and Wales began in 1837 and continues in the present day. Consequently this should be the first source that a new family historian should tackle, as the information contained in the certificates should initially be used to verify data obtained from your initial research phase within the family. Soon you will be generating names of yet undiscovered relatives…

BACKGROUND

The rapid population expansion of the early nineteenth century, coupled with concerns over the implications of urban growth on public health and poverty, led to the creation of the Office of the Registrar General. Its remit was to collect statistical data on demographic trends, which would be used to govern the country more effectively. One of the most important strands in this policy was the introduction of civil registration for births, marriages and deaths in England and Wales from 1 July 1837. Previously, the task of recording people's journey through life had remained the prerogative of the church, whether Anglican, Catholic, non-conformist or foreign; registers of baptisms, marriages and burials were compiled at a local level, but were not collated centrally.

With the introduction of civil registration, the state took responsibility for recording personal information. Local Registration Districts and Sub-Districts were created, initially based on Poor Law Union boundaries, with each district covering a defined geographical area. The boundaries of these districts were altered in 1852, and again in 1946, to reflect demographic and administrative changes; a further amendment to the registration system occurred in 1983, when annual lists were compiled, rather then four quarterly lists.

Essentially, civil registration of a birth, a marriage or a death was (and remains) a local phenomenon. Whereas, previously, record keeping was a by-product of the ceremony, and thus the responsibility of the presiding official in the local church, the onus was now on the individual to inform the authorities of the event.—

Above: A proud bride on her wedding day; this can be used to track down the wedding certificate.

Imagine your ancestor had just got married, given birth to a child or lost a partner. A trip to the local register office was required, where the officials would be notified that the event had taken place. The informant would be given a certificate recording the key facts, and a copy of the certificate made in the register. After three months, an index of all registered events would be made, and the information recorded in the local registry office was forwarded to the Registrar General's office. Central indexes incorporating all registration districts were compiled, and were cross-referenced by the official code allocated to every local district.

In theory, it should be possible to identify the date of any birth, marriage and death in England and Wales between 1837 to date. However, in practice this is rarely the case. There are several reasons why an event might not be recorded. For a start, errors are known to have occurred during the transfer of data from

Opposite: A full birth certificate showing the child's name, date of birth, and details of both parents.

the district registries to the Registrar General's Office, and so the central lists may be incomplete or incorrectly indexed. Perhaps more significantly, penalties for non-registration before 1875 were not strictly enforced, and therefore there was less compulsion for people to come forward with information. The law was eventually tightened up and the enforcement of stringent fines for non-registration after this date ensured more events were recorded, although it is quite alarming that recent studies based on other sources indicate that up to one-third of all births between 1837 and 1875 probably went unregistered. Some families were more diligent than others, so if one event was recorded, the chances are high that others would have been as well.

WHAT THE CERTIFICATES CONTAIN

Your task as a family historian is to locate certificates relevant to your ancestors using either the local or centrally compiled indexes; but before the processes are described, it is important that you understand exactly what each certificate is going to contain, so you can use them more effectively to find other relatives further back in time.

BIRTH CERTIFICATES

The information provided on a birth certificate is perhaps the most useful if you are attempting to trace data about earlier generations. The date of birth is invariably recorded, along with the address of the birth. The name of the baby is also given – although this data is usually the starting point of the search, it can sometimes throw up surprises such as unknown middle names or even the fact that your ancestor was one of a pair of twins. Of more importance is the full name and maiden surname of the mother; and usually (but not always) the full name and occupation of the father of the child, if he was the husband or was present at the registration. The name and address of the informant was also recorded, plus their relationship to the child. An additional entry from 1969 records the place of birth of both parents.

CAUTION—Any person who (1) falsifies any of the particulars on this certificate or (2) uses a falsified certificate as true knowing it to be false, is liable to prosecution.

CERTIFIED COPY OF AN ENTRY
Pursuant to the Births and   Deaths Registration Act 1953

NHS Number	LJASS 165 **BIRTH**	Entry No. 165

Registration district	**CAMDEN** Administrative area
Sub-district	**CAMDEN** LONDON BOROUGH OF CAMDEN

CHILD

1. Date and place of birth — Sixth July 1982. Royal Free Hospital Camden.

2. Name and surname — Natalie Lucienne Hunt   3. Sex — Female

FATHER

4. Name and surname — Roy Arthur Hunt

5. Place of birth — Middlesex

6. Occupation — Architect

MOTHER

7. Name and surname — Nicole Marie-Louise Hunt

8. Place of birth — South Wales

9. (a) Maiden surname — Parry   (b) Surname at marriage if different from maiden surname —

10. Usual address (if different from place of child's birth) — Flat 3. 142 Goldhurst Terrace. NW6

INFORMANT

11. Name and surname (if not the mother or father) —   12. Qualification — Father.

13. Usual address (if different from that in 10 above) —

14. I certify that the particulars entered above are true to the best of my knowledge and belief — R.A. Hunt.   Signature of informant

15. Date of registration — Sixth August 1982   16. Signature of registrar — M J Wotherspoon Registrar.

17. *Name given after registration, and surname —

* See note overleaf

Certified to be a true copy of an entry in a register in my custody

W J Wotherspoon. Registrar   6th August 1982 Date

B. Cert.
R.B.D.

DV 570411

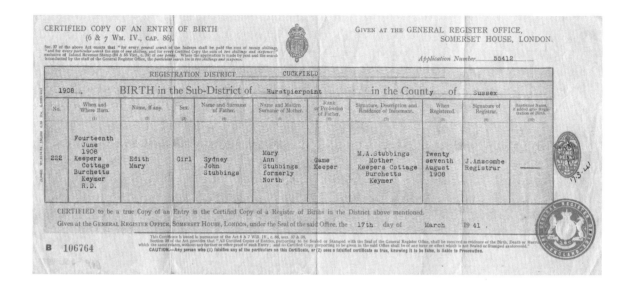

No.	When and Where Born.	Name, if any.	Sex.	Name and Surname of Father.	Name and Maiden Surname of Mother.	Rank or Profession of Father.	Signature, Description and Residence of Informant.	When Registered.	Signature of Registrar.	Baptismal Name, if added after Registration of Birth.
222	Fourteenth June 1908 Keepera Cottage Burchetts Keymer R.D.	Edith Mary	Girl	Sydney John Stubbings	Mary Ann Stubbings formerly North	Game Keeper	M.A.Stubbings Mother Keepers Cottage Burchetts Keymer	Twenty seventh August 1908	J.Anscombe Registrar	—

REGISTRATION DISTRICT CUCKFIELD

1908 BIRTH in the Sub-District of Hurstpierpoint in the County of Sussex

CERTIFIED to be a true Copy of an Entry in the Certified Copy of a Register of Births in the District above mentioned.

Given at the GENERAL REGISTER OFFICE, SOMERSET HOUSE, LONDON, under the Seal of the said Office, the 17th day of March 19 41 .

B 106764

Above: This birth certificate reveals that the father worked as a gamekeeper, probably on the nearest large estate.

Therefore birth certificates provide a gateway to the preceding generation through parental name data. Residential addresses might also be useful to cross-reference with other sources, such as census returns, to locate other siblings, whilst the inclusion of an occupation allows you to make further enquiries at other archives and institutions about social status and professional standing.

MARRIAGE
CERTIFICATES

When verifying parentage, it is useful to obtain a copy of the marriage certificate. This should contain the date and place of the marriage, and whether it was performed by banns, licence or certificates. The marital status of the bride and groom are recorded, which can be of interest if you suspect this was a second marriage (look for 'widow/er' or 'divorcee'). Yet the crucial nuggets of information are the names and ages of the bride and groom – though in early certificates you may find 'full age' listed to indicate they were over 21 – and the names and occupations of their fathers. This data can be used to start a search for birth certificates for the bride and groom. Keep an eye out as well for witnesses – they can often be members of the family, or close friends – whilst the religious beliefs of the family can be discerned from the certificate, for example if the wedding took place in an Anglican church, a Methodist chapel, according to the rites of the Roman Catholic church or in a synagogue.

Above: **The marriage certificate of the gamekeeper and his wife, featured on the opposite page.**

❦

Death certificates can often be the most useful starting point for research, especially if you know little about the individual you are looking for. As well as confirming the name, date, cause and place of death of the deceased, you will find out their given age, allowing you to look for a birth certificate and thus parentage. After 1 April 1969, death certificates record the date and place of birth of the deceased, their last known address and, if a married/widowed woman, their maiden name. In addition, you are likely to find the occupation of the deceased man, or that of the husband of a married or widowed woman. Although this might be of no immediate use, it can give you an insight into the lives of your ancestors, and might be useful in verifying other source material.

   The age at death is probably the greatest use to a family historian, as you can use this to work out a date of birth. Similarly, a death certificate permits you to search for other associated records, such as a burial entry or a will. However, the cause of

DEATH
CERTIFICATES

IV 898780

The statutory fee for this certificate is 3s. 9d.
Where a search is necessary to find the entry,
a search fee is payable in addition.

CERTIFIED COPY of an ENTRY OF DEATH.
Pursuant to the Births and Deaths Registration Act, 1953.

[Printed by authority of the Registrar General.]

D. Cert.
R.B.D.

Registration District   ST. MARYLEBONE

1958   Death in the Sub-district of ALL SOULS   in the METROPOLITAN BOROUGH OF ST. MARYLEBONE

Columns:— 1	2	3	4	5	6	7	8	9
No.	When and where died.	Name and surname.	Sex.	Age.	Occupation.	Cause of death.	Signature, description, and residence of informant.	When registered.	Signature of registrar.
268	Twentyfirst June 1958 Middlesex Hospital St Marylebone	Harry Victor Prior	Male	55 years	of 29 Keswick Avenue Kingston Vale Malden Survey Road Porter (Hospital)	Coronary atheroma Certified by W.B.Purchase Coroner for County of London after post mortem without Inquest	W. Webster Causing this body to be cremated 61 Linnell Road S. E. 5.	Twenty fifth June 1958	E.R.Sanders Registrar.

I, ROBERT R. SANDERS   , Registrar of Births and Deaths for the Sub-district of   ALL SOULS   , in the METROPOLITAN BOROUGH OF ST. MARYLEBONE
do hereby certify that this is a true copy of Entry No. 268 in the Register Book of Deaths for the said Sub-district, and that such Register Book is now legally in my custody.

WITNESS MY HAND this   25th day of   June   . 19 58 .   E.R.Sanders

CAUTION.—Any person who (1) falsifies any of the particulars on this certificate, or (2) uses a falsified certificate as true, knowing it to be false, is liable to prosecution.

Registrar of Births and Deaths.

Above: Death certificates can tell you a great deal about your relatives, including biographical data such as age and cause of death.

death can be of great interest, particularly if you feel that there is a pattern starting to emerge concerning a line of your family tree. Secrets can also be unearthed on a death certificate – unusual circumstances surrounding a death often resulted in a coroner's inquest, many of which were reported in the local newspapers.

HOW TO SEARCH FOR CERTIFICATES

Opposite: Associated documents, such as this cremation invoice, are often found amongst family papers.

Certified copies of entries in the English and Welsh registers can be obtained from either the local registry office, or the central register which is now held at the Office of National Statistics, Southport. The first step is to identify an entry in the indexes, which are free to consult. If you know where your family came from, you may want to start with the local registry indexes; but most people gravitate towards the central register, for which there are quarterly indexes from 1837 (March, June, September and December, with each including the two preceding months), and after 1983 there are annual volumes. It is important to remember that the local and central indexes do not correlate, so never order a certified copy from the central register using an index reference obtained from the local registry – otherwise you will receive the documentation of a complete stranger!

STANLEY LEVERTON, J.P.
DERRICK W. LEVERTON, T.D.

LEVERTON & SONS LTD.

IVOR H. LEVERTON
BASIL L. LEVERTON

(Incorporating GREEN AND EDWARDS)

CAMDEN TOWN	90 Parkway, N.W.1	
REGENTS PARK	81 Albany St., N.W.1	
HAMPSTEAD	30 Heath St., N.W.3	
GOLDERS GREEN	624 Finchley Rd., N.W.11	
SWISS COTTAGE	1 Rosemont Rd., N.W.3	

FUNERAL & CREMATION DIRECTORS
MONUMENTAL MASONS
ALL COMMUNICATIONS TO

ESTABLISHED IN THE REIGN OF
KING GEORGE THE THIRD

TELEGRAMS: "RESTING" NORWEST LONDON

TELEPHONE: EUSton 1810

(Private Branch Exchange)

Head Office: 210-214 Eversholt St., EUSTON, N.W.1.

Mrs. Edith M. Prior.   4th. July 1958.

494/712.

27th. June

To the Funeral of the late

Mr. Harry Victor Prior.

Providing a furnished 'Feltham' Cremation Shell,

Embalming the Remains, and conveying to Kingston Crematorium,

Cremation Fees,

Hearse and two Limousines,

Attendance of Mr. Basil Leverton and Assistants,

	£	s	d
as arranged, 45 gns.	47	5	0
Announcement in The Times,	2	8	0
Use of Organ and Organist's Fee,	1	1	0
Gratuities at the Crematorium,		5	0
	£ 50	19	0

The indexes to the central register are located at the Family Records Centre in Islington, London, but microfiche copies are usually accessible at most county record offices and Family History Centres run by the Church of the Latter Day Saints. Alternatively, online access is available via a number of websites – www.1837online.com, www.familyrelatives.org and via the Free BMD project associated with www.ancestry.co.uk

Once you have located a relative in the index, make a note of the reference next to their name. This will consist of the registration district, usually a number/letter combination, or prior to 1852 a number in Roman numerals, followed by the page in the register on which the certificate was copied. Complete an application form at the FRC, pay the appropriate sum and you should receive the document posted to you within four working days of application, or it will be ready for collection if you prefer. Always remember to apply for a FULL certificate rather than a SHORT one, as the latter will contain less information. Full certificates currently cost £7 and take four working days to prepare, although there is a 24-hour service that costs £23 and requires collection in person. Alternatively you can make an online application via www.gro.gov.uk

Below: You can use birth certificates to find out about previous generations, provided you make use of the mother's maiden name to find a marriage certificate.

Whilst the indexes cannot provide the same information as the certificate, at various stages additional information was recorded that makes searching much easier. The index to births began to include the maiden name of the mother from September 1911, whereas marriages were cross-referenced against the name of the partner from March 1912. Yet of most use are the index to deaths, which record the age of the deceased from March 1866 and the actual date of birth from June 1969. This might be sufficient to start a search for a birth certificate without the need to order the death certificate, depending on the purpose of your search.

ॐ Handy Hints

The following notes provide guidance on structuring certification research.

RESEARCH STRATEGY

- ॐ As with all research, start from a known date and work backwards. This may mean looking first of all for the death certificate of a relative to obtain their age, and then using this information to trace their birth certificate.

- ॐ Wherever possible, try using other source material, such as ecclesiastical records, passports, notices in newspapers, or census returns, to locate initial data, especially if the event occurred prior to 1875. This will make searching the indexes much easier.

- ॐ Use basic maths to work out possible dates of births of siblings, bearing in mind that the minimum age gap between births would be nine months. It is unlikely that there would be a subsequent birth listed within the same calendar year, unless the first birth took place in the March quarter.

- ॐ If you suspect your ancestor was one of a twin or multiple birth, you should see several entries in the index under the same surname that share the same registration details and page number; alternatively order the certificate before and after the known relative, as there is a strong likelihood that registration would have been consecutive.

❧ If you have only a rough idea of when an event occurred, start with the suspected date and then expand your search to two to three years either side. Age data from other sources, especially census returns, can be unreliable.

PROBLEMS WITH NAMES

❧ If you are having difficulty locating the event of a known relative, always check to see if they are entered under a different first name; we often refer to relatives by their nicknames, pet names or by an abbreviated version.

❧ Similarly, always try looking for an alternative surname spelling, as they were often recorded phonetically.

❧ If you are researching a common name – for example Smith in England, or Jones in Wales – it is important to find a unique personal identifier. This might be a middle name, a mother's maiden name or a particular registration district.

❧ If the surname is unusual, you may be able to compile a list of all birth, marriage and death events within one region and thus start to connect some of the individuals to produce an extended family; some of these individuals may be relevant to your research, and you can use other sources such as census returns to corroborate your findings.

❧ First-born children often bear a traditional family name, either that of the father/mother or grandfather/grandmother (depending on whether it's a boy or girl). Similarly, unusual middle names may reflect a mother's maiden name or a place of birth.

REASONS FOR NON-APPEARANCE IN THE INDEXES

❧ Aside from clerical error and non-registration prior to 1875, there are other reasons why a name might not appear in the lists. For example, some people never married, yet recorded the same surname on children's birth certificates. Others were married after the birth of their children, so you may have to search for the registration under the mother's maiden name.

❧ Families in the army used a separate registration system. Indexes are available for consultation at the FRC.

- Similarly the registration of births, marriages or deaths of British citizens abroad were sometimes recorded in British consulates, and a variety of indexes is also available at the FRC.
- The FRC also holds a separate set of indexes covering births, marriages and deaths at sea, with additional records at The National Archives.

REGISTRATION IN OTHER PARTS OF THE UK AND IRELAND

Scottish civil registration was introduced on 1 January 1855, but certificates carry the additional information.

SCOTLAND

BIRTH CERTIFICATES
- time of birth
- date and place of parents' marriage

MARRIAGE CERTIFICATES
- mother's name and maiden name

DEATH CERTIFICATES
- marital status
- name of spouse
- father's name and profession
- mother's name and maiden name

The central registers and indexes are housed at the General Register Office, in Edinburgh (see Resources at the back of this book).

Irish civil registration was introduced on 1 January 1864, but the registers and indexes are split between two archives. Records for the whole of Ireland up to 1921, and the Republic of Ireland thereafter, are located at the General Register Office of Ireland in Dublin, with online copy certificates available for purchase at http://www.groireland.ie. Indexes and registers for Northern

IRELAND

PLACE	HOUSES		NAMES of each Person who abode therein the preceding Night.	AGE and SEX		PROFESSION, TRADE, EMPLOYMENT, or of INDEPENDENT MEANS.	Where Born	
	Uninhabited or Building	Inhabited		Males	Females		Whether Born in same County	Whether Born in Scotland, Ireland, or Foreign Parts.
Upper Wharton P			Emely D.		month		Y	
			Eliza Rowe		15	F S ✓		N
29		1	William Casper	30		Linen Draper	Y	
			Jane Do		30			N
			Edward Do	2			Y	
			Jane Do		month		Y	
			Mary Lunden		30	F S ✓		N
			Wm Clive		15	F S ✓		N
30		1	Eliz.th Hernsley		30	Ind		N
			Ellen Sullivan		25	F S ✓		I
Cumberland Cottage		1	Wm Turnadge	50		Porter ✓	N	
			Martha Do		50			N
			Charlotte Do		10			N
Cumberland Place No 1		1	Clark Tomalin	50		Clerk ✓	N	
			Isabella Do		35		Y	
			Henry Do	15				N
			Mary Mahagan		20	F S ✓		I
2		1	Joseph Wilson	30		Merchant		N
			Joseph Do	1			Y	
			Sarah Sayer		20	F S ✓		N
3		1	Charles Pat	40		Ribbon M.y	Y	
			Ellen Connoly		25	St S ✓		I
4		1	Henry Dunster	55		Solicitor ✓		N
			Rich.d Do	55		Accounting		N
			Frederick Do	20		Procter		N
TOTAL in Page 19	1			11	14			

Ireland are located at the General Register Office in Belfast, with a duplicate index at the FRC. It is possible to purchase copy certificates from

http:///www.groni.gov.uk

You will also find civil registration for the Isle of Man and the Channel Islands began at different dates. The registers can be seen at the relevant registrar's office.

🎴 CENSUS RETURNS

The best approach if you are new to research is to employ a stepping stone approach to your initial searches, focusing on one relative at a time and using birth, marriage and death certificates to obtain enough data to search for the previous generation. Careful research enables most people to reach the beginning of the twentieth century with relative ease; and whilst this process can be continued back to the introduction of civil registration in 1837, there are limitations. For instance, it becomes more difficult to locate events prior to 1875 when registration was not strictly compulsory. Furthermore, it is a linear research technique, as the process only provides data about the preceding generation rather than information about siblings, uncles, aunts or grandparents. Consequently, family historians who have tracked down ancestors to the end of the nineteenth century broaden their research by utilising another product of the state's interest in population statistics – the decennial censuses, first initiated in Britain in 1801. The information contained in census returns enables the diligent researcher to discover additional data about non-linear family members, as well as place ancestors in the local communities in which their daily lives took place.

Opposite: An entry from the 1841 census, the first set of returns to list the names of each person living in every household.

BACKGROUND

Right: Census returns can often reveal an ancestor who served in the military, such as this soldier pictured in the photo.

From the time of the Roman Empire, governments across the world have used the headcount as a means to obtain statistical data about the population for administrative and taxation purposes. Yet in Britain, the first formal census was taken on 10 March 1801 for military reasons; the fear of invasion by the forces of Napoleon Bonaparte prompted the government of the day to assess how many people could be mobilised in the event of French troops landing on British soil, as well as preparatory planning for general civil defence. Thereafter, a census was taken every 10 years, with the exception of 1941 due to the intervention of another period of military fear, the Second World War.

To make administration easier, England and Wales were sub-divided into census regions; from 1841, these regions correspond with the districts and sub-districts created for civil registration. This makes it easier for you to move from one source to the other. Each sub-district was divided into smaller enumeration districts, and an enumerator took responsibility for collecting standardised data from everyone within the area on the night of the census. These schedules were then copied into census enumerators' books, which are the records you will be accessing during your research.

The censuses taken in 1801, 1811, 1821 and 1831 are of little relevance to the family historian, as the exercise was intended to obtain limited statistical data based on the total number of people living in each house, broken down into categories reflecting age, gender and status. The exercise was quintessentially English, with local enumerators appointed to wander the streets of their district, recording numbers of people in response to a fairly basic list of questions.

Yet in both 1821 and, more particularly, 1831, some enumerators took it upon themselves to make more extensive personal notes, such as the names of the heads of households. A good example is Richard Stopher, the 1831 enumerator for Saxmundham, Suffolk. As well as the simple statistical data he was required to collect, he not only recorded the names of the heads of household for every property in the village, but also a potted history of the occupancy of each house, listing the names of previous residents and general biographical miscellanea in his notebook – now preserved in the Suffolk Record Office.

RICHARD STOPHER TOOK MORE DETAIL

Men like Richard Stopher helped generate an important change in the questions that were asked in the next census, taken on 6 June 1841, in which, for the first time, the names of every household occupant were recorded. Further data was requested in the returns issued on 30 March 1851, which created an important source of social and genealogical material. There are

Left: Entire streets can be researched through census records, as the enumerators would walk from door to door, collecting information.

limitations to the information contained in census returns, which are explained later in this section, but the most important drawback is that the records are closed for 100 years for confidentiality purposes. The next census returns to be made public are those of 1911, currently due for release on 1 January 2012. This is the main reason why researchers turn to the census only after they have used registration data to get back to the turn of the nineteenth century.

WHAT THE CENSUS RETURNS CONTAIN

CENSUS RETURNS 1801–1831

The dates of the first four censuses are 10 March 1801, 27 May 1811, 28 May 1821 and 29 May 1831. Only the following totals were required for each parish: occupied and unoccupied houses; families; men and women; occupations; and baptism, marriage and burial statistics. However, local record offices are likely to hold any extensive personal returns that were created by enumerators.

THE 1841 CENSUS

On 6 June 1841, information about individuals was requested for the first time, recorded in columns on a grid-like form. They can be difficult to read, as the enumerators used pencil to record the information and the quality of handwriting varies. In theory, the enumerators obtained the following data from every resident within his district:

- Forename and surname
- Age, rounded down to the nearest five years if over 15
- Sex
- Occupation
- Where they were born, either in the county of residence (Y or N – yes or no), Scotland (S), Ireland (I) or foreign parts (P).

The undermentioned Houses are situate within the Boundaries of the

Civil Parish [or Township] of	Municipal Borough of	Municipal Ward of	Parliamentary Borough of	Town or Village or Hamlet of	Urban Sanitary District of	Rural Sanitary District of	Ecclesiastical District of
Kensington		St John & St James	Chelsea				All Saints

Page 4]

No. of Schedule	ROAD, STREET, &c., and No. or NAME of HOUSE	HOUSES	NAME and Surname of each Person	RELATION to Head of Family	CON-DITION as to Marriage	AGE last Birthday of Males	AGE last Birthday of Females	Rank, Profession, or OCCUPATION	WHERE BORN	(1) Deaf (2) Blind (3) (4)
			Lizzie Johnson	Serv	Un		28	Cook	Liverpool Lancashire	
			Mary Canfield	do	do		27	"	Brighton Surrey	
217	29 Arundel Gardens	1	Maurice Schwabacher	Head	Mar	54		Diamond Mer.	Bristone Hungary	
			Rosa do	Wife	do		37		Vienna Austria	
			Isidore do	Son		16		Scholar	Paris	
			Fanny do	Daur			13	do	do	
			Antoine do	Son		12		do	do	
			Lily do	Daur			8	do	do London	
			John do	Son		6		do	do	
			Ernest do	Brother	Un	30		Diamond Mer.	Vienna	
			Joseph Latz	Serv	Mar	33		Shop Serv.	France	
			Wilhelmine Schmuntz	do	Un		22	Cook do	Hamburg Prussia	
			Annie Butler	do	do		20	Dom Serv.	Essex	
			Agnes Young	do	do		19	do	Southampton	
218	27	1	Wolf Myers	Head	Mar	38		Clothing Contractor Tailor	Essex Chelmsford	
			Esther do	Wife	do		30		Surrey Stockwell	
			Charles J do	Son		8		Scholar	Middx Kensington	
			Stephen do	do		7		do	do do	
			Arthur P do	do		5			do do	
			William W do	do		3			do do	
			Henry G do	do		1			do do	
			Elizabeth Clarke	Serv	Un		23	Dom Serv.	Bressingham Norfolk	
			Susannah Walker	do	do		24	do	Middx Islington	
			Eliza Miles	do	do		19	do	Berkshire	
2	Total of Houses.. 2				Total of Males and Females..	13	15			

NOTE.—Draw the pen through such of the words of the headings as are inappropriate.

Relationships between family members are not noted. Although an address for each property was required, it is rare to find anything other than the name of the hamlet in rural areas, or the street name if situated in a town or city. Similarly, take great care with the recorded ages. They are usually very misleading, as people aged 59 and 61 would be recorded as 55 and 60 respectively, and it is possible to find two or more children listed as aged 15, whereas in fact they may have been aged 19, 17 and 15. Therefore you will have to use other sources, such as later returns or ecclesiastical registers, to obtain accurate data.

Above: Census returns offer a tantalising glimpse into the workings of a Victorian household.

CENSUS RETURNS 1851–1901

The returns for the censuses taken on 30 March 1851, 7 April 1861, 2 April 1871, 3 April 1881 and 5 April 1891 all contain roughly the same information, much expanded from the 1841 returns. They are also in general far easier to interpret, having been completed in ink. The format was still a grid-based enumeration form, though greatly expanded from 1841 to take the additional information. The following data can be expected for each individual:

- forename, middle name (often an initial) and surname
- relationship to head of household
- marital status
- age at last birthday, including how many months for infants under one year old
- gender
- occupation or source of income
- county and parish of birth if in England or Wales; or country of birth if outside
- any medical disabilities they might have suffered from
- from 1891 in Wales: language spoken

Although the level of detail provided was still at the discretion of the enumerator – and the willingness of the householders to co-operate – an increasing amount of information is provided about property addresses. More house names or numbers are increasingly used as time progressed, though earlier returns for rural areas still tend to group houses by hamlet or street. Each property is separated from the next by double parallel lines in the margin, with households within a single property separated by a single line.

THE 1901 CENSUS   The returns of the 1901 census, taken on 31 March, were made public on 1 January 2002. They contain the same data as those from 1851–1891, with the following additions:

- whether an employer or employee
- language spoken in Isle of Man

The enumerators' returns for England and Wales were sent to the Registrar General's office, and the archives are now held at The National Archives. Although the originals cannot be viewed, the returns have been made available on microform (film or fiche), and can be consulted at a number of locations. The Family Records Centre, Islington, London, holds national returns on microfilm from 1841–1891, plus 1901 on microfiche, and most local record offices retain relevant county copies. It is also possible to hire extra-county census returns from the nearest LDS Family History Centre.

The popularity of family history has led a number of companies to digitise the census returns and create searchable name databases, available online. The main place to visit is www.ancestry.co.uk, as you can gain access to all census returns from 1841–1901, as well as the Free BMD (Births, Death and Marriages) database for civil registration indexes. The site requires you to register as a user for an annual subscription, but thereafter you can look at all their datasets including the census returns. However, Ancestry have partnered with The National Archives, and you can search and view census images free of charge at either TNA or FRC – the only cost you will incur is when you print out all your findings! Other websites allow you to view some census records, but only Ancestry has all returns in one place.

1841–1901

CENSUS RETURNS

ONLINE

A search field allows you to type in information about someone you suspect should appear in the records, though it is sometimes a good idea to put less information in. The SOUNDEX function allows you to search for people with similar-sounding names – often a good idea, as transcription errors occasionally occur in the database so you might have to try several surname combinations if you cannot find the person you are looking for. A list of possible matches appears, with some basic biographical information that allows you to select a likely candidate. You can either view a transcription of the entry, or see the original census return.

1841–1901
CENSUS RETURNS
AT THE FRC

Most county record offices hold fairly comprehensive means of access to their copies of census records, so the following explanations refer to the FRC only.

If you do not have access to the Internet, or cannot find the person you are looking for in the database, then you should look on the microfilm in person – this is something you should consider doing even if you have found someone, because a search of the wider area can often throw up other family members in the same village, whilst at the same time gaining a sense of who lived in the parish and what the principal professions were.

Census returns are arranged by registration district, sub-district and enumerators' districts, so a degree of local knowledge is essential. First, you will need to check the Place Name Index, which lists every place, hamlet, village or town in England and Wales, cross-referenced to the Registration District. The exception is the 1841 census, where you are directed to a page number in the Reference Books.

Below: Names, ages, occupations and places of birth are given for every household from 1851 onwards.

Next, locate the page number or Registration District in the Reference Books and identify the place you are looking for. The far left-hand column will contain The National Archives document reference for this place, and all you need to do is to select the relevant roll of microfilm bearing this reference. A summary of The National Archives series codes is provided:

1841: HO107/1-1465
1851: HO107/1466-2531
1861: RG9/1-4543
1871: RG10/1-5785
1881: RG11/1-5632
1891: RG12/1-5643
1901: RG13/1-5338

In addition to the Place Name indexes, larger towns or cities are likely to have Street Name indexes. This provides a useful shortcut if you have a known address, perhaps from trade or residential directories, or certification data.

Of even greater use are retrospectively compiled name indexes. The most comprehensive in terms of national coverage is for 1881, which contains 26 million names across England and Wales, arranged by surname at county and national level. Access is also available online at http://www.familysearch.org – the website of the Church of the Latter Day Saints.

Additionally, there are numerous ad hoc surname indexes prepared by local family history societies or groups, with the returns for 1851 having greatest coverage. At the FRC, reference is made to these additional finding aids in the Place Name index next to the registration district, and separate paper lists are available for consultation. The surname indexes are arranged differently according to the group that compiled them, but reference to the document, folio and page number is normally made, providing a neat shortcut to the relevant census return.

❧ Handy hints

RESEARCH STRATEGY

❧ As with all other types of research, start with more recent data and work backwards. However, in common with all name index databases, errors will have crept in, and thus it will be hard to locate ancestors if their names have been incorrectly transcribed in the indexes. In these instances you will have to conduct a manual trawl.

❧ Always conduct simultaneous research in both census returns and civil registration indexes, as you can use information from one search to facilitate research in another. For example, age from census returns can be used to locate a marriage or birth, whilst addresses on certificates can narrow down where to look in the census records. However, bear in mind that census ages are not always accurate, and therefore you should proceed with caution in the civil registration indexes, searching a year or two either side of the probable date.

❧ Careful manipulation of census and certificate data in tandem should enable you to not only work back towards ancestors who were born in the late eighteenth or early nineteenth century, but widen your family tree to include siblings of direct antecedents located through certificate searches.

❧ In urban areas you can use additional sources, such as trade or local residential directories, to narrow down your search to a particular street or residential district.

❧ From the occupation data contained in the census returns, it is possible to find out more about the daily lives of your ancestors – where they worked, whether a family trade was passed through the family, or if their status rose or fell over time.

❧ Finally, when you have found a relevant entry, make sure you note the full census reference for your records. This should include the folio and page number from which you extracted data, as well as The National Archives reference (RG11, HO107, etc.)

REASONS FOR PEOPLE'S NON-APPEARANCE IN THE RETURNS

இ If your relative does not appear in the expected place, it could be that they were away from their residence on the night the census was taken. This a major drawback of census returns – they represent a mere snapshot of residency for only a single night in a 10-year period.

இ Even with name indexes, it can still be very difficult to trace people who travelled the country to seek work, or moved away from the traditional family location, between census years.

இ In rural areas, it is always worth considering a search of the neighbouring parish, particularly if an ancestor got married in the intervening years and went to live near their partner's family.

இ Similarly it is always worth checking institutions, such as barracks, prisons, schools, workhouses or asylums, and vessels at sea, which are included separately in census returns from 1851.

OTHER DRAWBACKS TO CENSUS RETURNS

இ Remember that householders voluntarily provided the data recorded by the enumerators. Incorrect information is therefore likely to have been passed across, particularly amongst people suspicious of state interest in their private lives.

இ In particular, some names have been recorded erroneously on census forms, particularly if the enumerator wrote them down phonetically. Alternatively, householders might provide 'pet' names instead of their real ones, or swap first and middle names over.

இ You will often find that ages of family members may fluctuate between census years. Once again this is due to incorrect information provided by the householders or through enumerator error.

இ You may find that other data can be wrong, such as the place of birth. Indeed, even relationships between family members can be inaccurately recorded, as terms such as 'cousin' and 'brother' were used to describe distant blood relatives or relations through marriage.

CENSUS RETURNS FOR SCOTLAND AND IRELAND

Scottish census returns are held at the General Register Office, Edinburgh, and can be viewed on appointment for a fee.

Even though a census was taken in Ireland from 1821-1911, few nineteenth-century Irish census returns have survived. Those for 1861–1891 were deliberately destroyed, whilst only a few for 1821–1851 survived a fire at The National Archives in 1922. Those for 1901 and 1911 are available in the Republic of Ireland at the National Archives, Dublin, with copies in the Public Record Office of Northern Ireland, Belfast.

(See contact details for the above in Resources at the back of this book.)

Below: A snapshot of rural life adds colour to the bare bones of a census return.

✢ Probate records

The death of an ancestor is an important event from
the perspective of a family historian, as the potential
for generating written evidence is far greater than any
other life event. We have seen how a death certificate
was issued in England and Wales after 1837,
providing the age at death or even date of birth; and
parish registers can provide data on burial, sometimes
leading to a gravestone with additional family
information inscribed upon it. This section deals with
a third possible line of research once the death of an
ancestor has been established in England or Wales –
the disposal of their possessions after death through
wills and letters of administration. Of these sources,
the last will and testament is usually the most
valuable, as it may record family relationships and
provide names of the deceased's partner, siblings or
children, as well as giving an insight into their
possessions, address, wealth, circle of friends and
occupation. Such crucial information can be used to
initiate searches in other records, and will almost certainly enrich your
knowledge of the way your ancestor once lived.

HELLIS & SONS.

Above: **Probate
records and wills can
tell us a surprising
amount about our
ancestors.**

   The following information is intended to provide basic guidance to the most
useful and readily accessible documents that are available to the family historian;
however, it does not cover a vast range of associated topics, such as contested
wills, court disputes and the mechanisms of probate. These are areas that you
may well need to investigate at a later stage of your research, but obtaining access
to and extracting information from the documents should be your first goal.

WHAT A WILL
CONTAINS

Today, we are expected to make and update wills on a regular basis, such as when we buy a house, get married, or have children. Our ancestors did the same, but the last will and testament was often literally just that — made when death seemed inevitable, often drawn up on their deathbed. The most pressing reason for making a will was religious belief, and thus most people began by commending their soul to Almighty God, asking for forgiveness of their sins, and arranging for Christian burial in their local parish churchyard. Some people were more meticulous than others: it has been known for detailed instructions to be left concerning the depth of the grave, materials to be used for the coffin, and the precise burial time.

Next, the testator would make specific bequests, usually starting with charitable gifts and then proceeding to members of the family and friends. It is this information that makes a will such an important source for family historians, as you can find out the circle of acquaintances, favoured children and siblings or treasured possessions and heirlooms — some of which may still be passed down within your family. Care has to be taken when interpreting this information, as basic descriptions such as brother, sister, father, mother were used indiscriminately for relatives through marriage, and not just blood kin. Furthermore, people may be omitted from the will for no other reason than that previous provision had been made for them, and so no further instructions were necessary.

Finally, the residue of the estate would pass by right either to the heir at law or the next of kin, unless specified in the will by the testator; and an executor or executors would be appointed to carry out the testator's instructions, with possibly an overseer also named to ensure the terms of the will were carried out. After the death and burial of the testator, the executors would seek official permission to administer the deceased's estate. Before 1858, the Church presided over the process, known as 'probate'. The executors took a copy of the will to the relevant ecclesiastical court, where a probate act would be granted. The seal of the court was attached to the will, signifying that the executor had authority to carry out its

Below: An official seal, used to authenticate important documents, including some medieval wills.

No. _16/222_   (Accts. 4.)   Effects.—Form 107.

I, _Miriam Abbott_

declare that _Alfred Abbott_

of _4/5 Yorks. Regiment_

who died on the _25th_ day of _April_   19_18_

If no Will was left insert "no" before "Will," and strike out the words in brackets. Any Will which it is not intended to prove should be forwarded for inspection.

left _a_ Will [which it is not intended to prove], and that Letters of Administration of this Estate or Confirmation have not been, and are not intended to be, taken out.

The only near relations left by the said _Alfred Abbott_

were as follows :—

Insert "None" if that is the fact in either case.

Relationship	Names in full		Addresses in full
Widow	_unmarried_		—
Children		Age	
—	_none_		—

Give degree of relationship.

Other relations			
Tom Abbott	_father_		_6 Alexandra R., Thorne_
Miriam do.	_mother_		_do._
Jane Catherine do.	_sister_		_do._
Alice do.	_sister_		_c/o T. Lawrence, Thorne?_
Hector do.	_brother_		_6 Alexandra R., Thorne_
Tom do.	_brother_		_do._
Evelyn do.	_sister_		_do._
Abbott do.	_brother_		_do._
Lily do.	_sister_		_do._
Alexander do.	_sister_		_do._

was born at _Thorne on Apr. 15th 1895_   _Miriam Abbott_

Alfred Abbott
Signature of the Applicant.

CERTIFICATE

I hereby certify that the above Statement made by _Miriam Abbott_
and signed in my presence is complete and correct, to the best of my knowledge and belief.

Dated at _Thorne_ this _17th_ day of _November_ 19_19_

Signature of Minister or Magistrate } _Rd. Servant_   Qualification _c.J.P. for W.R.Yorks._

Address _Thorne_
Doncaster

(4 6 62) W10115—RP3910 5000 5/19 H&V(P1227) H1209

Left: A letter of administration granted to the widow of a man who died without leaving a will, allowing her to dispose of his possessions.

terms. The probate act would be copied into the court's act book and, if requested, a copy of the will was recorded in separate will registers.

Of course, there is no guarantee that a will was ever made. Initially only personal estate – cash, belongings, furniture or leases – could be bequeathed (or 'devised') in a will, and thus real estate – land – was excluded until changes in the law in the sixteenth and seventeenth centuries. For this reason, many people did not make wills, as real estate would descend by right to the heir at law or next of kin, or prior provision had already been made for daughters' dowries. Many people simply had no personal possessions to bequeath, or died too suddenly to make a will.

Wills were usually written in the presence of witnesses; but, on rare occasions, the verbal requests of someone near death were noted by witnesses and then registered in the normal way. They are termed 'nuncupative' wills. In such cases when someone died 'intestate', that is without having made a will, the next of kin or heir at law would seek letters of administration from the relevant ecclesiastical court, which meant that they could distribute the possessions of the deceased as they saw fit. In many instances, the deceased's widow or next of kin was empowered by a probate court to distribute the estate as he or she saw fit; while anyone with a claim to the estate of the deceased could apply for a similar letter of administration. The estate of a deceased with no next of kin reverted to the state.

The original wills brought back from the ecclesiastical court were retained by the family or executor, and thus if they survive they are most likely to be amongst personal or private papers, usually deposited in the relevant county record office. Most are now lost, which means that records created by the ecclesiastical courts where the probate act was granted are the best place to look for information. Therefore you will require a basic knowledge of the historic structure of the ecclesiastical courts, which were based on the Church's hierarchy.

Opposite: Photos of the deceased were sometimes included on memorial cards circulated to friends and family.

WHERE TO FIND PROBATE MATERIAL

Where a will was proved or letter of administration granted depended on the value of the estate, and where the deceased's lands were situated.

- Probate for goods and property held solely within an archdeaconry was granted at the archdeacon's court. This was the norm for people of little property or wealth.
- Probate for goods and property held within more than one archdeaconry, but within one diocese, was granted at the bishop's diocesan court.
- Probate for goods and property valued at over £5, or held within more than one diocese or jurisdiction, was granted within the archbishop's Prerogative Court. Consequently the Prerogative Courts became much busier as more people found their estates valued above £5.
- There were two Prerogative Courts, one for the northern province of York (PCY) and another for the southern province of Canterbury (PCC). The former covered the counties of Yorkshire, Durham, Northumberland, Westmorland, Cumberland, Lancashire, Cheshire, Nottinghamshire and the Isle of Man; the remainder of England and all of Wales was in the latter.
- Probate for goods and property held in both provinces was granted in both.
- In addition, peculiars operated their own separate courts.
- After the English Civil War, a civil probate court was established in London in 1652 to hear all probate cases from both provinces. The court was abolished at the Restoration in 1660.

It is therefore important to know where your ancestor lived, so you can head for the relevant archive where the probate records are deposited. However, as the real value of money declined throughout the eighteenth and nineteenth centuries, more wills were proved in the Prerogative Courts.

The records generated by grants of probate are fairly complicated, but the source that family historians find to be of greatest use are the will registers, as they contain copies of all wills proved at an ecclesiastical court. Most will registers below Prerogative Court level are now deposited at the relevant Diocesan Record Office or County Record Office. In contrast, the records of the PCY (along with a number of separate courts for Yorkshire) are at the Borthwick Institute, York, whilst PCC material from 1383 is held by The National Archives, Kew. As there is no single name index that covers all these courts, you may need to visit several of these archives before finding an entry for your ancestor – if indeed they ever made a will. Nevertheless, the end results of a successful search are almost always worth the time and trouble taken, as the contents of a will reveal intimate details about the lifestyle and circle of friends and relatives of your ancestor.

Most will registers employ some form of internal reference system – for example, PCC registers are arranged by quire number, a block of eight folios or sixteen pages, and listed by the name of the Registrar rather than by year. Your task as a researcher is to extract this information from an index, use it to find

WILL REGISTERS AND ADMINISTRATION ACT BOOKS BEFORE 1858

Left: A street scene from London in the nineteenth century, showing just how different life was for our ancestors.

the relevant register and then hunt for the will within the specified block of pages. Although there is no central name index that covers all ecclesiastical courts, various cataloguing projects have produced indexes to local will registers at diocesan level or below, whilst the Borthwick holds indexes to PCY material. There are also calendars to the PCC Acts, which give access to both will registers and administration act books. From these, printed indexes have been compiled; and The National Archives has created an online database searchable by name for all PCC registered wills to 1858, with access to images of the wills for a small fee (though as with census records, you can view wills free of charge at both The National Archives and the Family Records Centre in person). This is a tremendously important resource, representing the first attempted complete name index of all PCC will registers.

If you can't find a will for your ancestor, it is worth checking to see whether there was a grant of letters of administration. The best place to start your search is within the administration act books, created by the relevant ecclesiastical authority. Apart from confirming that your ancestor died intestate, the letters of administration will tell you little more apart from the name of the person granted the power of administration, the address of the deceased and their relationship with the administrator. As with will registers, separate indexes are usually available for consultation.

ADMINISTRATIONS AND WILLS AFTER 1858

On 12 January 1858, important changes were made to the registration of grants of probate or letters of administration. The establishment of a central Probate Registry led to the abolition of the PCC and PCY; and from 1875 the Registry has been part of the Supreme Court. All grants of probate were registered at local probate courts under civil authority, with national name indexes to the registers compiled. The best source is the National Probate Calendar from 1858–1943, available on microform from CROs, which provides details of the

FURTHER RESEARCH

In addition to will registers and administration act books, other important documents were created during the probate process. One of the most interesting was the probate inventory, a list and valuation of the personal estate of the deceased, made by the executors and administrators. These are usually to be found in the relevant county record office or The National Archives, and provide a unique insight into the personal possessions of the deceased. You may recognise some of their belongings amongst your own treasured heirlooms!

The probate process was not always without problems. One of the most frequent difficulties was a disputed will, especially if one part of the family felt that underhand tactics had been used to 'change' a former bequest or promise of goods at the last moment; and even fraudulent alteration of wills was known to have occurred. Contested grants of probate were generally dealt with by the ecclesiastical courts, and the legal papers generated by the process can be usefully searched for further information on family feuds.

The introduction of a duty on the estate of deceased people above a certain limit in 1796 provides a useful way of searching for the relevant probate registry before 1858, as well as providing information on bequests, administration of estates and addresses of the deceased and their executors. The records are now at The National Archives, with indexes at the Family Records Centre in London, and might be worth checking if you are experiencing difficulty locating where a will was proved or letters of administration granted.

name of the deceased, details of the date and location of the grant, address at death, value of the estate and names of the executors. Indexes beyond 1943 are available from the main search room at the Principal Probate Registry of the Family Division, located at High Holborn, London (see Resources at the back of this book), where you can also order duplicate copies of probate grants and letters of administration. You can also access wills registered in local District Probate Registries.

SCOTLAND AND IRELAND

A separate system developed in Scotland, where testaments were created. These included an inventory of the deceased's possessions, and where a will was attached they are described as 'testament testators', the equivalent to the English grant of probate; where no will was attached they are called 'testament dative', similar to a grant of letters of administration. From 1515– 1823, commissary courts handled the process; and from 1824 the responsibility devolved to sheriffs, all commissary courts, with the exception of Edinburgh (which continues to function), having been abolished.

Most original Irish wills before 1900 were destroyed in Dublin in 1922. Surviving material is held at the Public Record Office of Northern Ireland from 1900, with indexes to will registers from 1858. Surviving local will registers prior to 1858 can be viewed on microfilm, and name indexes are also available.

✳ PARISH REGISTERS

Most researchers use certificates generated by civil registration and census returns to start their investigation, tracking back in a linear fashion via information on dates of birth, marriage and death to add new generations to the family tree. With diligent research, and perhaps a little bit of luck, it is possible to extend this process to discover ancestors who were born in the early nineteenth or late eighteenth century. At this point people often hit the dreaded 'wall'; their research grinds to a halt because there are no civil records with comprehensive nationwide coverage or access to name indexes before 1837.

If you are interested in going any further back in time, it is at this stage that the focus of your research will switch from national sources to the local area in which your ancestors lived, and thus utilise records generated by the daily activities of a community. The most important sources are known collectively as 'parish registers', where the key events in our ancestors' lives are reported – their baptism, marriage, and burial. If you want to use these records, now is the moment to gather the geographical clues that you have collected from civil registration and census returns – especially the place of birth – and use them to step back into a world before the Industrial Revolution, where people rarely moved outside their local parish unless they had to seek work in the nearest town or married into a family from a neighbouring community. If you are very lucky, the sources at your disposal will not only allow you to understand how your ancestors lived, but also to trace your roots as far back as the Middle Ages.

BACKGROUND

Ever since Christianity was first introduced to the British Isles, the Church dominated people's journey through life. The focal point of every hamlet, village or township was the parish church, and in addition to regular services of worship, special ceremonies were performed when infants were baptised into the religious community, couples were married, and upon death the deceased was laid to rest in consecrated ground in the churchyard. The dramatic theological changes of the Reformation altered the content and meaning of church services, but baptism, marriage and burial continued as before – with one important change. From 1538, the government decreed that every parish church must keep written records of these special ceremonies. The documents produced as a result of this decision – the parish registers – are the most important source for the genealogist wishing to research their ancestors before civil registration arrived three centuries later.

The registers were written by the parish priest and kept in the parish chest with other important documents used in the maintenance and administration of parochial life. Although registration was introduced in 1538, only a few parish registers have survived this far back, and on average the majority of English records begin in the early seventeenth century, and for Wales in the early eighteenth. The early registers are rarely complete; not every event was always recorded, and even in parishes where there is good sequential survival of records, there can be gaps where fire or flood has damaged or destroyed the documents. However, a copy of the parish registers was required by law to be made and forwarded to the bishop of the diocese in which the parish was situated, and

Right: Preparing the ground for the latest addition to a family tomb.

these copies can often provide supplementary information where the original registers have been lost.

Ecclesiastical registration continues today, but as a genealogical source parish registers become much harder to use once civil registration takes hold from the late nineteenth century. There are numerous reasons for this – the decline of the Anglican Church as a place of worship, the supplanting of religious ceremonies by civil ones (such as cremation instead of burial) and wider social changes, such as greater population movement prompted by the Industrial Revolution and transportation networks, that drove people away from 'traditional' communities, with the result that parish registers recorded fewer and fewer ceremonies. However, the initial overlap with the onset of civil registration from 1837 is particularly important – until the introduction of financial penalties for non-registration in 1875, many people did not bother to register a birth, marriage or death, particularly in rural communities where ties with tradition and locality were stronger, and therefore ecclesiastical records can be the only surviving record left of a person's journey through life.

The most important point to remember is that parish registers are records of ecclesiastical ceremonies – baptism, marriage and burial – rather than birth, marriage or death, and therefore the information they contain must be interpreted with care. People were not always baptised at once, and a number of months may have passed between the birth and the baptism ceremony; indeed, adult baptisms are frequently recorded in the registers, as are entire family baptisms, and in these cases you may find the age of the baptism. The registers are a particularly good place to track illegitimate children, usually described as 'base born' or 'bastard', as well as the burial of 'strangers' who normally resided outside the parish. A private baptism is likely to have taken place at home, usually because the child was too ill for the ceremony to be conducted in church; this is an indication that death was feared, and you may find another entry shortly afterwards for an infant burial.

Initially, one register was used to record all baptisms, marriages and burials, jumbled together in loose chronological order, but by the eighteenth century separate registers were introduced for each event. In general, more information is contained in the registers the closer to the present day you look, although the level of data will vary from parish to parish. In general, by the mid-eighteenth century you are likely to find the names of both parents of a child being baptised, or the age on burial along with some information on next of kin (for example, Mary Smith, widow of John Smith; Helen Jones, wife of David Jones; or Roger Baker, son of Michael Baker). Similarly, witnesses to marriage ceremonies are recorded, an important source for friends and family. The introduction of standardised printed volumes in the early nineteenth century provides some conformity, when space was made available for additional information such as addresses and occupations of participants.

You may find some of the earliest parish registers very difficult to read. Handwriting can be tricky to decipher, early entries were often written in Latin and levels of literacy mean that spellings can fluctuate widely. Many local and family history societies have provided transcripts of the records, and the Harleian Society has published transcripts from many London parishes. Another important point to bear in mind is the use of the ecclesiastical year,

READING PARISH REGISTERS

Opposite: **You may be surprised by some of your ancestors' occupations - this gentleman found a career in the church.**

which began on 25 March. The Catholic Church reformed its calendar in 1582 to start the New Year on 1 January, also cutting 10 days out of the year 1582. This system, known as New Style, was not adopted in England until 1752. Thus all English dates before 1752 may seem out of kilter – a parish register will record consecutive events on 31 December 1700 and 1 January 1700, whereas today we would consider this to be 1 January 1701. You will often find such entries referred to as 1 January 1700/01, which indicated the ecclesiastical year followed by the New Style year. This sounds confusing, but there are publications, such as Cheney's Handbook of Dates to help you untangle the problem.

LOCATION OF THE RECORDS

Most historic parish registers and bishops' transcripts have been deposited at the relevant county or diocesan record office. In some cases the registers may still be held at the parish church, along with modern registers, in which case you would need to contact the church direct if you wished to view the records. There are also two important published sources to help you locate the whereabouts of historic parish registers – The Philimore Atlas and Index of Parish Registers and the Society of Genealogists' National Index of Parish Registers. Remember that you can always order microfilms of records held outside your county of residence at family history centres run by the Church of the Latter Day Saints (LDS).

SHORTCUTS

Although there is no single comprehensive name index to parish register entries, there is one extremely important resource that provides an excellent means of reference – the International Genealogical Index (IGI). This has been compiled by the Church of the Latter Day Saints (LDS), based at Salt Lake City in the USA, and is essentially a collection of genealogical sources from around the world. Of particular prominence are extracts from English parish registers.

The English IGI is arranged by county, and is available on microfiche at most local record offices or LDS family history centres. Entries are mainly for baptisms, with some marriages and only a handful of burials, reflecting the interests of the LDS. Not every parish is included in the IGI, nor is there any consistency in the period of extraction for each parish. In general, fewer nineteenth-century entries appear on the IGI, and consequently you should bear in mind that the failure to find a reference in the IGI does not mean there is not a parish register entry waiting to be discovered in the relevant record office.

The advent of new technology has transformed the use of the IGI, and it is now available to search online at http://www.familysearch.org. A powerful search engine enables you to search for a named ancestor, and provides information not just from the IGI but also other genealogical resources such as the 1881 census and submitted pedigree resource files. These are research notes and family trees compiled by other researchers, so always beware when considering incorporating this data into your research – you should never simply accept data as fact, and always try to verify an online source against the original from which it was taken. In addition to the IGI, the British Isles Vital Records Index (BIVI) contains entries solely from vital records – baptisms, marriages and burials – from not just England and Wales, but also Scotland and Ireland. It is available on CD-ROM from standard genealogical research centres – FRC, county record offices, national institutions and LDS family history centres – but like the IGI is not fully comprehensive.

Another useful national index is Boyd's Marriage index, again based on extracts from parish registers and bishops' transcripts, arranged chronologically by county and cross-referenced by name of groom andbride. About 12 per cent of all marriages in England are included between 1538 and 1827, and the Society of Genealogists have made large sections available online at www.englishorigins.com.

There is a similar resource for London, the Pallot marriage and baptism index, covering the period 1781–1837. The Institute of Heraldic and Genealogical Studies hold the index and will conduct a search for a fee; it is also available online at www.ancestry.co.uk, but a charge is also applicable.

Finally, the Federation of Family History Societies has extracted burial data from over 4,000 registers to create the National Burial Index. This is an ongoing project, and is most useful if you are looking for deaths between 1800 and 1840, though the scope of the project includes burials from 1538–2000. Although some counties are not yet included, cataloguing work continues and the present results can be viewed on CD-ROM from most county record offices and national institutions.

The sixteenth-century Reformation challenged the teachings of the Church of Rome, and consequently new forms of worship were established across Europe. When Henry VIII broke from the jurisdiction of the Pope and established a separate Church of England, new Anglican forms of worship were introduced over the next 60 years. However, not everyone chose to accept them. Adherents to the Catholic faith continued to observe their own practices, whilst other religious groups and sects pursued more radical forms of congregational worship, particularly during and after the English Civil War. In addition to flourishing groups such as the Quakers, Independents, Congregationalists and Methodists, foreign emigrants, such as the Huguenots, fleeing from religious persecution abroad came to England and set up their own churches; and Jewish communities became re-established in Britain in the nineteenth century.

NON-CONFORMIST REGISTERS

Most of these religious groups established their own records, including registers of baptism, marriage and burial, although some did use Anglican churches for some of their ceremonies. Non-conformist registers, as they have collectively become known, were established under two government commissions, dated 1837 and 1857, and are now deposited at The National Archives in the collections of the Registrar General. There are indexes arranged by place and religion to help you identify which set of records you need to view.

In addition, two non-conformist central registries of births were set up, namely the Protestant Dissenters' Registry at Dr William's Library, Stafford, from 1742–1837; and the Wesleyan Methodist Metropolitan Registry from

1818–1838 in London. Indexes and records are available at The National Archives. You will also find that specialist libraries exist for many of these groups, where you are likely to find additional information about how your ancestors lived and worshipped. Similarly, Huguenot, Jewish and Catholic genealogical societies have been established to assist researchers in tracing their roots among these communities.

✿ HANDY HINTS

The following short notes are intended to assist you in your research.

RESEARCH STRATEGY

- ✿ The first step is to use existing data, from census returns or certificate data, to locate where the event took place.
- ✿ Use national indexes such as the IGI (available online) to see if a record of the event has been made.
- ✿ Consult a printed source to check the availability of parish or non-conformist registers.
- ✿ Visit the local county diocesan record office and consult the registers, remembering to keep an eye out for printed transcripts or name indexes, which will be easier to work with.

RESEARCH TIPS

- ✿ Never assume a link between generations or families – always try to use corroborating sources (such as wills, bishops' transcripts and other local records) to provide concrete evidence of a connection. If you are unsure, remember to place a question mark against the event on your draft family tree or research notes.

- With this in mind, it is far better to work back in time from the last known piece of information. This is especially important if you have found a clue from the Internet – no matter how tempting it may be to connect with a pre-researched family tree, you have to ensure the links are correct. This means starting with a verified 'fact' and painstakingly working back, step by step.

- Look out for other families with the same name – they may be siblings, uncles or aunts of the person you are trying to track down.

- However, common surnames may cause confusions, and it is important to use all genealogical data available to ensure you have the correct people, such as the mother's maiden name when looking for baptisms, cross-referenced against marriage records. Maiden names often appear as middle names, providing important clues when you are unsure about lineage.

- If your family 'disappears' from the parish, always check the registers for neighbouring parishes or the nearest large town. Relocation was most common at marriage; the groom often moved to join the bride's community for a while before returning to his roots, perhaps on the death of his parents if he was the oldest son.

- Similarly, try looking in non-conformist registers, especially if your ancestors lived in a part of the country where non-conformity or independent worship was prevalent.

- It is worth linking parish records with other related sources, such as marriage licences or gravestones. The latter are a striking visual source, and often contain epitaphs or information on other family members (particularly in family graves) that are especially poignant.

CHAPTER 5

Getting Help

During the course of any research project, and especially with family history, there comes a time when a particular line of enquiry grinds to a halt and there appears to be no way forward. When this happens, it is important to realise that you are not alone, and that the problem or obstacle facing you is not unique. Countless other researchers have probably reached the same dead-end as you have, and consequently you can draw upon their collective experience to get you started once again. The follow suggestions are provided to encourage you to seek help at these moments, and remind you that however insurmountable the problem may seem, all hope is not lost!

Opposite: A relative in mourning, wearing the black dress worn by widows, often for a specific time after the death.

EDUCATION

With the popularity of family history reaching new levels, there has been an explosion of taught courses, diplomas and certificates in family history at a number of institutions. It is probably worth checking for details at your local library, as many local authorities publicise Adult Education programmes, whilst WEA courses (Worker's Educational Association) and evening classes are often available. Accreditation can also be acquired from many universities, often as long-distance learning courses via the Internet, and the Institute of Heraldic and Genealogical Studies www.ihgs.ac.uk provides courses in family history. As already mentioned, many Family History Societies run programmes of events, talks and seminars, whilst the Federation of Family History Societies maintains a database of teachers of family history. Archives and institutions often run day conferences on aspects of genealogy, sometimes stretching to week-long summer schools for the real enthusiast.

❧ HAS SOMEONE DONE THE WORK ALREADY?

Below: Styles and fashions changed over time, which can help you to work out the period in which the photo was taken, and how fashion conscious our ancestors were!

It may be that someone has already done some work on your family's history. You may want to start by asking around the Family History Society network (see box) to see if there is someone working on a particular branch of your family – you will quickly discover that people are only too keen to exchange information that they have uncovered, particularly if it turns out that you share a common ancestor!

However, perhaps the most important organisation for deposited research is the Society of Genealogists, London (see Resources at the back of this book). Their library contains a wide range of genealogical publications, as well as various microfilm copies of datasets collected over the years, duplicate census records, civil registration indexes, union name indexes to parish registers and associated resources, and research that has been undertaken into families and their origins by private individuals over the centuries. This means that the Society of Genealogists holds a large collection of pedigrees and family trees; and you can find out more about their organisation online at www.sog.org.uk

FAMILY HISTORY SOCIETIES

Around the country you will find locally organised Family History Societies, and if you are new to genealogical research it is a good idea firstly to join the nearest group. Membership fees are usually charged, but most societies produce journals and put on talks that are either free or heavily subsidised for members. By belonging to one of these you will gain access to a wider research network, where fellow enthusiasts are more than willing to share their experience, tips and techniques, and may even have research notes that are relevant to your own studies. With this in mind, it is also probably worth joining Family History Societies that are local to where your ancestors originated, so that you benefit from expertise across the country when tracing branches of your family. Many societies undertake their own cataloguing work for records relevant to the area that they cover, and as a member you would have access to many of these indexes.

To find out where local societies are located, you can contact the Federation of Family History Societies (FFHS), who co-ordinate and regulate the activities of member organisations, undertake cataloguing and listing work (for example, the National Burial Index), run Internet resources such as Family History Online, and produce publications on family history (such as the *British Isles Genealogical Register*, which contains information on surnames and locations currently being researched). For further information about their work, visit the FFHS website at http://www.ffhs.org.uk

Also based at the Society's premises is the Guild of One Name Studies. They specialise in co-ordinating research into single surnames and maintain a Register of One Name Studies. This can be a useful resource if you are looking for researchers looking into the surname as your family, and you can find out more about them online at www.one-name.org

Finally, you might also want to seek out pedigrees of well-known families if you suspect that you may have a connection to the higher echelons of society among your ancestors, perhaps through stories of noble birth passed down through the years. One place to start is the British Library, as they hold a number of records that pertain to heraldic visitations and aristocratic pedigrees. Alternatively, you could approach the College of Arms to commission some research, though you would need to set up a meeting with one of the royal heralds, and there is a research fee for this process. (See Resources for both of these at the back of this book.)

BOOKS AND OTHER PUBLICATIONS

Family history is a popular subject, and to cater for the growing interest there is a wide range of general and specialist books on the subject. You have already invested in this book, *The Family Detective*, and it may be well worth looking at one or two of the following, in addition (many of these titles are available from your local library or can be purchased from county record offices, national institutions and standard booksellers):

- D Hey, *The Oxford Guide to Family History* (Oxford, 1993)
- D Hey, *Family Names and Family History* (London, 2000)
- P Christian, *The Genealogist's Internet* (TNA, 2005)
- M J Burchall, *National Genealogical Dictionary* (annual publication)
- M Herber, *Ancestral Trails: The Complete Guide to British Genealogy and Family History* (Society of Genealogists, 2000)
- A Bevan, *Tracing Your Ancestors at The National Archives* (TNA, 2006)
- S Colwell, *The Family Records Centre: A User's Guide* (TNA, 2002)
- S Colwell, *The National Archives: A User's Guide* (TNA, 2006)
- R Pols, *Family Photographs* (PRO, 2002)

There is an equally varied range of weekly, monthly and bi-monthly magazines and journals that provide information on the latest research, with feature articles on specialist lines of research; you will also find advertisements for specialist family history software and professional researchers. Some of the most popular titles include:

- Ancestors
- Family History Monthly
- Practical Family History
- Your Family Tree
- The Genealogists Magazine

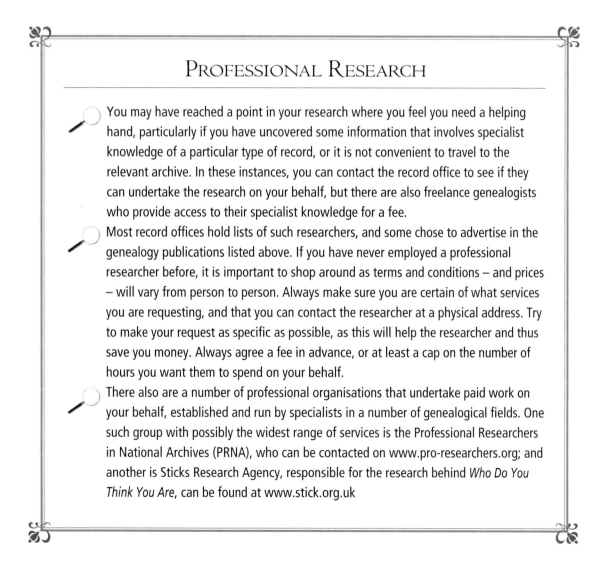

PROFESSIONAL RESEARCH

You may have reached a point in your research where you feel you need a helping hand, particularly if you have uncovered some information that involves specialist knowledge of a particular type of record, or it is not convenient to travel to the relevant archive. In these instances, you can contact the record office to see if they can undertake the research on your behalf, but there are also freelance genealogists who provide access to their specialist knowledge for a fee.

Most record offices hold lists of such researchers, and some chose to advertise in the genealogy publications listed above. If you have never employed a professional researcher before, it is important to shop around as terms and conditions – and prices – will vary from person to person. Always make sure you are certain of what services you are requesting, and that you can contact the researcher at a physical address. Try to make your request as specific as possible, as this will help the researcher and thus save you money. Always agree a fee in advance, or at least a cap on the number of hours you want them to spend on your behalf.

There also are a number of professional organisations that undertake paid work on your behalf, established and run by specialists in a number of genealogical fields. One such group with possibly the widest range of services is the Professional Researchers in National Archives (PRNA), who can be contacted on www.pro-researchers.org; and another is Sticks Research Agency, responsible for the research behind *Who Do You Think You Are*, can be found at www.stick.org.uk

✇ COMPUTER SOFTWARE

In this electronic age, there are numerous software packages designed specifically for the family historian. Many provide name databases, but the primary function is to allow you to organise the data that you find. Family trees can come to life, as these packages make it possible to scan or upload photographs, audio clips and video footage of your grandparents, uncles, aunts and immediate family. It is worth reading about the various products first, so always check out the latest software reviews in some of the magazines listed above.

Alternatively, it is possible to download material from specialist websites such as www.ancestry.co.uk or www.thefamilyhistoryproject.co.uk, where you can organise your data and submit your results to other users, who may be able to add information from their own research.

✇ INTERNET RESEARCH

An increasing number of websites promise online access to millions of names, pre-researched family histories and other genealogical data. Before you log on, you should consider the following general advice:

✇   The golden rule of Internet research is that just because it is online, it is not necessarily correct. You should never take the findings of other people at face value without attempting to verify their data. Always look for a document reference that leads to an original source for the piece of information; if there is no reference you cannot be sure of the authenticity of the data.

✇   In any case, if you want to use data from someone else's website, remember that you are benefiting from their hard work. There are copyright laws to protect information posted online, and you should make every attempt to contact the site host or content provider.

❧ Always make a note of the Internet address of the site you are visiting – the URL. This will help you to establish whether the site is compiled by an accredited organisation, or is simply the work of an enthusiastic amateur. Ensure that a website has a physical address or contact details that you can track down or verify, and look out for the credentials of the site author. This is especially important if the site is offering to sell name data.

Broadly speaking, there are three types of family history website that you will encounter – personal websites that are compiled by individuals; commercial websites that are offering access to name data in exchange for a fee; and the websites of genealogical organisations or institutions holding records that provide free access to catalogues, name indexes or research information. Generally speaking, the last two categories are the ones to aim for, as at least you will receive bona fide advice or access to data that you can then analyse to see whether it is relevant.

One of the best websites is Cyndi's List www.cyndislist.org as it acts as a portal for millions of genealogical resources across the globe, with a directory that covers virtually every subject under the sun. More relevant resources can be found a bit closer to home, focusing more on British records such as www.rootsweb.com and www.genuki.co.uk, linking to other websites in the UK where you can find records. Sites that offer access to images and original records include www.nationalarchives.gov.uk, www.ancestry.co.uk, www.1837online.com, www.familyrelatives.org.uk and www.origins.net. Many organisations now maintain their own web presence, such as www.sog.org.uk www.ihgs.ac.uk and www.ffhs.org.uk. There are also sites such as www.familysearch.org and www.genesreunited.co.uk that bring you access to other people's research and indexes but, as noted above, voluntarily submitted information should always be treated with extreme care, especially in the case of the latter website where the whole point is to connect people with one another, as opposed to the use of original records to construct accurate family trees. As the saying goes, don't believe the hype!

USEFUL WEBSITES

2

Going Furthur

Opposite: You can find out about who our ancestors were with a bit more detailed research.

In the first section of this book, I've explained how you can start out on the research trail, and introduced you to the main sources you'll work with to build a basic family tree. Until recently, many researchers have been satisfied with simply collecting the names of their ancestors, and focused their attention on going as far back in time as they possibly can. Personally, I think there are two problems with this approach. First, the further back you go, the fewer comprehensive records survive and you start to enter a 'zone of probability' concerning the links from one generation back to the next, since it becomes much harder to corroborate sources and verify that you've found the right person unless you have a family with an unusual surname, or find that they stayed put in the same place for hundreds of years. However, the second problem concerns relevance. Even when it is possible to go back centuries to the start of parish records and beyond, and you've created an impressive family tree with hundreds of branches on it, this approach doesn't really tell you who your ancestors were, which to me is the whole point of starting the research in the first place. TV shows such as *Who Do You Think You Are* have demonstrated that in many cases it's the journey that's the exciting part just as much as the final destination, and the excitement felt by the celebrities revolved around finding out about where their ancestors lived, what jobs they had, and the period of history through which they lived. It's often better to focus on one generation at a time, and investigate them thoroughly, before haring back to the sixteenth century; and you'll be amazed at how much information exists to place your relatives in their historical context.

The starting point for this journey of discovery lies in the basic documents you used to find out who your ancestors were in the first place. Census records, certificates and wills all contain valuable clues besides the names and ages of your relatives – addresses, occupations, clues about 'hidden' lives that you might not have ever heard about. All of this information can be used to propel you into the past, as you step back in time to a bygone era. Many people who have embarked on research into their personal heritage have found that they became interested in the history of the period in which their ancestors lived, as much as the people they discovered, often saying that they wished history at school had been as interesting. The reason for this is that history books have traditionally focused on the leading figures of the age – politicians, monarchs, aristocrats and military leaders – rather than the everyday folk who lived through momentous events. Yet family history allows you to see the same events through the eyes of your ancestors, and the understanding the historical context of your family is a crucial part of working out who they were, what they did and why they did it.

The second section of this book shows you how to investigate the social and local history that surrounds the people you uncover from the basic sources. I've identified four main areas that might be of interest – occupations, military careers, migration and family secrets – and provided an overview of the likely documents and archives where material may be held. In the main, I've focused on the period immediately before the Industrial Revolution towards the end of the eighteenth century, partly because you should be able to find people born at this time from census records and parish registers, but also because daily life before this date for a large percentage of the population working in the agrarian sector remained largely unchanged. I've provided a brief overview of the history and context of each theme, alongside more specific advice about relevant document sources, archives, museums and online resources so that you can start your own research with a degree of confidence. Interspersed are case studies that are relevant to each theme, drawn from the celebrities, politicians and sports stars of today.

Below: Formal poses often reveal a great deal, especially if you can identify the clothes that are being worn.

However, I'll start by showing what steps you should take when the main sources described in Section One run out, as well as looking at the new resources you can use if you intend to work further back in time.

81

Thomas
Harvard

at her luce chum ingrant debene et fideliter Administrand eadem Ad, x
sancta dei evangelia Jurat &c

In the name of god Amen the fowrteenth

Daie of July, Anno domini one thousand six hundred, thirtie and six
And in the twelveth yeare of the raigne of our soueraigne Lord Charles by
the grace of god kinge of England Scotland Fraunce and Ireland Defender of
the faith &c J Thomas Harvard of the parish of Saint Olaue in Southwarke in the
Countie of Surrey and Cittizen and Clothworker of London beinge att this presente
sicke and weake in bodie but of good and perfecte mynde and memorie all laude and
praise be given to Allmightie god therefore and consideringe with my selfe the
fraieltie and instabilitie of this present life and the certaintie of death, And to
the end that J may bee the better prepared and setled in my mynde, whensoever
it shall please god to call me out of this transitorie life J doe by the permission of
god make and declare this my last will and Testament in manner and forme followinge, That is to saie, First and principally, J comend my soule into the
handes of Allmightie god hopinge and assuredly, beleevinge through the death and
passion of Jesus Christe his only sonne and alone Saviour to obtaine remission
and forgivenes of all my synns and to be made ptaker of everlastinge life my
bodie J will to the earth from whence it came to be decently buried att the
discretion of my executors here under named, And as concerninge all such
worldly goods Chattells and psonall estate as it hath pleased god to endue me in
this life J give and bequeath the same in manner and forme followinge, That is
to saie Inprimis J give and bequeath unto my deere and welbeloued wife Elizabeth
Harvard the some of fower hundred poundes of lawfull English money to be
paied unto her within six monthes next after my decease More J give and
bequeath to my said lovinge wife all my plate and houshold stuffe excepte only my
best standinge bowle of siluer guilte and my greate Chiste with trunck locke Item
J give and bequeath unto my said lovinge wife Elizabeth Harvard one Annuitie
or yearly payment of thirty poundes of good and lawfull English money to be
yearely due goeinge out issuinge and payable unto my said wife out of all
those mes suages and Tenemente with thapp ntenance, And the rente issues and
proffittes of them seituate lyinge and beinge att or neere Tower hill in the parrishe
of All Saints Barkinge in London which J hould ioyntly togeather with my
brother John Harvard by vertue of a lease to vs thereof made by the me
brothers and sisters of the hospitall of Saint Katherine neere the Tower of
London, To haue and to hould the said Annuitie or rente charge of Thirtie poundes
J giue vnto my said lovinge wife for and duringe the tearme of her naturall life
to be paied vnto her att fower feaste or tearmes in the yeare, That is to saie att the
feaste of Saint Michaell Tharchangell, the birth of our lord god, Thannuntiacon
of the blessed virgin Marie and the nativitie of Saint John Baptist or within one
and twenty daies nexte ensuinge everie of the same feast daies by equall and even
porcons, The first payment thereof to begin and to be made att the feaste of the
feaste aforesaid which shall first and next happen and come after my decease Or
within one and twentie daies then nexte ensuinge with power to distreyne for the
same Annuitie in and vpon the said tenemente or anie of them, if the same annuitie
shall happen to be behinde and vnpaied contrary to this my will, Provided
that my father in law me Nicholas kinge or his heires att any time duringe
the tearme of my naturall life doe assure and conveie vnto me and my heires or
within six monethes after my decease to my executors hereunder named or to such
pson or psons as J the said Thomas Harvard shall by anie writinge under my
hand name and appointe, And theire heires and assignes, And to such vse and
vses as J shall thereby lymitt and declare and in such good sure and sufficiente

CHAPTER 6

Going Back Further in Time

There will come a time during your research that 'national' sources, such as civil registration certificates and census returns, are no longer of any use if you want to trace relatives who were born before the mid nineteenth century. At this point, you must gather together all the clues you have found from the national sources, such as place of birth or occupation, and start to sift through records created by or about the local communities in which they lived. Most people head straight for parish registers, as these contain biographical information such as baptisms, marriages and burials. Used in combination with probate records, you can often achieve spectacular results. Yet although there is often immense satisfaction to be gained from seeing how far back in time you can go, the end product is likely to be little more than a list of names on a family tree.

This is something you can rectify by finding out more about the communities in which they lived, the local industries where they found work, the house in which they brought up their family, and how changes to society at large affected their daily lives. It is often easy to forget that events such as the industrial revolution or the coming of the railways in the nineteenth century had a massive impact on our ancestors, and that before such momentous changes the vast majority of people worked on the land, and rarely moved far from their place of birth.

Once you have a fix on where your ancestors were based, through census returns or parish records, it is worth taking time to read about the area in which

Opposite: This will names relatives and friends, as well as providing information about occupation and social status.

CONSIDER HOW THEY LIVED

To understand how your ancestors lived before the nineteenth century, you need to strip away the modern transport infrastructure – no cars or trains – and remove the industrial towns of the north and midlands. Apart from London, the main 'urban' centres were ports such as Bristol and Liverpool, and regional centres such as Norwich, for many years England's second city in terms of population. You have to visualise a world in which your ancestors rarely moved more than a few miles from where they were born; to reach the nearest large town or city, they would need to afford to keep a horse or pony, or save up enough money to ride on a mail-coach via the king's highway – a time-consuming, dusty and often dangerous way to travel. Yet you can bring this lost age back to life through your research, and begin to understand exactly what the simple phrase 'agricultural labourer' or 'miner' meant in reality through the grind of daily life.

they lived. First, you will see how the community developed, what the prevalent industries were, and the structure of the society in general. This last aspect is particularly important, as you will need to start thinking in terms of historic 'administrative areas' when looking for records about your ancestors – not just ecclesiastical parishes, but also poor law unions, hundreds or other county divisions such as wapentakes, and manors. Many local records were created at this administrative level, and consequently you need to be armed with this information if you want to track down relevant information about your family. The best place to start looking is the relevant local studies centre or county record office, where important literature will be stored. In particular, look out for any Victoria County History volumes that cover your area, or antiquarian works. The county record office is where you will also find the vast majority of records relevant to the local community.

The next step is to look into the way in which the community was organised. One of the oldest social units was the manor, dating back to the Norman Conquest in the eleventh century, and the records generated by the manorial court, in which the administration of the manor was handled, can be of great interest to the family historian. If your ancestors held land according to the custom of the manor – copyhold tenants – then there is every chance that the court rolls may record information on inheritance from one generation of your family to another. Even if they were not copyhold tenants, then freehold tenants or lower-status members of the manor could be recorded in other documents, such as lists of rent due to the lord of the manor, or fines paid for offences. Alongside manorial records are the documents created by large estate owners, who often employed many local people in the community to run or work upon their lands. Stewards accounts, pay books and surveys can provide a rich source of information.

After the death of an important tenant of the Crown, or prominent local landholder, an inquisition was taken by a local jury under the guidance of a royal official called an escheator to determine any rights or – more usually – financial payments due to the Crown. The records of the process were returned to central government, and provide a fascinating insight into the workings of the middle to upper levels of English society up to the middle of the seventeenth century. The subject of the inquisition would have his or her lands listed, the terms under which they were held; and, crucially, the date of death and the next heir. Often property inheritance through the family was recorded, along with marriages, details of prior property transactions or details of other family members. Even if your ancestor was not the subject of an inquisition post mortem, they may still be listed as one of the jurors, an indication of their status or circle of acquaintances. The records are stored at The National Archives, Kew, and are primarily written in Latin. Some name indexes and calendars (partial translations) are available.

Above: Colourful characters sometimes emerge, lifting the lid on a bygone age of flamboyant styles!

22 THE CRIMINAL AND CIVIL COURTS

The British judicial system has undergone dramatic changes over the centuries, and was totally reorganised in 1971 as a result of the Courts Act, which introduced the system we know today. So documents covering legal proceedings before this time are likely to feature concepts and terminology that are unfamiliar to many people and can seem mystifying. Even professional researchers often find the bafflingly complex legal procedures of the past both fascinating and frustrating.

Until 1971, the principal criminal courts were Magistrates Courts (or 'Petty Sessions'), the Assize Courts and the Quarter Sessions. Magistrates Courts have retained a broadly similar function over the years. Their main role is still to try lesser criminal offences, and consider whether there is sufficient evidence to send serious cases to a higher court. Quarter Sessions had a limited range of powers relating to criminal and civil matters and some appeals. They were usually held every three months – or 'quarterly', hence the name. Most of the civil functions of the Assizes and Quarter Sessions are now carried out by the County Courts, their criminal jurisdiction is covered by the Crown Courts, and appeals are dealt with by the High Court.

A judicial system that was anything like what we would recognise today only began to take shape with the Assizes ('sittings') that were set up in the fourteenth century. These were organised into four to six Assize Circuits covering all the counties of England and Wales. Pairs of judges, whose job was to administer both civil and criminal law, were given responsibility for each circuit. At regular intervals, they would call at each county town within their circuit, in turn, to hear the cases that had occurred since their last visit. In London and its surrounding counties, the functions of the Assizes were carried out by the Old Bailey Sessions – later the Central Criminal Court – which met once a month. The Old Bailey also tried the most serious cases, including 'piracy on the high seas'.

Minor crimes were known as misdemeanours and dealt with by specially appointed magistrates, often local landowners, sitting at Petty Sessions. Those found guilty were usually punished with a fine or sometimes jail ('gaol'). The most serious crimes, such as murder, manslaughter, rape and the theft of any goods worth more than one shilling (5p), were called felonies. Before a case could be heard, a Grand Jury consisting of 24 men was summoned to decide whether there was a case to answer. This system, which is still used in the USA today, was ended in the UK by the Criminal Justice Act of 1948.

Felonies were tried in the Assize Courts, Quarter Sessions or Old Bailey, and defended cases required a 12-man jury. In earlier times, jurors were made up of the people who had direct knowledge of the alleged crime, such as witnesses, and were there to give evidence in the case. It was the judge that decided the defendant's guilt or innocence. Over time, however, this changed so that issues of fact came to be decided by the jury, while only issues of law were the province of the judge.

If a guilty verdict was returned, the sentence was death by hanging and forfeiture of all goods and estate. During the late eighteenth and early-to mid-nineteenth centuries, this was most often reduced to transportation to the colonies. Many of those sentenced to transportation never made it to their destination, having succumbed to typhus ('gaol fever') in the prison hulks they were confined in.

By modern eyes, early judicial systems can seem monstrously unfair. Until the late seventeenth century, a judge could jail or fine a jury if he disagreed with their verdict. Torture was commonplace, and it was not until almost the end of the nineteenth century that defendants could actually speak in their own defence. Before then they had to present a written statement, and leave it to others to give evidence on their behalf.

PLACES OF CORRECTION

Jails were usually located close to the court building in each county town and at first used solely to hold a defendant while awaiting trial. Over time they became 'places of correction' in their own right. It was only following a massive expansion of prison capacity during the Victoria era, made necessary by the ending of transportation, that jail became the main method of punishment for serious offences, often involving back-breaking manual work called 'hard labour'. Many records on criminal proceedings and punishment in the UK are held at The National Archives.

THINK THE TAXMAN!

We may all grumble about paying our taxes, but be thankful if your distant ancestors did! From the late thirteenth century onwards, taxation in the form of lay subsidies, poll and heath taxes were called to fund the administration of the state. The returns are crammed full of names. Although few relationships are clearly defined, the records can be used to show who was living in an area at a given time. Many people earned too little to be included, or managed to find reasons for 'exemption'; but enough returns survive to provide useful snapshots of a community over time. Some local or family history societies have produced transcripts of medieval lay subsidy returns, and the originals are primarily stored at The National Archives.

If ancient criminal jurisprudence seemed complex, it was simplicity itself compared with many of the cases dealt with under civil law. This is where the family researcher will find some of the choicest morsels of information about distant relatives. Whereas criminal courts dealt with relations between the individual and society – breaches of common law – the civil courts adjudicated over disputes between individuals.

Most commonly, these involved claims for damages, breaches of trust, contested contracts, or disputes over property ownership. The civil courts had to decide whether the civil wrong, or 'tort', that was claimed actually existed in law, as well as who – if anyone – was responsible and what the remedy should be. In the criminal court, guilt had to be determined 'beyond reasonable doubt', but a civil case was (and still is) determined 'on the balance of probabilities', so that the slightest shift in the weight of evidence might tip the case towards one side or the other. This could make for very-long-drawn-out legal wrangles.

As today, many family squabbles over inheritance ended up in civil courts. The development of equity courts in the fourteenth century provided a means by which people with grievances could seek redress. They set out their case and the defendants were then asked to respond. This process was called 'pleading', and the documents produced – bills, answers, rejoinders and replications – are full of genealogical information. Furthermore, the stages of the suit through court generated other forms of document, such as witness statements (depositions), orders, decrees and affidavits. In some cases, evidence was brought into court and never collected, so personal possessions, wills, title deeds and pedigrees can still be found. As the equity courts were under Royal jurisdiction, the records are to be found at The National Archives. Most of the documents are in English, and some name indexes are available.

The principal court dealing with the most complex civil litigation, especially over property, was the Court of Chancery in London. By the nineteenth century, the volume of work – and the hierarchy of clerks and other officials needed to deal with it – was causing the Chancery to become mired in its own bureaucracy. This was described most graphically in Charles Dickens' novel *Bleak House* (1853). Cases could drag on for many years and

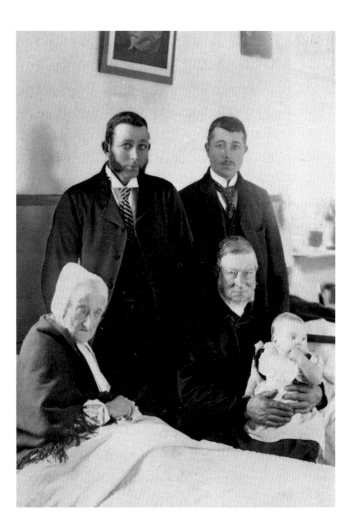

Right: Care of the elderly was very different in the past, and unless you could work or had a sympathetic family, you could end up in the workhouse.

involve succeeding generations, for as one claimant died then his or her sons, daughters, siblings, grandchildren and even distant cousins could become embroiled in the case. Each claim was liable to involve deeds and documents, secondary claims, counterclaims, and depositions, all meticulously copied, filed and miss-filed by the clerks and their assistants. For the family detective, tracking a relative through the labyrinthine paperwork thus created can be a monumental task. Yet in such reports of criminal and civil proceedings, all human life is found, tragic and sometimes comic, and whether or not you are successful in tracing one of your relatives via these records, they offer a fascinating insight into the lives of our predecessors.

☙ LATIN LEGAL TERMS

Ancient legal documents often hold important clues about our ancestors and the events they were caught up in. They might include business contracts, wills, judicial findings, land disputes and reports of inquiries and commissions. However, in earlier times they were usually written in Latin, and even later documents are likely to be peppered with obscure Latin phrases. Even a familiar expression, such as 'ad infinitum', can have a special legal meaning that differs markedly from the more common usage we are familiar with.

Many Internet web sites can help you translate Latin terms, but you should always check that these include legal definitions. Bear in mind, too, that even though Latin has been a dead language for many hundreds of years, this does not mean Latin definitions are set in stone. Even legal terms change meaning over the years, and continue to evolve today, as lawyers adapt them to fit a specific context. So, when trying to interpret a phrase in a document, try to gauge its meaning in the broadest possible sense. To help you, here's a list of common Latin phrases you may uncover in law documents dating from before the twentieth century, along with their legal definitions.

ab extra – from outside

ab initio – from the beginning

actio in distans – acting from a distance

actus non facit reum – the action alone does not prove guilt

actus reus – guilty act

ad colligenda bona – restricted grant of letters of administration

ad diem – until the appointed day

ad hoc – for this purpose

ad idem – of the same mind, in agreement

ad infinitum – without limit

ad litem – for the suit or litigation

ad sectun – at the suit of

ad valorem – according to the value

aemulatio vicini – out of spite against a neighbour

aliunde – from a different source (elsewhere)

alias dictus – otherwise called

aliter – otherwise

amicus curiae – friend or adviser of the court

animus – intention

ante – before

ante litem motem – before litigation started

assizes – sittings

assumpsit – breach of promise

auctor in rem suam – agent (acting) for personal gain

audi alteram partem – hear both sides

bona fide – sincere, in good faith

bona vacantia – goods without an owner

brevi manu – without application to a court, a short cut ('by short hand')

cadit quaestio – there is no further argument to be made

causa causans – immediate or direct cause

causa sine qua non – indirect cause, contributory factor

caveat emptor – let the buyer beware

certiorari – a writ from a higher to a lower court

certum est quod certum reddi potest – it is only certain if it can be proven

cessante ratione legis, cesat ipsa lex – if there is no longer a reason for a law, the law lapses

ceteris paribus – other things being equal

clare constat – it clearly appears

condicto indebiti – reclaiming wrongful payment

consensu – by common consent, unanimously

consensus ad idem – agreement on an essential point

contra – to the contrary

contra bonos mores – contrary to good morals

coram non judice – before one who is not a judge

corpus – body

corpus delicti – main body of the offence

curia regis – the king's court or council

custos morum – guardian of morals

damnum sine injuria – loss or injury without legal wrong

de bonis asportatis – goods carried away

de die in diem – from day to day

de facto – in fact

de futuro – in the future

de integro – regarding the whole

de jure – rightful, lawful, according to law

delegatus not potest delgare – delegated authority cannot be passed to others

de lege ferenda – what the law ought to be (i.e. rather than what the law is)

de lege lata – what the law is (i.e. rather than what the law ought to be)

de minimis non curat lex – this matter is too trivial to be dealt with in law

de novo – starting anew

desseisin – regaining possession

doli incapax – not capable of a criminal act

donatio inter vivos – gift between living people (i.e. not a legacy)

donatio mortis causa – gift made at the point of death

dominium – ownership

dubitante – doubting the correctness of the decision

dum casta – allowance given to an estranged wife for as long as she remains celibate

dum sola – allowance given to a young woman before marriage

incumbit probatio qui – the onus of proof rests with the individual

et cetera – and so on

ex cathedra – with official authority

ex concessis – that which has already been accepted

ex gratia – out of kindness, voluntary

ex parte – application made in the absence of one of the parties involved

ex post facto – by reason of a subsequent act

ex turpi causa non oritur actio – an unlawful contract is unenforceable

faciendum – something that must be done

factum – act or deed

habeas corpus – where is the evidence? ('where's the body?')

id est (i.e) – that is

idem – same person or thing

in articulo mortis – on the point of death

in camera – heard in private or secretly

in curia – heard in open court

in custodia legis – held by the court (e.g. money or securities)

in delicto – at fault

in esse – existing

in extenso – in total, at full length

in extremis – at the last gasp

in faciendo – in doing

in flagrante – in the act

in flagrante delicto – in the act of committing a crime

in forma pauperis – not required to pay legal fees ('in the form of a pauper')

in futoro – in the future

in gremio legis – under the protection of the law

in invitum – against an unwilling person

in limine – at the outset, threshold

in loco parentis – in place of a parent or legal guardian

in media res – the heart of the matter

in omnibus – in every respect

in perpetuum – for all time, in perpetuity

in personum – affecting one person, personal liability

in pleno – in full

in situ – in place

in solidum – for the whole sum

in terrorem – as a warning

in toto – without exception

in utero – in the womb

indicia – indications, marks, signs

inter alios – between other people

inter partes – between the two parties concerned

inter se – between themselves

interim – temporary, provisional

intra vires – within legal authority

ipsissima verba – the very words

ipso facto – by the fact itself

ipso jure – by the law itself

item – just so

jure divino – by divine right

jus naturae – natural law

latitat et discurrit – write to arrest an absconder in another county (where he 'lurks and runs about')

litera scripta – written word

literatim – literally

locus poenitentiae – opportunity to withdraw from a contract

locus sigilli – the place where a seal is attached to a deed

locus standi – right to be heard or legally recognised ('place of standing')

mala fides – bad faith

mens rea – criminal state of mind

mora – delay in asserting a right

mutatis mutandis – making necessary changes

ne exeat regno – a writ to restrain an absconder

nemine contradicente (nem. con.) – if all agree ('with no one contradicting')

nemo dat quod non habet – no one can give what he does not have

nemo tenetur seipse accusare – no one can be forced to incriminate himself

nexus – a legal bond

nisi – unless, not final, according to set conditions

nisi prius – unless before

nolens volens – whether willing or not, willy nilly

nominatum – by name

non compus mentis – not of sound mind

non est factum – not done, invalid

non est inventus – he has not been found (absconder)

non sequitur – does not follow

obiter dictum – non-binding legal opinion

onus – duty, burden

onus probandi – burden of proof

pari passu – equally, without preference

particeps criminis – accomplice or accessory to a crime

per capita – shared out equally ('per head')

per curiam – by the whole court

per infortunium – through mischance

per se – in itself

post factum – *after the event*

post hoc, ergo propter hoc – after this, therefore because of this

post mortem – after the death

post partem – after the birth

prima facie – at first sight

pro bono publico – for the public good, for free

pro rata – in proportion

pro tempore (pro tem.) – for the time being, temporary

proferens – party that proposes a condition or contract

quaere – inquire, query

quaesitum – answer

quantum – amount (of damages), sufficient amount, extent

quantum meruit – fair payment for work done

quia timet – preventive action

quid pro quo – one thing (in exchange) for another, compensation

quoad hoc – as to this matter

ratio decidendi – central principal of a case

re – concerning

res – an item or issue

res communis – common property

res gestae – facts of the case

res integra – an issue that has not been dealt with

res ipsa loquitor – self-evident, presumed ('it speaks for itself')

res judiciata – an issue that has been adjudicated

res nullius – no one's property

residuum – residue of an estate

restitio in integrum – restore to the previous state

sederunt – a sitting of a judicial body

semble – apparently

seisin – possession, ownership

sine die – to another day, indefinitely

sine prole – without issue

sub silentio – in silence

suggestio falsi – misrepresenting the truth

sui generis – unique

summus jus – highest law, maximum severity of the law

suppressio veri – suppressing the facts

tenendum – to be held, tenure

terminus ad quem – final point of a (legal) argument

terminus ad quo – starting point of a (legal) argument

totitem verbis – in so many words

uberrima fides – utmost good faith

ubi jus ibi remedium – where there is a right there is a remedy (in law)

ultra vires – beyond legal powers or authority

verbatim – word for word

vide – consult

vi et armis – by force of arms

volens – willingly, consenting to risk

Right: Property records can reveal ancestral homes that were passed from one generation to the next, showing you how families were related.

❧ DATING DOCUMENTS

Dating conventions changed over time, as did the start of the year, so it may not always be clear when a document was written. Survival of material is often patchy, so one area may have a good series of administrative records whilst a neighbouring district might have none at all. Place or surnames will change over time as scribes wrote down what they heard; standardisation of regional spelling on a national level is a remarkably late phenomenon, so make sure you are

Above: One of the most famous documents in British history is the Domesday book, but you would be very lucky to prove a link to anyone listed there.

tracking the right family. Furthermore, many people below a certain level of society will simply not leave a trace in the records at all, so you should really prepare yourself for disappointment. It is most unlikely that you will be able to find ancestors in the Domesday Book! (See box.)

Yet it is definitely worth persevering with this challenging line of work – your results can often be spectacular, and the very act of looking through older material will enhance your historical skills and make research in the later era that much more rewarding. The apparent barriers listed above can be overcome. There are Latin dictionaries, phrasebooks and formularies which show you how the most common documents are set out, leaving you to look for names or places. Many documents normally written in Latin were, by Parliamentary decree, produced in English during the Interregnum between 1649–1660, so you might be able to locate a clearer 'worked example' from this period. The abbreviations and handwriting – the 'paleography' – can be decoded using similar volumes, such as Trice-Martin's Record Interpreter. Dates that incorporate a regnal year (for example, 2 Elizabeth for 1554), a feast day (St Michael the Archangel for the 29th September), or references to the start of the

THE DOMESDAY BOOK

The Domesday Book, also known as 'the Great Survey', was England's first major census and the most comprehensive assessment of a nation's wealth that was ever undertaken in Medieval Europe. The survey was instigated by William the Conqueror and gives a unique 'snapshot' of England in the period around 1086. It was carried out principally so that William could find out how much his recently acquired kingdom was worth. He would then know exactly how much tax he could exact. But William's aims went further than that. The Norman king also wanted to consolidate his hold over his new Anglo Saxon subjects, who he had conquered after defeating their king, Harold, and his troops at the Battle of Hastings. During his 21-year reign, William imposed his will on the people with ruthless efficiency, brutally putting down a series of uprisings. The 'Great Survey' enabled William to bring England's system of law and government into line with the legal and feudal systems of his native Normandy, in northern France. Once the Domesday Book was completed, all land and property in England would be regarded as belonging to the King, or held on his behalf by his Norman overlords. The book was only completed after William's death, in 1087. Although it is called the Domesday 'Book', it is actually in two volumes, with the information set out by shire (county), hundred (an ancient subdivision of a shire), village and hamlet. During the two years it took to complete, the King's officials visited each shire at least twice using a standardised questionnaire to record all landowners and their tenants and note down the ownership of all property, equipment and livestock in minute detail – even down to the number of cows, pigs and hens. The survey caused deep resentment and even led to riots in some counties. The Domesday Book is now held at The National Archives at Kew.

ecclesiastical year (25 March instead of 1 January) can be checked in Cheney's Handbook of Dates. Most archives stock these useful aids.

There are many other sources available, which will vary from region to region, family to family; this is only a flavour of what is out there. It may take you a little time to find your feet, but it is certainly worth plugging away at the records — you never know quite what you will find. If you get really stuck, it might be worth contacting a local history group in addition to your usual family history society.

Case study 1

David Attenborough

When you think of iconic television moments, perhaps one of the most memorable in recent years was David Attenborough's piece to camera surrounded by a family of gorillas. Indeed, almost all of his recent series about life on our planet have provided a unique insight into a world that most of us have never imagined, whether he is talking about the oceans, plants, mammals or birds. There seem to be few places left on the planet where he hasn't delivered his breathy sense of wonderment when confronted with another remarkable wildlife specimen. Yet his travels around the world are a far cry from the journey his family has taken over the years.

David Attenborough was born in 1926, three years after his brother Richard – the actor and director. Their parents, Frederick Levi Attenborough and Mary Clegg, were married in Paddington in 1922, which belies their roots in Stapleford, Nottinghamshire. Frederick was born in 1887, so married quite late in life at the age of 35, following a period of service during the First World War. Thereafter he followed an academic career path, and at the time of his marriage was a fellow of Emmanuel College, Cambridge. Mary Clegg was clearly a good match for Frederick; her father, Samuel Clegg, was a schoolmaster having trained at Manchester, whilst her grandfather, Alexander Clegg, had enjoyed success in the same profession years before.

Yet previous generations of Attenboroughs had struggled to give Frederick Levi the benefits of a good education. David Attenborough's grandfather was Frederick Augustus, a baker and grocer who lived and worked in Stapleford, Nottinghamshire, whilst his mother, Mary Saxton, came from a weaving family based in Hucknall. It is clear that they were a very forward-thinking family, as revealed by their occupations listed in the 1901 census are interesting; Frederick Levi's sister, Ada, was working as a typist in an office, still a relatively unusual profession for a woman and especially so given her parents' backgrounds.

Frederick was the son of an ironstone labourer, George Attenborough, and at the age of twelve was working as a winder in a silk mill along with his older brother Charles. George appears to have been disabled, in all probability during an accident at his work, and his wife Sarah stayed at home to look after him. Yet even at the age of 80, George had to find work of sorts, acting as a clerk at the iron works where he had previously found employment as a young man. This demonstrates vividly the nature of society before the welfare state – there was no retirement age if you could not afford to live on your own means. On the Saxton side of the family, the main profession seems to have been in the wool manufacturing trade, though Mary's father Levi Saxton appears to have been making Shetland wool shawls in 1881 – even though he was hundreds of miles from the isles and had probably never visited in his life, being born and bred in Hucknall.

Even the Clegg line can be traced back to similar roots; Alexander Clegg's father, James, had worked as a power loom weaver in Bolton in 1861 – a difficult time, given the cotton famine caused by the US civil war – and the occupations of the rest of the family suggest times were hard. His wife, Margaret, was a paper finisher whilst his thirteen year old son, William, worked as a paper maker. Alexander, on the other hand, went to school even though he was only one year younger and can perhaps count himself lucky not to have been called into work as well to help the family earn a living. On such small decisions is the fate of a family decided, and without this decision to turn to teaching the entire Attenborough family tree would have been very different, and consequently our understanding of the natural world greatly diminished.

RESEARCHING EDUCATION RECORDS

David Attenborough's father was a fellow at Emmanuel College, Cambridge, and many universities maintain lists of their former undergraduates, postgraduates and staff. Oxford and Cambridge in particular have published the names and dates of their alumni (former students), whilst many other higher education institutions can provide access to their archives if you suspect a family link with a specific college – perhaps from a photograph or certificate that you've found somewhere within the family.

Teaching records, though, are harder to come by and a lot will depend on the school. Many of the larger public schools have their own archives, and the School Archivists Group should be able to assist you to track down relevant papers or staff records. The National Archives holds a large amount of material relating to schools and education policy, although local authority records may be of use as well if you broadly know where your ancestor was teaching. Many towns and villages would have had only one school, so if you can find your family on the census and they are listed as a teacher, the chances are that they would have worked in the nearest institution.

CASE STUDY 2

DAME ELLEN MACARTHUR

As an island race, the British have always been associated with the sea. Ever since Alfred the Great established a small fleet to repulse the Danes, the importance of protecting our shores has been all to clear. The height of British naval power came in the nineteenth century, and for a century after the Battle of Trafalgar in 1805 the Royal Navy ruled the waves. Yet alongside this awesome military power, an even longer tradition of maritime exploration and trade has existed. Men such as Sir Francis Drake and Sir Walter Raleigh figure prominently in our history books, whilst for centuries an even larger navy of trading vessels and fishing fleets have brought goods from far-flung places and fish from our waters into our ancestors' shops and markets.

Ellen MacArthur is regarded as one of the greatest British sailors, and in recognition of her exploits in traversing the globe single-handed in record-breaking time, she was created a Dame earlier this year. Despite the fact that she grew up in landlocked Derbyshire, there are clues to her affinity with the open seas hidden in her family's past.

The MacArthur surname is steeped in Scottish history, tracing its origins back to the originator of the clan, a man called Arthur whose name in Celtic is associated with 'the courage of a bear'. It has been claimed that there are links to the Celtic King Arthur of legend, but the earliest clan histories refer to a 6th century chieftain who named his son Arthur. It is without dispute the MacArthurs are certainly amongst the most ancient of Scottish families, as reflected in an old Gaelic saying 'as old as the hills, MacArthurs and the Devil'. The clan appear throughout the annals of Scotland's history at key moments, particularly during the Jacobite risings against the Hanoverian monarchy after which many leading MacArthurs chose to leave the country. Famous émigrés include John MacArthur, who arrived in Australia in 1790 and whose sons planted the first vineyards; and General Douglas MacArthur who commanded the US forces in the Pacific during the Second World War.

Sub-branches (or septs) of the MacArthur clan spread throughout Scotland, with one sept ending up on the Isle of Skye where, in the eighteenth century, they became the hereditary pipers to the MacDonalds. There is a MacArthur tomb on the Isle near to that of Flora MacDonald, of Bonnie Prince Charlie fame.

Ellen was born in rural Derbyshire in 1976, and was brought up near Whatstandell by her parents

Ken and Avril, both of whom were teachers. Her father specialised in craft design and technology, and Ellen's childhood home was surrounded by sheds full of tools and equipment – an association with DIY that perhaps stood her in good stead during her months alone on the high seas.

Ellen's family were very close knit, with her paternal grandparents John and Oriel MacArthur living with Oriel's father, Peter King, close to Ellen's home. Peter King's background was in the Derbyshire mines, and he would often tell Ellen stories of pit-ponies and the canaries that were taken down to warn the workers of noxious gases. Yet it is on the other side of the family that Ellen's love of the sea can be traced.

The MacArthurs had lived in the Belper area of Derbyshire for several generations. Ellen's grandfather John worked as a stonemason in his later years, surrounded by tools of the trade. However, before he enlisted to serve with the Royal Fusiliers during the Second World War, he had found employment as a hosiery framework knitter and his forebears had worked in similar industries in the Belper region of Derbyshire for several decades. They had journeyed from Scotland towards the end of the nineteenth century, where the family profession had originally been in the fishing industry, earning a living as fishermen from their home at Luib, Strath. Generations of MacArthurs had worked on the seas around Skye, including Peter MacArthur (baptised in 1827), as was his father John MacArthur before him. The break from the sea seems to have occurred in the late 1870s or early 1880s, when members of the family first start to appear in the Belper area of Derbyshire recorded on the 1881 and 1891 censuses.

Ellen discovered her links to the sea whilst on holiday to Skye, and was even able to visit the ancestral family home having done some research at the Portree archives. Local archives and county record offices are often the best place to discover the history of our sea-faring ancestors, where you can examine parish registers and census returns that often record professions such as fisherman. Related sources such as newspaper clippings, articles and memoirs can provide an insight into the dangers of working with the sea for a living.

National institutions are another excellent source of information too. Records of the merchant navy are likely to be divided between The National Archives, Kew (www.nationalarchives. gov.uk) which holds records of service, ships crew lists and agreements and inquests into maritime disasters; and the National Maritime Museum, Greenwich (www.nmm.ac.uk), which holds more crew lists, Lloyds Shipping records and background material on maritime history. You can also use The National Archives to investigate ancestors who served in the Royal Navy and coastguards.

CASE STUDY 3

TONY BENN

The political career of Tony Benn is well chronicled, not just in the press but also through his own published journals. A champion of the left wing of the Labour party, he was first returned to Parliament in 1950 following a by-election in Bristol South East. He comes from a family with a long history in politics - indeed his son Hilary Benn has followed his father into the House of Commons and is the present Secretary of State for International Development - but as a consequence of inheriting his father's hereditary peerage, granted by Winston Churchill in 1942, when his father died in 1960, Tony was forced to leave Parliament, even though his former constituents re-elected him at the subsequent by-election caused by his elevation to the House of Lords. His attempts to abandon his peerage led to reform and in 1963 legislation was passed to allow individuals to renounce their hereditary titles; within a month of the law being changed, Tony Benn was back in the House of Commons. This is the story about the origins of this remarkable politician.

Anthony Neil Wedgwood Benn was born in London in 1925, the son of the Liberal MP for Leith William Wedgwood Benn and his wife Margaret Eadie Holmes. In 1942 William was created 1st Viscount Stansgate, and was elevated to the House of Lords, a title that was hereditary. It was tragic circumstance that led to Tony inheriting the peerage, as his older brother Michael was killed in action during the Second World War leaving him next in line. Tony's education reveals a great deal about the status of his family, as he was educated at Westminster School and New College, Oxford; and it appears that his radical politics come in part from his mother, who was a dedicated feminist and supporter of the ordination of women priests; for example, she was a member of the League of the Church Militant. The couple had married in 1920 at St Margaret's Church, Westminster and the occasion was graced by the great and good from the world of politics; for example, the former Liberal Prime Minister Herbert Asquith was one of the witnesses on the marriage certificate. Both of Tony's grandfathers, Sir John Williams Benn and Daniel Turner Holmes, were also MPs for the Liberal Party. Sir John was first elected to Parliament in 1891 and was created a Baronet in 1914, and led the Progressive Party until ill health forced him to relinquish the role in four years later.

Generations of the Benn family were heavily involved in helping the poorer classes of society, particularly in London. John Benn was elected to the newly formed London County Council in 1889 and was involved in the dockworkers strike late in the same year, whilst his father Julius Benn was a congregational minister who founded the Home in the East, an institute for homeless boys in the East End of London. However, the Benn line hailed from the industrial north and it is clear that before he moved to London to carry out philanthropic work, Julius had attempted to make his influence felt from within the establishment, having previously worked as a schoolmaster in Hyde near Stockport, where his son was born in 1851. Quite a wide range of professions appear in later generations - John was variously described as a draughtsman, cabinet and furniture designer, journalist and author (having established a trade journal, The Cabinet Maker) and eventually publisher, whilst one of his siblings, William, can be found working as a clerk at East India House in 1871 when the British Empire was at the height of its influence on the sub-continent. In contrast, John's wife Lily (Elizabeth) Pickford came from a line of manufacturers turned landowners who were also from Hyde, whilst she also claimed a distant family link to Josiah Wedgwood, the famous potter and Unitarian, via a common ancestor Gilbert Wedgwood.

Virtually every generation of Tony's direct family boasts larger than life characters, and by studying their lives it is possible to draw comparisons with Tony's own beliefs. For example, his father William was studying at University College, London when the Boer War broke out, and held strong anti-war beliefs. During one debate at Union Debating Society, his views so enraged some of his audience that a group through him out of the window! It is therefore perhaps no coincidence that his son would later take a leading role protesting about Britain's role in the war in Iraq, eventually becoming President of the Stop the War Coalition. Although in his eightieth year, Tony Benn remains a powerful voice in British politics, championing the case for the oppressed and thus echoing the beliefs of his forebears down the centuries.

Chapter 7

Working Life

Working life in Britain has changed out of all recognition over the last thirty years, so just imagine the impact the Industrial Revolution had on our ancestors over two centuries ago! The shift from a predominantly rural, agricultural society to the world's industrial powerhouse in the nineteenth century altered the face of Britain and created the urban-based society that we know today. Birmingham, for example, was a tiny hamlet in the Domesday Book and remained relatively small until the Midlands became one of the major manufacturing centres in the mid nineteenth century; its population rapidly expanded as factories and mills spread, until it cemented its current position as England's second city. Contrast that with the fate of Norwich, for centuries second in population to London and the centre of one of the richest regions in the country, having derived its wealth from the profits of the wool trade with the Continent. With the coming of mechanised industry and manufacturing, England's economic base shifted from its predominantly agricultural base and moved to the north and west, and the rural population went with it, leaving East Anglia as one of the poorest regions by the end of the nineteenth century. Hand in hand with the spread of industry and engineering came the rise of the professional classes – lawyers, accountants, bankers and merchants – as well as the growth of occupations such as teaching and healthcare as government sought to improve the living conditions in the newly developed cities and towns. We should not forget that Britain is an island and consequently many of

Opposite: **Many of our ancestors worked long hours in difficult conditions, such as these miners emerging from a long shift underground.**

our ancestors found a living from the sea as directly as fishermen and sailors, or working in one of the support industries such as dockyard labourers and ship-builders. The key to unlocking Britain's rich social history lies in the occupations listed in census returns and certificates – and you can experience these changes through the eyes of your ancestors by investigating the background to their daily work.

🏵 AGRICULTURE

In the eighteenth century, the bulk of the 'working classes', for want of a better term, were tied to the land as agricultural labourers, usually depicted as 'ag labs' in census returns. Most of our ancestors would have worked on the land prior to the Industrial Revolution, although the greatest factor that influenced change was an earlier social phenomenon known as the enclosure movement – a term used by historians to describe a whole range of measures whereby landowners changed the way land was cultivated, with consequences for the communities that it affected. For centuries, the old system of manors with common land, open pasture and uncultivated 'waste' land had existed, though some changes had occurred; yet there was an acceleration towards private ownership and farming of land in the eighteenth century. Private acts of Parliament 'enclosed' open fields and common land, with private landowners gaining the most out of the process and forcing many smaller tenant farmers off their land as their farms quickly became uneconomic and unprofitable. Many left their communities and joined the exodus to the emerging mill towns to find work in the newly industrialised Britain, particularly the poorer agricultural labourers who were unable to secure seasonal labour as once they had.

Yet it would be incorrect to say that agriculture in Britain declined; from the perspective of the landowners, it was even more profitable than ever and large areas of Britain remained under cultivation. Furthermore, the sector was still a

major employer particularly the further south you went, with less competition from factories that tended to be situated more in the north west and midlands. Seasonal labourers were still required to gather the harvest, and the population still needed to be fed. It was only during the latter half of the nineteenth century, when the import of cheap north American wheat made Britain more dependent on overseas cereals, that the labour market in the agricultural sector

Above: Before the Industrial Revolution, a large proportion of our ancestors worked on the land, with the majority described as 'agricultural labourers'.

Right: Traditional ways of farming survived well into the twentieth century, and often as late as the 1950s or 1960s.

started to collapse. By the end of the century, more people had flocked to the towns to find work and the face of Britain was transformed forever.

There are a number of resources you can use to find out about an ancestor that worked on the land, either as an agricultural labourer or a farmer. The National Archives holds a series of important land surveys that should allow you to trace the owner and occupier of a farm, and start to establish how the property might have changed over time. Working forward chronologically, you can build up a snapshot of a bygone age. The first source you can look at is the tithe apportionment survey (copies are also usually stored at the relevant county archive as well); they were created after the 1836 Tithe Act as part of a re-assessment of the medieval system of providing the local parish church with a tenth of all produce grown on land, in response to complaints from farmers that they were receiving an unfair burden given the redistribution of wealth during the Industrial Revolution. The surveys were made for each parish that continued to levy tithes in kind, and were intended to commute payments into a monetary amount. Consequently, in the decades following the act, local agents were sent round to make the assessment, and in consequence maps and

SOURCES

If you find that your ancestor was once an agricultural labourer, it's very unlikely that you'll find out which farm they were working on unless they are listed as being resident with the farm owner – which often happened. If this is the case, you can use the above sources to find out more about the property. However, one of the best ways to ascertain the conditions under which your relatives worked is to contact a relevant local museum that focuses on the agricultural way of life. One of the best is the Rural History Centre and Museum of English Rural Life, University of Reading, Whiteknights, Reading www.rdg.ac.uk/rhc

apportionment schedules were drawn up. Where they survive, you can find out who owned and occupied each plot of land in the parish, and start to work out the size and shape of the farm.

A similar exercise was carried out under the terms of the 1910 Valuation Office Survey, though this time the purpose was to raise tax for the government based on the rateable value of all property. The survey was conducted from

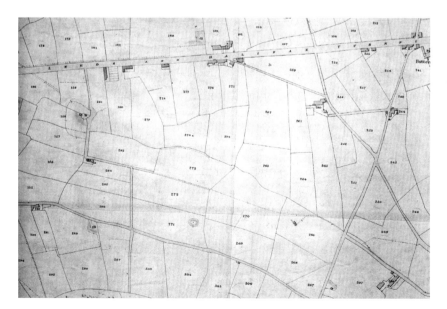

Left: You can work out where your rural ancestors lived from sources such as this Tithe Apportionment map.

c.1912 onwards, but was curtailed by the First World War so not all areas are covered, with also some destruction of documents in the Second World War. The records work in a similar way, with maps created that denote each plot of land, referenced by a number; these can be looked up in accompanying field books, which again tell you the name of the owner and occupier. Finally, as part of the war drive in the 1940s, the Government decided to survey the state of the country's farms to assist with food production. The resultant National Farm Survey was conducted in 1943, and once again the extent of farms can be plotted on a map and compared to a range of assessment files noting the size, extent, productivity and ownership of each farm. All relevant records are at The National Archives, Kew.

COMMERCE, INDUSTRY AND REGIONAL IDENTITY

Throughout British history, certain regions have been linked with particular skills, trades and forms of industry and commerce. Even before the start of the Industrial Revolution, which is usually thought to have started around 1750, many parts of the country were already associated with specific goods and the specialised skills needed to produce them. By tracing your ancestor to an area of the country during a specific period of history, you will be able to flesh out their lives by studying the types of industry they would have been involved in. Censuses, birth, marriage and death certificates and other public records often include occupation details, and this can help you to build up a more rounded picture of the person. Industrial museums and heritage centres try to keep this Britain's working history alive. They are well worth a visit to help you gain a feeling for the sort of life distant relative lived and the conditions they had to cope with.

Until the late seventeenth century, Britain was sparsely populated, mostly living in rural communities, little changed since medieval times. Two-thirds of the population worked in farming and related industries, such as wood, flax (used in rope-making), and leather goods. Vast swathes of the south Midlands and the southern and eastern counties were given over to cereals crops. The Midlands was also famed for its horses, and Wales and the Highlands of Scotland for cattle farming. Skilled and semi-skilled workers toiled in rural cottages and village workshops, as blacksmiths, weavers, spinners and tanners.

By far the most important industry, however, was sheep farming and associated woollen textile manufacture. At the start of the eighteenth century, it made up more than one-third of Britain's total industrial output and was worth an estimated £5 million to the country. Over the following century, the wool industry was to more than triple in size, to over £18 million. So there were few parts of the country that did not play some part in the production of woollen clothing. In 1700, Lancashire was already associated with spinning, but this was still literally a cottage industry at this time, with small groups of workers laboriously producing cloth by hand. Other forms of cloth manufacture were based in Cumbria, Devonshire, Essex, central Wales and Yorkshire.

Coastal regions mainly relied on fishing, coastal freight transport and international trade, and this pattern changed little right up to modern times. But some ports towns are famous for their shipbuilding heritage, now sadly in decline. In 1700, shipbuilding was mainly associated with Newcastle, Sunderland, Hull, London and parts of Essex, Portsmouth, Southampton and Plymouth. The coal mining industry was still relatively small, producing around 3,000 tons a year in the late 1600s. It was mainly located in Cumbria, Durham and Northumberland, the Forest of Dean, the Midlands, South Wales, Scotland, and parts of Yorkshire. Iron production, which was still in its infancy, was based primarily in the West Midlands. Staffordshire was already famous for its pottery, as was Sheffield for its cutlery, Lancashire for cotton goods, Derbyshire for silks and Nottingham for hosiery. Bristol grew rich on imported goods, especially wine and tobacco.

Cotton remained a minor industry until late in the eighteenth century, when an amazing social transformation took place. The Industrial Revolution owes its origins to many factors, including the development of mechanisation, steam power, more efficient methods of iron production and the rapid expansion of overseas trade. But the principal effect that it had on society, throughout the latter half of the eighteentth century and well into the nineteenthth century, was to bring about a dramatic change in the work and living patterns of ordinary British people. The principal occupations switched from mainly agricultural labour, based in small, scattered rural communities, to factory-based skilled and semi-skilled jobs, densely concentrated in dedicated industrial towns and cities.

Below: Small cottages started to spring up in the emerging industrial towns to house the workers from cotton spinning factories and the foundries.

The movement of the population from rural communities to towns had been a gradual process, beginning with the breakdown of communal farming in the middle ages. This was accelerated by the various Enclosures Acts, which removed large areas of open land from communal ownership and gave it to a relatively few large landowners. Displaced agricultural workers headed for the towns in search of new employment opportunities.

Higher wages and improved housing and health care brought about a population boom. This, in turn, led to a huge rise in the number of people living in urban areas, seen most vividly in the growth of four principal port cities during the course of the Industrial Revolution. Within 150 years, from 1700 to 1851, Bristol grew from 20,000 to over 130,000, Glasgow from 12,000 to 350,000, Liverpool from 6,000 to over 370,000 and London from half a million to two and a half million inhabitants. Norwich, by contrast, could do little more than double in size, from 30,000 to 68,000. With this growth in industrial population came increasing prosperity, with total national income increasing more than ten-fold, from £45 million in 1700 to over £570 million in 1851.

There was a massive expansion in coal production, from just 3,000 tons in 1700 to more than 240,000 tons by the end of the nineteenth century, matched by huge population growth in the principal mining areas. The application of new technology and water-powered and then steam-powered machinery to spinning and weaving brought about a rapid expansion in textile manufacture. By the end of the eighteenth century, cotton was Britain's most important industry and principal export. It was concentrated in Glasgow, Lancashire and the East Midlands, where workers lived in vast, sprawling factory towns. Later, the woollen industry, too, became mechanised, and based in Gloucestershire and the West Riding of Yorkshire. From the census of 1851, it is clear just how

Above: A row of coal miners waiting to start their shift.

SOURCES

A good source of information on working life in Britain through the ages is the local reference library, which may have copies of local trade directories from around 1800 giving lists of tradesmen and professionals, or search the database at www.historicaldirectories.org. The People's History Museum (www.peopleshistorymuseum.or.uk) has information on the history of British working life. Trade associations, trade unions and employers' archives are held at The Modern Records Centre (www.warwick.ac.uk/go/modernrecordscentre)

many regions relied on specific industries for their prosperity, such as linen and flax in Southern Scotland, lace in Devon, Nottingham, Oxfordshire and Northamptonshire, footwear in Leicestershire, and hosiery in Northamptonshire. The silk industry had switched to London. Steel making – and most especially cutlery – was based in Sheffield. Iron mining and manufacture were concentrated in Cumbria, Durham and Northumberland, South Wales, and the West Midlands. Britain was now being described as the 'workshop of the world' and could proudly show off its industrial heritage at the Great Exhibition of 1851.

⚜ INDUSTRY

It is a terrible oversimplification to state that the working population was split between town and country – clearly, a whole host of trades, occupations and professions existed back to medieval times, and continued to thrive and flourish alongside agriculture and industry throughout the nineteenth century and beyond as a glance at any census record will show you. Yet it is also clear that there was a clear shift from the rural working class to those who spent their days in the mills and factories, mines and foundries, that sprang up all over the country.

The growth of the cotton industry was perhaps the most striking. Whilst spinning and weaving existed as a means to earn some additional money amongst the yeomen farmers in the north west – hence the name 'spinster' for unmarried women who would spin from home – the mechanisation of the process through inventions such as the 'spinning jenny' prompted the construction of large sheds to house the new machinery. As these grew in size, so did the accompanying workforce that was required to operate them, and the 'manufactory' was born. Women and children as young as five or six would work long hours at the mechanised looms, and the 1802 Factory Act shows just how tough life was before this initial attempt to regulate conditions; for example, children's hours were restricted to 'only' 12 hours a day, with some provision for their education. Conditions in some factories were dangerous, with little lighting and occasionally poor ventilation. Given that the tasks that each employee performed were hard and repetitive, and that people worked long hours, tiredness led to lapses in concentration, which in turn produced horrific injuries.

Below: A small spinning loom - a piece of machinery that many of our ancestors would have been familiar with.

The rapid expansion in the number of mills, coupled with the associated move from country to the growing mill towns, meant that legislation was often ignored

Left: Mother and son pose for the cameras, their black dress suggests this might be a funeral or memorial service.

by unscrupulous mill owners and worked alike, and further pieces of legislation were required to raise the age of mill workers, reduce the hours that children could work, and increase the amount of education they were to receive. It's not completely true to say that this was the result of pressure by the workers — many opted to cram as many children into the mills as possible to support large families — whilst on the other side, many mill owners attempted to go beyond the terms of the various factory acts to insist of better standards of education for its workers.

Most people pick up clues about their family's employment from census records, which provide an indication of what they did for a living. Although few specify a particular mill or factory, it can be possible to narrow down from where they were living the most likely place of work, bearing in mind they would have walked a short distance to the nearest mill. Thereafter, factory records may survive, but they can be difficult to track down because they were essentially private records created by the companies concerned. It is rare to find employment records that give the names of individuals, though other documents can be found that shed light on other aspects of mill work, such as co-operative societies, friendly societies and other organisations set up to improve conditions for the workforce during times of hardship. Such material is usually deposited in the relevant county archive, although some specialist collections exist in university libraries. To gain a flavour of what life was like in one of the mills or factories, you should also seek out museums – most industrial towns have their own collections relating to life in the mills. Organisations such as the Weavers Triangle Visitors Centre, Burnley, also allow you to step back in time, whilst there are a range of websites – www.spinningtheweb.org.uk for example – that will also be of assistance with your research.

Alongside the rise of the mills, other major industries flourished in Victorian Britain, in particular steel and iron – the principal construction components behind many of the amazing feats of civil engineering that shaped the world, in particular the railway networks and the great iron ships that traversed the

SOURCES

As with many factory records, precise employment records rarely survive for coal mines as they were created for and retained by the mine owner, before the industry was nationalised; any administrative records of post-nationalisation can be found at The National Archives. You can use census records and civil registration documents to make an assumption as to the most likely place of employment, and then look into the history of the pit. Alternatively, you can piece together a very clear idea of what life in a pit was like from 'working mines' and museums such as the National Coal Museum, Caphosue Colliery, New Road, Overton, Wakefield www.ncm.org.uk.

Above: Child labour was prevalent in industrial Britain before legislation was introduced to limit their hours.

oceans. Many thousands of people found work in iron foundries and other forms of factories associated with the production of goods that were in demand not just domestically but also across the globe, as Britain established itself as the leading global industrial and economic power. However, these factories required fuel on which to operate, and one that was relatively abundant and therefore cheap – coal. The main areas of supply were in Wales, the Midlands around Nottinghamshire and Derbyshire, and the North East. Mining has been established in Britain for centuries, but as demand increased dramatically through the nineteenth century, so did the size and number of mines, which were sunk deeper and deeper.

If life in a factory was considered tough, then conditions could be even worse down a coalmine. Once again, young children – six or seven years old – would be sent down the mine, as their size meant that they could reach and hew coal seams that adults could not. At the coalface it was hot, cramped, dusty and dangerous, with constant fear of gas, flood or worst of all a tunnel collapse. Although mechanisation reduced some of the need for manual labour, for most people working in a mine the daily routine was punishing, and many miners ended their days in horrific accidents down the pit with crush injuries, or met a premature death with lungs coated in black coal dust.

THE CHANGING FACE OF TRANSPORT

A comprehensive search for ancestors is likely to send you all over the country. Throughout the eighteenth and nineteenth centuries, as the economy grew and transport links were steadily improved, the population became more mobile, ready and willing to move to any region that offered well-paid work and an opportunity for a better standard of living. As the British economy began its massive expansion in the early 1700s, this was matched by growing demand for a much better system of transport to carry raw materials and finished goods around the country.

Until the mid-1600s, the bulk movement of goods and passengers was a laborious process. Roads were poorly maintained and plagued by highway robbers, and so any journey by mail coach and cargo wagon was slow, arduous and dangerous. Consequently, most people rarely travelled farther than the nearest major town – and then only on market day. Most freight was carried in bulk by coastal shipping. Cargo boats and ships simply transported goods and materials from one port to another, hugging close to the shore. The principal ports at this time were East Lynn, Hull, Newcastle and London on the east coast, Dover, Portsmouth, Southampton and Exeter on the south coast, and Bristol, Liverpool and Glasgow on the west coast.

As international trade grew, these ports steadily developed to satisfy needs. Smaller craft were needed to carry goods inland along the 500 miles or so of navigable rivers. But this still left the bulk of the country more than 15 miles from any waterway that a cargo boat could safely negotiate and so effectively isolated from major trade routes. Over the next 100 years, an extensive engineering programme was carried out to more than double the amount of navigable waterway available – to over 1,100 miles. But this was still nowhere near enough to satisfy the rapid growth in trade and commerce that was in progress.

Another approach was to improve road transport. During the first half of the 18th century, parliament passed a series of Turnpike Acts intended to generate a boom in road building. These acts set up 'turnpike trusts' whose principal role was to build and maintain a network of major roads, paid for by toll charges collected from road users. In 1750, using the fastest stage coaches available, the journey from London and Bristol was nearly two days. It could take nearly four days to reach Manchester from London, and well over a week to get to Edinburgh. By the end of the century, the improved road network had effectively reduced journey times by up to half. The turnpike system did not cut the cost of transport, but shorter journey times encouraged more people to travel and to trade their goods in more remote parts of the country.

Although the improvement to the roads encouraged the movement of people and small quantities of goods, wagons were still unsuitable for transporting large volumes of freight. Bulk cargo still had to rely on the limited number of navigable rivers available. The obvious solution was to build more waterways. In the 1760s, the cost of transporting coal to the factories of Manchester was cut drastically by the building of the Duke of Bridgewater's Canal. This success story inspired a massive programme of canal building that effectively quadrupled the navigable waterway network to a total of 4,000 miles. Although slow, canals reduced the cost and vastly increased the capacity for moving raw goods and freight and gave a major boost to the Industrial Revolution. Now supplied with a cost-effective system for receiving raw materials and dispatching finished goods, the industrial regions expanded at an even faster rate, providing more employment and so requiring more housing to supply the growing workforce.

The labour-intensive canal building programme in itself provided a huge boost to employment, creating a new type of worker known as the navigator, or 'navvy'. Men travelled from all over mainland Britain and Ireland to join the labouring gangs building the new canals. Wherever navvies were working, huge temporary encampments sprang up, where the free-spending workers gave a welcome lift to the local economy. By the early 1800s, when the canal boom was loosing momentum, work was beginning on a new transport network. It was now the dawn of the railways.

The first major line, the Liverpool to Manchester Railway, opened in 1830. Over the following 20 years there were two major rail programmes creating a basic network of inter-city routes and increasing total rail track to more than 6,000 miles. By 1870, all the major lines were complete, doubling the total length of railway to more than 13,000 miles and the annual capacity to more than 300 million passengers and 150 million tons of freight. The final phase was the building of local routes and branch lines that, by the start of World War I had increased the rail network to 20,000 miles, each year carrying more than a billion passengers and five million tons of freight.

The growth of the railways also encouraged another mass movement of mainly younger people from rural areas to the major towns and cities. Yet more towns began to grow and expand, simply because they were strategically placed on a major railways line. Among the towns given a new lease of life by the

View from Railway Bridge. Belmont.

railways were Darlington, Doncaster, Edinburgh, Lincoln, Reading, Preston, Salisbury, Swindon, Stockton and Taunton. The railways were also responsible for a new social phenomenon, the suburbs, which sprang up around major cities and towns. The building of small local stations and branch lines feeding into the major cities encouraged many to return to the countryside to enjoy the best of both worlds – living in semi-rural locations while working in an urban conurbation. In London, workers had a choice of overland and underground railways, as the tube network began to develop from the late 1800s onwards.

Another social phenomenon, spurred on by the growth of the railways, was the increasing popularity of letter writing. This was aided by educational reforms that improved literacy rates, and by the launch of the 'penny post', which made letters much more affordable. This boosted trade and commerce, by making it much easier to order goods, and helped the increasingly widely dispersed population keep in touch with friends and relatives. When the postal service was at its height, from the late nineteenth to early twentieth centuries,

Above: The railway network transformed Britain into the world's leading industrial power in the nineteenth century.

it was possible to write a letter to a friend living locally inviting them to tea that afternoon – and even get a reply by return of post. That ease and speed of written correspondence wouldn't be seen again for nearly a century – and the development of the email.

The National Archive contains staff records of many public bodies including merchant seamen, and the railway companies. Other useful sources include the National Maritime Museum (www.nmm.ac.uk), which has a library and manuscript section, and the London Metropolitan Archives (www.cityoflondon.gov.uk/lma), the People's History Museum (www.peopleshistorymuseum.org.uk), and the British Library Newspapers (www.bl.uk/collections/newspapers.html).

Sources

 There are hundreds of places and industries in which our ancestors could have worked, each with its own sets of employment records and associated archives. Railways, for example, provided an opportunity for thousands of people to find work up and down the country, often relocating to places along the route of the line; many employment records are at the National Archives, with further material at the National Rail Museum, Leeman Road, York (www.nrm.org.uk). If no specific employment records survive for the profession in which your ancestor worked, you could always try to track them down through trade unions, which flourished during the industrial age to cater for the rights and conditions of the workers. Many of the records can be found at the People's History Museum, 103 Princess Street, Manchester (www.peopleshistorymuseum.org.uk) or Trades Union Congress Congress House, Great Russell Street, London (www.tuc.org.uk). Hand in hand with trade unionism came politicisation and the birth of the Labour Party; early records of the labour movement can be found at the Modern Records Centre, University of Warwick, University Library, University of Warwick, Coventry (modernrecords.warwick.ac.uk).

℘ PROFESSIONAL CLASSES

Alongside the growth of the workers in areas away from the countryside came the expansion of the middle classes, in particular in the growing civil service required to keep the country running; as teachers in the schools that emerged to educate workers children; plus a multitude of other white collar professions such as lawyers, doctors, architects, engineers and so on. Each will have its own professional body, with associated records – Institution of Civil Engineers, Royal Institute of British Architects, the Law Society for example – that you can approach for further information and archives.

Yet one driving factor shaped one of the main areas of activity that linked one of the most important economic sectors that created wealth and employment for many of our ancestors –

Above: The emergence of international trade led to the expansion of the professional classes - financiers, bankers, merchants and economists.

overseas trade, particularly in the golden age during the eighteenth and nineteenth centuries. This was a period of British history when London was at the heart of international trade, and the pool of London bristled with the masts of hundreds of ships unloading their cargoes into warehouses, ready to be moved to other destinations. The merchant classes had flourished throughout the 1700s, with an entire insurance industry supported on the back of the trade in exotic goods from around the world, specifically linked to the emerging British Empire in both the East and West Indies. Lloyds of London was originally one of many insurance houses operating at the time, but quickly gained a pre-eminence that has continued to the present day. Shipping was big business, and of course provided an excellent opportunity for the Crown to derive its revenue from customs duties – so as well as merchants, clerks and insurance agents, customs officials would also have operated at the docks to ensure no-one evaded

PLACES OF CORRECTION

There are a number of ways to research an ancestor who formed part of Britain's merchant classes. Trade directories – first published in the eighteenth century but surviving in greater numbers from the nineteenth century onwards – are an excellent place to begin your research, as they provide the name and address of individuals involved in trade and commerce. In a similar vein, Lloyds of London produced a range of annual publications, aimed specifically at the mercantile classes who were involved in shipping. Some of the most useful list vessels registered in Britain, along with the names and addresses of their owners or agents.

the proper dues set out by the Government. Closely linked to shipping, insurance and trade was the banking profession, which expanded dramatically from the eighteenth century onwards to establish London at the heart of international finance. This was a truly momentous period in British history, and created thousands of jobs for the emerging professional classes; not just in London, but also in ports all over the country, such as Bristol, Liverpool and Glasgow, where the mercantile elite based their operations and funded the construction of Georgian townhouses from the proceeds of their wealth.

It might also be worth investigating whether there is an official trade magazine or newspaper, as these often feature advertisements by key players in a particular industry, or include information about individuals. Thereafter, any records likely to survive will be of a personal nature, and so may be deposited in the local archive or county record office. It might also be worth checking to see if there is a guild or association linked to your ancestor's profession, as there might be admission records or other official records. Finally, though, one of the most important sources is wills or probate inventories, as they can not only provide an intimate perspective of a person's family, friends and treasured possessions, but also can shed light on what they did for a living, where they were based and how much they were worth when the died!

Opposite: **Even distinguished-looking ancestors might have secrets to hide!**

Case study 1 (occupation)

David Jason

David Jason has worked in television for many years on a range of series, yet he will almost certainly be remembered for 'Del Boy', the archetypal loveable wheeler-dealer from Nelson Mandela House, Peckham who always dreamed that next year he'd be a millionaire. One of the charms of the series was the family relationship played out between the Trotters, and the close family bonds kept them together through largely bad times. Have you ever wondered how much of David Jason's own background went into the creation of Del Boy? The clues from his family tree are quite intriguing…

David Jason was born David John White in 1940 in Edmonton, London. The comedic mainstay of *Only Fools and Horses* is the relationship between Del Boy and his brother, Rodney; so it is tragic to discover that David's twin brother, Jason, died just two weeks after birth and was secretly buried at home by their mother. David only discovered that he had a twin when he was fourteen, and was so affected by the news that when he started acting he adopted the surname Jason in memory.

David's background mirrors that of Del Boy to a certain extent, in the sense that he was born and bred in London. His parents were Arthur White and Olwen Jones, who, given her name, perhaps unsurprisingly hailed from Wales, and the couple married in 1932 in Barnet. The White family were butchers by profession, though when Arthur married Olwen he was plying his trade as a fishmonger's assistant. The ancestral business can be traced through the White family as far back as the 1850s, when David's great great grandfather James White was practicing as a butcher around Manchester. His son Henry Rowland White also worked as a butcher in 1877 at the time of his wedding to Theresa Beaumont, the daughter of a local gentleman – or so he was described on their marriage certificate – and the couple lived in Russel Square, Hulme where their son Rowland Beaumont White was born the following year. Rather strangely, Henry states on the 1881 census that he had been born in Sussex, which suggests quite a large degree of travelling was involved at some stage in the family history. This pattern seems to have continued; by the time of Rowland's marriage to Elizabeth Boots in 1899 he had moved to London, where he continued to live for the rest of his days as a butcher in a meat market.

So there is an apparent story of social mobility that would have impressed Del Boy – a direct relative marrying into the gentry, before moving to London to make good in the family trade. Yet all was not as it seemed; Rowland's father in law Richard Boots was a car man and caretaker, whilst his maternal grandfather James Beaumont appears to have worked as a painter and glazier rather than a gentleman; which seems to fit more with the social profile of the family. The reasons for the move to London in the 1890s are unclear, but they clearly settled in their new surroundings, making a home for themselves in Clapham – not a million miles away from Peckham…

As with so many television and film stars, David Jason's surname is actually something different, in this case White. Whilst not as common as Smith or Jones, there are still an incredibly large number of White families scattered throughout Britain, making life that bit harder when trying to track down the correct lineage. There are ways, though, of ensuring that you have found the right ancestors.

First, geography is always important. You can usually narrow down the area where your relatives came from by looking at the places of residence recorded on certificates, census records or parish registers, and you can use existing family knowledge to start this process. The next thing to watch out for is naming patterns, particularly if unusual middle names appear, as in the case of Rowland Beaumont White – this often indicates the inclusion of a female surname following a marriage, and helps you to distinguish one line of descent from another if your family tended to use a traditional Christian name from one generation to the next. Wills and probate documents can often help to untangle complicated family relationships – if, of course, they survive. Finally, a family trade can provide important clues, particularly if you are trying to corroborate data from other sources such as census records; for example, Henry White refers to himself as Rowland White (his middle name) on the 1881 census, yet his address and name of his spouse and children all fit; the crucial piece of evidence is the fact that he is a butcher. Trade directories, which survive in increasing numbers from the mid-nineteenth century onwards, can help you plot the movements of a family who rely on a job where local reputation was a vital part of business.

CASE STUDY 2

BOB HOSKINS

Made famous in the film *The Long Good Friday*, in which he played opposite Helen Mirren and gave a performance that many believe to have defined the British gangland film for decades, Bob Hoskins has always taken challenging roles of anti-heroes – another good example being *Mona Lisa*. He has always breathed life into the characters that he portrays on screen, creating rounded three-dimensional characters that the audience can empathise with. It's therefore rather ironic that in one of his best known films *Who Framed Roger Rabbit?* he starred opposite cartoons. Most recently, he has appeared with Judi Dench in *Mrs Henderson Presents*. Family detective sifts through Bob's background to see if there are any clues as to where he gets the inspiration for his characters.

WHO IS BOB HOSKINS RELATED TO?

Robert William Hoskins was born in 1942 in Suffolk – Bury St Edmunds to be precise – although his parents' normal address was north London. His father, Robert, was a lorry driver for Pickfords, the removal firm, and spent long periods shifting furniture from house to house. Before he married Elsie Lillian Hopkins in 1940, Robert lived in Islington, not far from the household of his future bride. This is the heartland of the Hoskins family, and explains why Bob associates himself most strongly with London characters despite his Suffolk birthplace. Yet if we move back another generation or two, the connection with street savvy 'gangsters' (for want of a better word) becomes even harder to fathom, because in terms of profession his ancestors had more in common with Steptoe and son than the Kray twins.

Bob's father, Robert Hoskins, was born in Brewery Road, Islington, in 1913, the son of William Hoskins and his wife Elizabeth Lord. William worked as a car man – an occupation that was very common in London from the Victorian age onwards, and although it can be described a number of ways, the most common usage was as a type of rag and bone man. Indeed, at the time of William's marriage in 1908, he described himself as a metal worker – whether this meant he worked in a metal beater's yard or traded in old scrap metal is a little hard to determine from the records, but it is clear that William's father – another Robert Hoskins – was listed on the marriage certificate as a scavenger. All of these professions were essential in keeping Edwardian London's streets free from rubbish, bearing in mind the revolution in domestic technology that had taken place in the decades following the Great Exhibition. Scavengers, carmen, metal workers, rag & bone men all collected the discarded scraps that society had no further use for, and where possible recycled the materials and sold them to other dealers and traders. They have always been considered amongst the ranks of the Victorian under-class along with less savoury scavengers who would scour the sewer networks for hidden 'treasure' – but today we would hail them as eco-warriors and put them at the forefront of those doing their bit for the planet.

It is probably fair to describe Bob's ancestors as working class – Elizabeth Lord's father James was a woodcutter, living in Marylebone amongst labourers, bricklayers and painters. An entry on the 1891 census marks out how difficult life must have been for James – he was described as a cripple, yet was forced to earn money chopping wood so that he could support his wife Eliza and seven children, two of whom were already at work aged 16 and 14. Fast forward ten years, and we find him at the same address, a widower with four children aged between 10 and 16 to feed; it is little surprise that he had taken in a lodger, James Lee, to help make ends meet. Yet the story becomes sadder still, as he came from quite well to do stock. His father, Charles Lord, was originally listed as a master tailor and draper living alongside other craftsmen and traders – a master boot maker, and fishmonger for example, all employing staff. One wonders if it was James's disability that restricted his chances in life, and if what the implications for his children might have been if he had followed in his father's footsteps. On such details do our current lives depend, and James's fate illustrates clearly that some clouds have a silver lining – without these events happening in the exact way that they did, his great-grandson Bob Hoskins is unlikely to be with us today.

CASE STUDY 3

DAME JUDI DENCH

Dame Judi Dench has enjoyed a glittering film career, with her latest offering, *Mrs Henderson Presents*. Her roles have been diverse and varied, covering period drama, such as *Pride and Prejudice*, quintessentially English ladies in *Ladies in Lavender* and *Tea with Mussolini*, biography (Iris Murdoch in *Iris*), or the intelligence officer M in James Bond films such as *Die Another Day* and the forthcoming *Casino Royale*. She has even found time to play royalty – twice – as Elizabeth I in *Shakespeare in Love* and, to great acclaim, the grieving Queen Victoria in *Mrs Brown*. Yet for many, she is equally recognisable at the heart of a family sitcom, playing opposite her late husband Michael Williams in *A Fine Romance* and more recently the generational comedy *As Time Goes By*. So, what influences for her characters can be found in her family tree? Are there spies, royalty, or a plethora of very nice middle-class ladies? It's time to reveal all...

Judith Olivia Dench was born in York in 1935, the daughter of Reginald Arthur Dench and his wife Eleanora Olave. Reginald worked as a doctor in York, and both he and his wife were very keen amateur actors. Judi was first taken to see a play at the age of four, and within a year she had secured her first role – as a snail! Her parents sent her to a Quaker school in York, where she continued to be drawn to the stage. She appeared in several productions including *Richard II*, playing the part of the Queen – a taste of things to come? Reginald had studied medicine at Trinity College Dublin where he met Olave, the daughter of Haeey Jebb Jones, who was a native of Dublin. After marrying, the couple moved to York to set up a practice and raise a family.

Reginald's own origins were not as grand as you might expect from someone who went on to train as a doctor. He was born in 1897, the son of George William Dench, a printer and stationer living in Southampton. George had married his wife Bessie Oak Smith in 1887, and raised three children, William, Mabel and Reginald, but one suspects that additional income was welcome to help support the family – in 1901, the family had taken in a lodger, George Fraser, who worked as a marine engineer, and a quick check of the other tenants in their block suggest the family were living amongst artisans and labourers – occupations included grocer, tailor, school caretaker and a flour agent, not quite the same calibre as one of the professional classes that Reginald was later to aspire to. Although living in Southampton by 1901, George had been born in Melcombe Regis, near Weymouth, in 1866 and can be found with his family on the 1881 census where he was apprenticed to become a printer. Once again, there is evidence that the family were not exactly thriving; George's father George Joseph Dench is not listed as being at home when the census was taken, whilst his wife Emily was described as a dressmaker, indicating that two incomes were required to look after the family. An additional cause for concern would have bee her eldest daughter Florence, who had been deaf since she was 7 years old.

Yet further investigation reveals one possible reason for George Joseph Dench's absence from the census records in 1881, as ten years earlier his occupation was that of an outdoor officer for HM Customs. A career linked to the see clearly ran in the family, as George Joseph's father William had worked as a porter on the quayside at Weymouth since at least the 1850s, if not earlier, whilst as a child George Joseph has earned some pocket money running errands Customs officers were civil servants, and can be relatively easy to trace at The National Archives providing you have some idea of where they were serving. By the middle of the nineteenth century, most of the danger had gone out of the profession, but even sixty or seventy years earlier it could have been potentially hazardous, particularly on some of the remoter parts of the coast when smugglers were prepared to kill customs officers to prevent capture of their goods or themselves.

Bessie Oak Smith was born in the same year as Reginald Dench just a few miles down the road in Wyke Regis, but came from a very different background. Her father Thomas was a journeyman confectioner and pastry cook, a skilled profession that in the late 1800s was often associated with German-born families. Yet it is clear that his roots lay firmly within Dorset, and that there was probably a strong connection with the sea. Here the trail ends for now, as the genealogist's nightmare begins to unfold: the 1861 census return shows from the various family relationships that Thomas Smith had previously married Susan Jane Smith, and lived with his in-laws, William and Susan Smith, next door to a Frederick Smith and family who may – or may not – be related. There are simply too many Smiths to untangle in just a single attempt!

CASE STUDY 4

MICHAEL CAINE

Michael Caine's screen credits make for a long and impressive read – indeed, many of his most famous roles have now been remade, most prominently *Alfie*, *Get Carter* and *The Italian Job*. He was the original cool Brit in the 1960s, turning his considerable talent to a range of films covering many genre, from war epics (*Zulu*), via gangster films (*Get Carter*) to less serious roles in the 1980s (such as *Jaws 4: The Revenge*). More recently he has turned his hand to play slightly darker characters – who can forget his memorable turn at the end of *Little Voice*? – plus serious roles (*Cider House Rules*), and still remains one of the most recognizable names and voices of British cinema. In 2000, the BBC and BAFTA teamed up to accord him a tribute show, and in the same year he was knighted in the Queen's Birthday Honours List. However this stellar filmography masks a very humble background.

The line 'my name is Michael Caine' has been used by impressionists over the years as an opener for their take on his inimitable style, but strictly speaking it is not true. The man we know as Michael Caine was actually born Maurice Joseph Micklewhite in Rotherhithe in 1933, the son of Maurice Micklewhite senior and his wife, Ellen Frances Maria Burchell. Yet his birth certificate reveals that even this might have been different, as his original first name was recorded as John, but was crossed out by the registrar as a mistake. One wonders what difference this would have made to his stage name had the error been allowed to stand. At the time of Maurice's birth, his parents were working as a council road labourer and charwoman respectively, living in one of the poorer parts of Bermondsey, south London. Previously Maurice senior had worked as a fish porter, following in the footsteps of his father Joseph. This was a fairly common profession in the area, given the proximity of the docks and the continued reliance on the import of fresh fish to supply the needs of the City and beyond. Indeed, in 1891 Joseph was actually listed as a dock labourer.

Yet before Joseph transported fish around the docks of south London, he had previously worked as a more general mover of goods – a journeyman carman, a very common profession and often loosely associated with the rag and bone trade. This occupation crops up again and again in the family tree; Maurice junior's maternal grandfather John Burchell was also a journeyman carman and hawker at various stages of his career, whilst his father John was described as a porter. He too was involved in fish, working at the famous Billingsgate Market for most of his life. The intrinsic link between the Burchell family and the docks can be extended back one further generation, where James Burchell – Maurice junior's two times great grandfather – was listed in 1851 as a dock labourer, whilst his wife Jane also found work as a sail cloth maker, whilst living at their home in May Pole Alley, Southwark, raiding their three children. The census return gives a remarkable insight into the family, as their youngest daughter, Catherine, is listed as being only one day old! As was common in the poorer parts of town, the family also took in lodgers, including a costermonger called Mary Regan from Ireland. To underline the poverty of the family, many of the signatories to birth and marriage certificates simply left their mark, a standard indication of illiteracy. The story of Michael Caine's family reflects the experience of thousands of people in south London during the nineteenth and early twentieth centuries, earning their living either from the docks or through hard graft, and it makes Michael's rise to international superstardom even more remarkable.

CASE STUDY 5

STEPHEN HAWKING

Stephen Hawking's remarkable book *A Brief History of Time* popularised some of the most complex theories that humanity has yet developed about such eternal puzzles as the nature of the universe, black holes and time itself. Stephen William Hawking was born at the Radcliffe Maternity Home, Oxford, in 1942, the son of Frank Hawking, a medical practitioner, and Isobel Eileen Walker. Although the family lived in Hampstead, a well-to-do part of London where Frank worked, it was decided that in the interests of safety the baby should be born outside the capital, given the increased dangers from German bombing raids during the war. Shortly afterwards, the family moved to St Albans where Stephen grew up.

Frank's career decision to become a doctor was a pivotal moment for the Hawking family, as for generations the family had found a living on the land working as farmers in Yorkshire; and it is not too much of an overstatement to claim that this probably changed the course of human history, given the influences that Stephen received growing up in a scientific environment rather than training for a life in agriculture. The Walker family also came from a medical background, as Eileen's father James also finding employment as a doctor.

Yet to find out about the Hawking roots, we have to travel to the rolling dales of Yorkshire and step back into a world far removed from the dreaming spires of Oxford where Stephen was born, and later studied as an undergraduate. His father Frank was born in 1905 in Aldborough, in the west riding of Yorkshire, to Robert Hawking, a farmer, and his wife Mary Lund Atkinson. The family were clearly making money out of agriculture, as they were able to pay two house servants to care for their first child John Lund Hawking, including the rather wonderfully named Cerise Bosomworth, a fifteen year old domestic nurse. In 1901, Robert's father John Hawking lived just down the road in Ellenthorpe, where he too farmed and employed several house servants to look after himself and three adult children, Elizabeth, Eleanor and Henry, all of whom worked from home – a term that a century later has found a new meaning throughout this summer as a euphemism for 'watching the Ashes'.

The Hawking family can be traced through successive census returns as far back as 1841 to Linton upon Ouse, where they worked as farmers; indeed in 1851, John's father Henry Hawking had 480 acres of land under his cultivation, employing nineteen labourers to work the farm as well as two household servants – clearly the family liked their domestic chores taken care of by others. Parish registers can be used to take up the story, with the Hawking line traceable in the area for at least a further century to the 1740s. However, there are exceptions in the unbroken chain of census records. For example, in 1871 John Hawking appears with his wife Hannah as a border at the Liverpool Street Hotel, Pancras. Given that they had married only just prior to when the census was taken, it is highly likely that this return reveals where they went on their honeymoon! Ten years previously, John was listed once again as a border, this time as a twelve-year-old scholar in the care of his teacher, Carvus Bedford.

But agriculture did not just run through the Hawking family. John's daughter in law, Mary Lund Atkinson, also came from a farming family who originally hailed from Linton. Whilst working as a teacher in 1891, she was living with her grandfather Hebdon Groves, who can also be traced through census records back to 1861. At 104 acres, his farm was smaller than his neighbour Henry's but still a considerable amount of land to attend to, especially in 1891 when he was approaching 80 years of age. Hebdon's children included James Lund Groves, who worked 157 acres of land in Kirk Deighton and lived with his grandmother Mary Lund, aunt Jane Lund and no less than four servants. Similarly, as with the Hawking line, it is possible to trace the Groves and Lunds back through earlier census records and parish registers into the eighteenth century.

Tracing your Yorkshire roots

Whilst there are no really dramatic incidents that jump out of the records relating to Stephen Hawking's family, the devil lies in the detail and illustrates several aspects of Yorkshire family history. Outside of towns and cities, particularly before the population movements of the mid nineteenth centuries, communities retained their identity and families tended to stay relatively local – as the Hawkings, Groves and Lunds prove above.

Yorkshire has always had a unique and strong identity, dating back from the Dark Ages when it was first a separate kingdom, then a centre for Viking settlement, and finally a site of resistance to the Normans in the eleventh century. Each of its administrative divisions – or Ridings – has at least one record office, and the Borthwick Institute, part of the University of York, holds a large collection of documents relevant to the pursuit of local and family history, such as northern wills. You can find out more online at www.york.ac.uk/inst/bihr.

Case study 6

Menzies Campbell

With the resignation of Charles Kennedy as leader of the Liberal Democrats, a contest between the three main contenders resulted in the veteran politician, Menzies Campbell becoming leader. It is unsurprising to find that his background lies in Scotland, but there is great diversity in his background.

Walter Menzies Campbell was born in 1941 in Glasgow, the son of a surveyor, George Alexander Campbell and his wife Elizabeth Jean Adams Phillips. George worked in the construction industry all his life, being listed as a building contractor at the time of his marriage nine months previously in 1940. Yet although there was a family tradition of employment in this field, George was the first to rise to such a position of prominence; by contrast, his father Walter Campbell was a joiner and grafted all his life, working his way up from journeyman status. Although he raised his family in Glasgow, he had been born in 1864 in Inverness and married late in life in 1907 at the age of 43; his wife Helen Hardie was 36 at the time. She worked as a telephone supervisor – quite an impressive position, given the fact that telecommunications were still a fledgling industry. Despite their relatively advanced ages, the couple settled down and raised a family, with George being born in 1909. Helen Hardie was clearly a woman of some substance, living to the ripe old age of 93.

There is a remarkable diversity of backgrounds and professions further back in the Campbell side of the family, yet evidence of continuity as well. Walter's father was another George Campbell, and he appears to be the first in the line to turn his hand to the arts and crafts of the building. He married Mary Menzies in 1863 – which is where Sir Menzies Campbell derives his name – a domestic servant living at Raigmore House in Inverness. Her family were closely involved in the service industry, her father James Menzies acting as the local gamekeeper on the same estate. He was also socially mobile, having worked his way up from a humble agricultural labourer hailing from the parish of Dull, perhaps an unfortunate placename bearing in mind his great grandson's chosen profession as a politician. Returning to George Campbell's background, it is clear that George achieved quite a prominent position, described on various census returns and certificates as a carpenter and clerk of works, someone who would have held authority and responsibility on any project he was employed on. The really interesting character in the

Campbell family lies one generation further back, though – Walter Campbell senior, George's father. At the time of his death aged 83 in 1899, he was described as a Gaelic teacher, having worked for most of his life as a schoolmaster. However, there is further evidence that he also found time to work as a lay missionary for the Free Church of Scotland, and that during the early part of his working life he traded as a merchant – quite a varied career, and therefore a man of versatility and intelligence. His ability to speak and teach Gaelic had been passed down through successive generations, as his father George also taught the language in his home of Dornoch, Sutherland.

The maternal side of the family tree also holds a variety of interesting occupations. Sir Menzies Campbell's mother, Elizabeth Jean Adams Phillips, was born in 1915 and worked as a post office sorting clerk and telephonist; her father, William Phillips was a dispensing chemist whilst her grandfather, Samuel Phillips, had worked as a gasworks labourer. William Phillips married Jane McGovaney in 1911, and in the light of my revelations about Charles Kennedy's ancestral connection with alcohol, her father John McGovaney's profession might send shivers down the spine of all prospective voters – he was a spirit salesman!

In summary, it is clear that Sir Menzies Campbell can trace his ancestry to some interesting and diverse characters, and that there is a great deal of social mobility in his family tree covering agricultural labourers, teachers, a wide variety of professions in the building trade, telecommunications, merchants and salespeople. There's something that everyone can relate to in his family tree, and from a politician's perspective he can draw upon these various elements to appeal to a wide section of the population.

Arthur L. Gillies.
Xmas 1920

CHAPTER 8

Military Ancestors

We've all heard stories told to us by parents, uncles, aunts or grandparents that began 'during the war...' but how many times have we switched off at this point? How much of that story can you now recall? It's easy to forget the fact that the entire course of the twentieth century was been shaped by the two world wars, and in particular by the changes to society that followed 'the Great War' of 1914–1918. Most families were touched in some way by the conflict, either directly through active service in the Army, the Royal or Merchant Navy, or the newly created Royal Air Force; or at work on the home front in munitions factories or on the land. Although most of this generation have passed on, the memories of this traumatic period in British history survive in oral accounts, handed down to children and grandchildren who are still alive. In most communities there is at least one war memorial that commemorates the names of local men and women who fell during the conflicts, and we would be fortunate indeed if there was not at least one member of our family listed somewhere in the UK, or in the mass graveyards in France and Flanders. There are also more personal and tangible pieces of evidence that have survived - medals, photographs, letters and postcards sent back from the Front Line, and remnants of military uniform such as regimental cap badges. These treasures, passed down through a family as heirlooms, or often still hidden in boxes waiting to be discovered in attics and cellars, will provide a gateway into the world of the professional and conscripted soldier, sailor or airman. With the

Opposite: This young soldier survived the Great War, but many of his friends and family would have fallen in combat.

Right: You can work out a soldier's rank and regiment from a photograph of his uniform.

release of service papers from the First World War at The National Archives, and the publication online of campaign medal index cards, you can now obtain crucial biographical information, as well as piece together their movements on the front line. Indeed, you can trace the career of almost any professional soldier or sailor before the Great War through records in the public domain.

I'll be using this chapter to sketch a basic introduction to the sources available for tracing a military ancestor, as well as explaining how you can use personal memorabilia, along with family tradition or census data, to investigate their life and times. The first and most obvious step is to work out which of the services your ancestor was enrolled in – and this is where you need to interpret the clues carefully. Then, if you want to look for service papers, you have to decide whether they were a commissioned officer, or a non-commissioned officer or other rank – this is how most service records are arranged. There are further divisions that you have to consider. For example, if your ancestor was a seafarer, he may have served with the merchant navy instead of the Royal Navy, or as a Marine or reservist. Many records of army service are organised by regiment; without this information your search for information could be

1931 200,000 7—10 H W V Forms
[No. 14*.]   E. 501.
—28 58 47   4

Army Form E. 501.

A

30.11.21

TERRITORIAL FORCE.

4 years' Service in the United Kingdom.

ATTESTATION OF

2148

No. 2326 Name *Ronald Charles Colman* Corps *London Scottish*

Questions to be put to the Recruit before Enlistment.

1. What is your Name?	*Ronald Charles Colman*
2. In or near what Parish or Town were you born?	2. In the Parish of *Ealing* ...... in or near the Town of ...... in the County of *Middlesex*
3. Are you a British Subject?	3. *Yes*
4. What is your Age?	4. *23* Years *5 6* Months.
5. What is your Trade or Calling?	5. *Shipping Clerk*
6. In whose employ are you?	6. *W.H. Walter & 7, Whittington Av: EC*
7. Where do you now reside?	7. *Denbigh Road Ealing W.*
8. Are you now an Apprentice? if so, please state particulars	8. *46 Lancaster Gate. W*
9. Are you married?	9. *No*
10. Do you now belong to the Army, the Marines, the Militia, the Militia Reserve, the Territorial Force, the Royal Navy, the Army Reserve (Regular or Special), or any Naval Reserve Force? If so, to what Corps?	10. —
11. Have you ever served in the Army, the Marines, the Militia, the Militia Reserve, the Imperial Yeomanry, the Territorial Force, the Royal Navy, the Volunteers, the Army Reserve (Regular or Special), or any Naval Reserve Force? If so, please state Corps and cause of discharge.	11. *Yes. London Scottish – Expiration of 4 years service*
12. Do you belong, or have you belonged, to any Cadet Unit?	12. *No*
13. Have you ever been rejected as unfit for the Military or Naval Forces of the Crown? If so, on what grounds?	13. *No*
14. Did you receive a Notice, and do you understand its meaning?	14. *Yes*
15. Are you willing to be attested for the term of 4 years (provided His Majesty should so long require your services) for service in the Territorial Force of the County of † *London* to serve in the ‡ 14th B COUNTY OF LONDON (LONDON SCOTTISH)?	15. *Yes.*
16. Do you understand that during the first year of your original enlistment you will be (a) required to attend the number of drills and fulfil the other conditions prescribed for a recruit of the arm or branch of the service which you have elected to join? ¶ (b) That in addition to such preliminary training you will be liable to attend the number of drills and fulfil the other conditions relating to training prescribed for the arm or branch of the service which you have elected to join, and be liable to be trained for not less than 8, or more than 15 days altogether, in every year, or, if belonging to a mounted branch for not less than 8, or more than 18 days altogether, in every year, as may be prescribed, ¶ and may for that purpose be called out, once or oftener, in every year? (c) That if you, without leave or reasonable excuse, fail to attend the number of drills required to fulfil the conditions relating to preliminary or annual training prescribed for your arm or branch of the service, you render yourself liable to a fine not exceeding £5? (d) That when a proclamation has been issued, in case of imminent national danger or great emergency, calling out the first class Army Reserve you will become liable to be embodied? (e) That, if your term of 4 years' service expires when a proclamation ordering the Army Reserve to be called out on permanent service is in force, you may be required to prolong your service for a further period not exceeding 12 months? (f) That you will be liable to serve in any place in the United Kingdom without further agreement, but not in any place outside the United Kingdom unless you voluntarily undertake to do so? (g) That you will be required to deliver up in good order, fair wear and tear only excepted, at such times and place as may be ordered by the Commanding Officer, all arms, clothing and appointments issued to you, being public property (including the property of the County Association)?	16. *Yes.*

¶ A further period of preliminary training may be prescribed during the first year of original enlistment by an Order in Council, the number of days being specified, and the period of annual training in any year may be extended by an Order in Council, due notice thereof having been given, and provided that neither House of Parliament has dissented, but the whole period of annual training shall not exceed 30 days in any year.

Under the provisions of Section 99 of the Army Act, if a person knowingly makes a false answer to any question contained in the attestation paper, he renders himself liable to punishment.

I, *Ronald Charles Colman* do solemnly declare that the above answers made by me to the above questions are true, and that I am willing to fulfil the engagements made.

Ronald E Colman SIGNATURE OF RECRUIT.

W Culverwell Sgt Signature of Witness.

OATH TO BE TAKEN BY RECRUIT ON ATTESTATION.

I, *Ronald Charles Colman* do make Oath, that I will be faithful and bear true Allegiance to His Majesty King George the Fifth, His Heirs, and Successors, and that I will, as in duty bound, honestly and faithfully defend His Majesty, His Heirs, and Successors, in Person, Crown, and Dignity against all enemies, according to the conditions of my service.

CERTIFICATE OF MAGISTRATE OR ATTESTING OFFICER.

I *William Harvey Anderson* do hereby certify, that, in my presence, all the foregoing Questions were put to the Recruit, above named, that the Answers written opposite to them are those which he gave to me, and that he has made and signed the Declaration, and taken the oath at *59 Buckingham Gate* on this *5th* day of *August* 1914 *WH Anderson 2/Lt* Signature of Justice of the Peace, Officer, or other person authorised to attest Recruits.

If any alteration is required on this page of the Attestation, a Justice of the Peace should be requested to make it and initial the alteration under Section 80 (6), Army Act.

The Recruit should, if he require it, receive a copy of the Declaration on Army Form E. 501A.

Right: Letters home from the front provide an intimate account of a soldier's life.

lengthy. It might be possible to get a positive identification from a cap badge, and most people enlisted to the local regiment, or regiment stationed nearest to them. A good starting point is J Kitzmiller, *In search of the 'Forlorn Hope': A Comprehensive Guide to locating British Regiments and their Records*. If you have a picture or note on which ship your ancestor served, there are similar publications to get you started, as well as specific records at The National Archives to confirm whether he served on board when he was supposed to.

I'll be introducing the main documents that are relevant for each branch of the armed forces, starting with records generated by the army.

乿 ARMY

During the eighteenth and nineteenth centuries, life in the army was seen as a career. Men joined up in the ranks for set periods of service, usually 14 years. On retirement, either through disability in the line of duty or after the expiration of service, many men were granted pensions. The surviving pension records, deposited at The National Archives, give many biographical details for each soldier, such as when and where they were born. In addition there are musters and pay lists, description books, registers of regimental baptisms, marriages and burials and other material that allow you to trace each man's career, often beyond British shores and into famous campaigns and battles. There are similar sources available for commissioned officers, as well as printed 'Army Lists' that can be used to compile an outline of service and dates of promotion. Indeed there are many printed regimental histories available, as well as museums that can held place your relative's career in its proper historical context.

Below: This photo reveals the rank and battalion of the soldier, which should be sufficient to start a search for records of service.

However, most people look for the military records of a soldier who fought in the Great War. Unfortunately a large proportion of records were destroyed by enemy action in the Second World War, but in addition to the surviving documents there are unit war diaries, trench maps and an index to campaign medal entitlement, the closest thing to a union name index for serving soldiers. For those who died in the conflict, the Commonwealth War Graves Commission is a good place to start your research; contact details are provided at the end of the article. Don't forget that many people served in the support services, such as the Royal Army Medical Corps or Queen Alexandra's Imperial Nursing Service Reserve.

Above: You can trace the history of a sailor's career in the Royal Navy as they moved from vessel to vessel.

⚓ NAVY

There is a similar division between Royal Naval officers and other ranks – known as ratings – with an equally wide range of source material available for each. Before 1853, naval ratings can be traced through musters and pay books, so you really need the name of the ship first – often a tricky task. Thereafter, service records were compiled, arranged by service number (which latterly reflected the role they were to play in the navy). There are surviving name indexes to the service registers, where you can find the names of all the ships that they served on, along with basic biographical data. Some pension records are also available. An even wider selection of records survive for naval officers. As well as service registers and pensions, there are separate pay registers, passing certificates, confidential reports and payments to widows, as well as the printed Navy Lists. Through these sources, it is possible to trace not only the service history of your ancestor, but also the ships on which they served, stations they were based and any naval engagements.

However, it is important to establish which branch of the Royal Navy they were with. For example, there are separate service ledgers for marines, as well as attestation forms, pension records and separate lists of births, marriages and deaths. Not all Royal Navy personnel were regulars – the Royal Naval Reserve and Royal Naval Volunteer Reserve were two pools of expert seamen who could be called upon in times of extreme need, such as the First World War. Be equally careful not to confuse Royal Navy with Merchant Navy – separate sets of records survive from the 1850s for masters, mates and seamen who worked on commercial vessels, and often served on Royal Naval vessels on occasion, or saw action during a war.

❧ RAF

The Royal Air Force is the newest of the services, formed on 1st April 1918 on the amalgamation of the army's Royal Flying Corps and the navy's Royal Naval Air Service. Before this date, service papers for men who served in these units will be stored with the relevant army and navy records where they survive. For those who joined the RAF, service ledgers were created, though these are closed after 1922. However there is a vast array of other data available, such as operation record books, base records and casualty reports to reveal the career of a pilot and support crew from the early 20th century onwards. As with the army and navy, there are additional printed Air Force Lists for officers, which can provide an outline career.

Above and right: A selection of RAF service papers telling us the airman's flight number and rank.

✂ MERCHANT MARINE

It's easy to overlook the fact that thousands of our ancestors worked on the seas in the merchant navy, finding employment on fishing boats or further afield, voyaging on one of the many trading routes that criss-crossed the globe. Many people would switch employment between royal and merchant navy, making them that much harder to trace in official records that start to survive from the mid-nineteenth century onwards. But at least records do survive, stored in a multitude of archives ranging from The National Archives, the National Maritime Museum, Greenwich, the Maritime History Archive, Newfoundland, Canada, and local archives. There is no central holding, and in many cases the records no longer survive. Most people in the merchant navy were seamen, and an identification system was introduced known as the register of seamen. Surviving records are at The National Archives; however, it was not comprehensive and was abandoned as unworkable in the 1850s, which meant that until its re-introduction in 1913 there is no way of tracing individuals unless you know the name of the ship they served on, in which case you can pick them up from crew lists and agreements. After 1921, when

Below: Cards such as this highlight Britain's historic position as a maritime power.

records for the so-called fourth register of seamen begin, ID cards, seamen's pouches and other documents exist at The National Archives, whilst the fifth register (which ends in 1972) provides details of voyages undertaken. Masters and mates were required to acquire certificates of competency (also at The National Archives), whilst information about the ships they sailed and crewed can be located from a wide range of printed sources. Medals for those involved in military conflict during the First World War can also be researched at The National Archives.

❧ WHAT THE MEDALS REVEAL

Families are, rightly, extremely proud of their relatives' military records. Campaign medals, gallantry awards, cap badges and other military insignia, framed photographs of uniformed ancestors, pay books and service documents are often passed on from one generation to the next. For those researching past military service, these items give the family researcher invaluable information about the branch of the forces their relatives served in, rank, any campaigns they fought in, and their conduct – both good and (perhaps) bad.

Armed with this information, you can hunt through public records, military archives and other sources to find out more about the person, and also study history books and visit military museums to gain an insight into the life they led. It is well worth while including a visit to the relevant regimental or service museum, including the Imperial War Museum, The National Army Museum. The Royal Navy Museum and the Royal Air Force Museum. All contain artefacts and displays depicting service life down the ages.

Service records and medal entitlements up to 1923 are held at The National Archives in Kew (www.nationalarchives.gov.uk). These archives also house information on other aspects of military service, such as pensions and pay lists. Records after this date are held at the Ministry of Defence. The Ministry has a useful

Left: Medals often contain important information about a soldier's rank and regiment.

website that can help you identify the cap badges of regiments that are still in existence (www.army.mod.uk/presscentre/badges/cap–badges). But for older, now defunct regiments, you may need to broaden your search, to include reference books and even collectors' web sites devoted to militaria. Information about those who died on active service are held by the Commonwealth War Graves Commission (www.cwgc.org).

For exceptional service in battle, a soldier, sailor or airman may have been 'mentioned in dispatches' – that is, referred to by name in the reports that senior officers sent back to headquarters. These, too, may be held at The National Archives. Published accounts of an individual's exploits appear in journals such as the London Gazette. If relatives performed an act of daring that caught the eye of the commanding officer, they may have received one of the top military awards. These include the Victoria Cross, 'for valour', the highest award that can be given for acts of courage under fire, the Military Medal, 'for bravery in the field', the Military Cross, the Air Force Cross, the Distinguished Flying Cross, the Air Force Medal, the Distinguished Flying Medal, the Distinguished Service Order (for officers) and the Distinguished Conduct Medal (for rank and file).

BRITISH CAMPAIGN MEDALS

British campaign medals are awarded to soldiers who took part in a specified military campaign. Only certain campaigns were commemorated in this way, and so absence of a medal does not necessarily indicate a lack of active service. Campaign medals over the last 200 years provide a fascinating insight into British and colonial history, revealing long forgotten military expeditions to far flung corners of the globe. They often feature a clasp naming a specific battle. This is attached to the ribbon just above the medal. Spellings were often very different from those we recognise today, and some seem little more than phonetic guesswork. So you may find, for example, Kabul shown as 'Cabul', Gujerat as 'Goojerat' and so on.

All medals are collector's items and those dating from before the nineteenth century are especially valuable. You are unlikely to find the older and rarer medals among the family relics, unless a member of your family is an avid collector. It is more likely you'll find a document or newspaper cutting describing the medal or, by the latter half of the nineteenth century, a photograph of the serviceman in full dress uniform, with battle honours proudly on display.

It is possible (although unlikely) that a member of your family has retained campaign medals dating as far back as the French Revolutionary Wars and Napoleonic Wars. These include the General Service Medal (1793–1814), which covered all service on mainland Europe including the 'Peninsular Wars', when the Duke of Wellington's forces defeated the French army in Spain, and the Waterloo Medal (1815) for service during the famous battle in June 1815, when Wellington's troops, aided by Field Marshall Blücher's Prussian army, defeated Napoleon once and for all.

THE INDIAN SUBCONTINENT

By the end of the nineteenth century, Britain's had gained control over most of the Indian sub-continent. But this came about only after a long series of very hard-fought military campaigns. British military service in India is marked by numerous campaign medals including the Army of India Medal (1799–1826), the Sinde Medal (1843), which commemorates the famous battle that brought the north-east India province of Sind under colonial rule, and the Punjab Medal (1848–1849) marking the British victory at the Battle of Gujerat, which gave Britain control of the Sikh homelands. The Indian Mutiny Medal (1857–1858) was awarded to troops sent to quell the mutiny by Sepoys in the Bengal Army of Northern India and relieve the besieged city of Lucknow. The India General Service Medal was given for campaigns from 1852–1895 and in 1909, 1936 and during World War II, after which (in 1947) India gained its independence.

OTHER CAMPAIGNS AROUND THE WORLD

There was barely a year in the nineteenth century when British troops were not in action in some part of the world. Indeed, Britain's forces were often fighting several campaigns at once. The First Burma Medal (1824–1826) marks the end of a now largely forgotten war that followed a threatened Burmese invasion of

Bengal, in India. A British counter-invasion captured Rangoon and brought the territories of Arakan and Tenasserim to the British. Later campaigns gained the whole of the country. The China Medal (1842, 1857–1860 and 1900) marks a series of trade wars with China, commonly known as 'the Opium Wars', and also a later uprising by the Taiping rebels, that was suppressed by a multi-national force led by General Charles Gordon (later killed at Khartoum). The New Zealand Medal (1847–7 and 1860–6) was given for quelling an uprising by the Maoris, the warlike native inhabitants of New Zealand, who had been angered by breaches of the treaty they signed with the British. The Crimea Medal (1854–1856) was awarded for action in the Crimean War, when Britain and her allies defeated the Russian Army at Sevastopol and Balaclava. This campaign included the infamous 'Charge of the Light Brigade' (October 1854) as well as the battles of Inkerman and Alma.

SOUTHERN AFRICA

As with India, Britain won control of southern Africa after a series of fiercely contested wars against native tribesman, especially the Zulus under their leader Cetshwayo, and the white Afrikaans settlers, the Boers, who were of Dutch ancestry. These battles were honoured by the South Africa Medal (1853–1879), the Cape of Good Hope Medal (1880–1897), the British South Africa Company Medal (1893–7), the South Africa Medal (Queen's) (1899–1902) and the South Africa Medal (King's) (1901–1902), and the Natal Medal (1906). Other African campaign medals included the Central Africa Medal (1894–98) and the West Africa Medal (1873–1899).

AFGHANISTAN

Afghanistan has long been a thorn in Britain's side, and continues to be so. Throughout the nineteenth century, a number of medals were awarded for military campaigns there. These included, the Cabul Medal (1842) given to mark the British retreat from Kabul after a combined Anglo–Indian force under General Elphinstone was heavily defeated by Afghan troops. Two medals were issued for the Defence of Jellalabad (1842). The Afghanistan Medal

(1878–79–80) was awarded to members of the British invasion force that secured the treaty of Gandamak, handing over territories to the British. Robert's March Medal – Kabul to Kandahar (1880) celebrates a famous event in which a 10,000-strong force under General Sir Frederick Roberts marched virtually non-stop for three weeks to relieve the garrison at Kandahar. The North West Frontier Medal (1908) commemorates later action on Afghanistan's border with Pakistan.

British troops saw service in 'Abyssinia' (now Ethiopia), Egypt and the Sudan to quell nationalist uprisings by armies led by Arabi Pasha's and Mohammad Amed ibn Abdallah ('al-Mahdi' – 'the expected guide'). These campaigns are celebrated with the Abyssinia Medal (1867–1868) the Egypt and Sudan Medal (1882–1889), the Khedive's Star (1882–1890), the British Sudan Medal (1896–1897) and Khedive's Sudan Medal (1896–1905). During the 19th century, British forces were also in action in Canada, marked by the Canada Medal (1866–1870) and North West Canada Medal (1885), and in Gyangtse, in Tibet, for which they received the Tibet Medal (1903–1904).

ABYSSINIA, EGYPT AND THE SUDAN

The twentieth century was dominated by the two world wars. Commemorative medals for World War I were issued in sets of three for those who saw service from the start of the war, and sets of two for servicemen and women who joined after 1915. These were the 1914 Mons Star (with 'Mons' clasp) or the 1914–15 Star, and the British War Medal and Victory Medal. Territorial soldiers were awarded the Territorial Forces War Medal, and merchant seaman received the Mercantile Marine War Medal (issued by the Board of Trade) and the British War Medal.

THE WORLD WARS

Military personnel during World War II may have received the 1939–45 Star, the Defence Medal, and the War Medal (1939–1945), as well as any campaign medals marking the particular theatre of war in which they fought. These included the Africa Star, the Pacific Star, the Burma Star, the Italy Star and the France and Germany Star. Other awards included the Atlantic Star, and the Air Crew

			WAR DIARY		Army Form C. 2118.
			~~INTELLIGENCE SUMMARY~~		
			(Erase heading not required.)		

Instructions regarding War Diaries and Intelligence Summaries are contained in F. S. Regs., Part II. and the Staff Manual respectively. Title Pages will be prepared in manuscript.

Place	Date	Hour	Summary of Events and Information	Remarks and references to Appendices

NAME OF COMPANIES	UNIT TO WHICH ALLOTTED	TANK No.	ORDERS RECEIVED	HOW ORDERS WERE CARRIED OUT	CASUALTIES
2nd Lt H.G. Pearsall	N.Z. Div 15th Corps	D11	Same orders as for D10 (Lt Darby) but did not stop on CREST TRENCH	When this Tank reached FLERS and failed to find any Germans the officer reported to a NZ Officer who asked that Tank might protect his flank. Lt Pearsall took up this position & remained there till 7.15 PM. Tank was then asked to go forward to meet expected counter attack and remained forward till 6 A.M. next day (16th Sept.). Tank advanced with infantry at 9 A.M. & carried on till hit by H.E. shell which burst under belly of car blowing in the gear box. Lt Pearsall remained in Tank for some while using his Vickers guns on enemy & also took one Vickers gun into the trenches when he had to abandon Tank.	3 O.R. Wounded Caused by HE bursting under Tank blowing gear box to pieces.
CAPT. G. NIXON	N.Z. Div 15th Corps	D12	Same orders as for D11 Tank (Lt Pearsall)	Orders were carried out as given till Tank advanced through FLERS, when in village Tank was hit, putting tail out of action. Capt. Nixon decided under these circumstances to withdraw. In withdrawing Tank became ditched at 1936 D.9.9 & during digging operations Tank was again hit & caught fire crew brought back to camp with 1 man missing.	1 O.R. Missing No trace of his man who crew were returning to cover after having abandoned Tank.

2449 Wt. W14957/M90 750,000 1/16 J.R.C. & A. Forms/C.2118/12.

Above: As well as looking for service records, you can use regimental war diaries to work out what your ancestors did during their career.

Europe Star. Specific medals were given to Commonwealth servicemen, including the Africa Service Medal, the Australia Service Medal, the Canadian Volunteer Service Medal, the Newfoundland Volunteer War Service Medal, the New Zealand War Service Medal, the South African Medal for War Service, and the Southern Rhodesia Medal for War Service.

POST-WORLD WAR II

Campaign medals continue to be given for active service today. Post-World War II campaign medals include the Korea Medal (1951), the South Atlantic Medal (1982), which commemorates the Falklands Conflict, and the Gulf Medal (1992).

This is only a brief overview of how to trace an ancestor who found employment in one of the armed or associated services, as it would take a book in its own right to fully do justice to each branch. You will quickly find that there are many institutions, archives and museums available to help with your research; a few useful resources have been listed below to get you started.

Right: Preparing for
active duty.

✌ GENERAL RESOURCES

Contact details for the following, and many other relevant organisations, can be
found at the back of the book.

Nominal medal rolls (giving information on campaign medals and gallantry awards) and the London Gazette (where gallantry awards were published) can be examined at The National Archives.	MEDALS
The Commonwealth War Graves Commission provides burial information for all armed forces. You can also find nominal rolls of war dead, as well as regimental births, marriages and deaths, at The National Archives and Family Records Centre.	WAR DEAD
Context is an important part of your research, and military memorabilia can be found in shops specalising in the subject, and at local, regimental and national museums including the Royal Navy Museum, the National Army Museum and	MILITARY MEMORABILIA

the Imperial War Museum. In particular, photographs, uniforms, weaponry and equipment provide an indication of their life and times in the armed forces.

NEWSPAPER & MEDIA REPORTS Coverage of wars and military operations can be found in contemporary newspapers. From the twentieth century onwards, you should also look for television and radio coverage at places such as the National Sound Archive at the British Library.

USEFUL ADDRESSES

The National Archives
Ruskin Avenue, Kew, Richmond, Surrey
TW9 4DU
www.nationalarchives.gov.uk

The Imperial War Museum
Lambeth Road, London SE1 6HZ
www.iwm.org.uk

2

(1) SOLDIER'S NAME and DESCRIPTION on ATTESTATION.

Army Number T/230453
Surname (in capitals) STUBBINGS
Christian Names (in full) THOMAS JAMES
Date of Birth 8-8-15
Trade on Enlistment MOTOR DRIVER
Religious Denomination C. of E.
Approved Society Manchester Unity of Oddfellows
Membership No. 1076
Enlisted at BULFORD On 7-11-40
For the :— D of W.
~~* Regular Army.~~ ~~* Supplementary Reserve.~~
~~* Territorial Army.~~ ~~* Army Reserve Section D.~~
* Strike out those inapplicable.
For ...... years with the Colours and ...... years in the Reserve.
Signature of Soldier
Date

3

DESCRIPTION ON ENLISTMENT.

Height 5 ft. 6 ins. Weight 127 lbs.
Maximum Chest 35 ins. Complexion RUDDY
Eyes GREY BLUE Hair FAIR
Distinctive Marks and Minor Defects
SCAR BACK OF RIGHT CALF
A&S GROUP 29
PYTHON DATE (JULY 1944)

CONDITION ON TRANSFER TO RESERVE.

Found fit for
Defects or History of past illness which should be enquired into if called up for Service
Date ...... 19......
Initials of M.O. i/c.

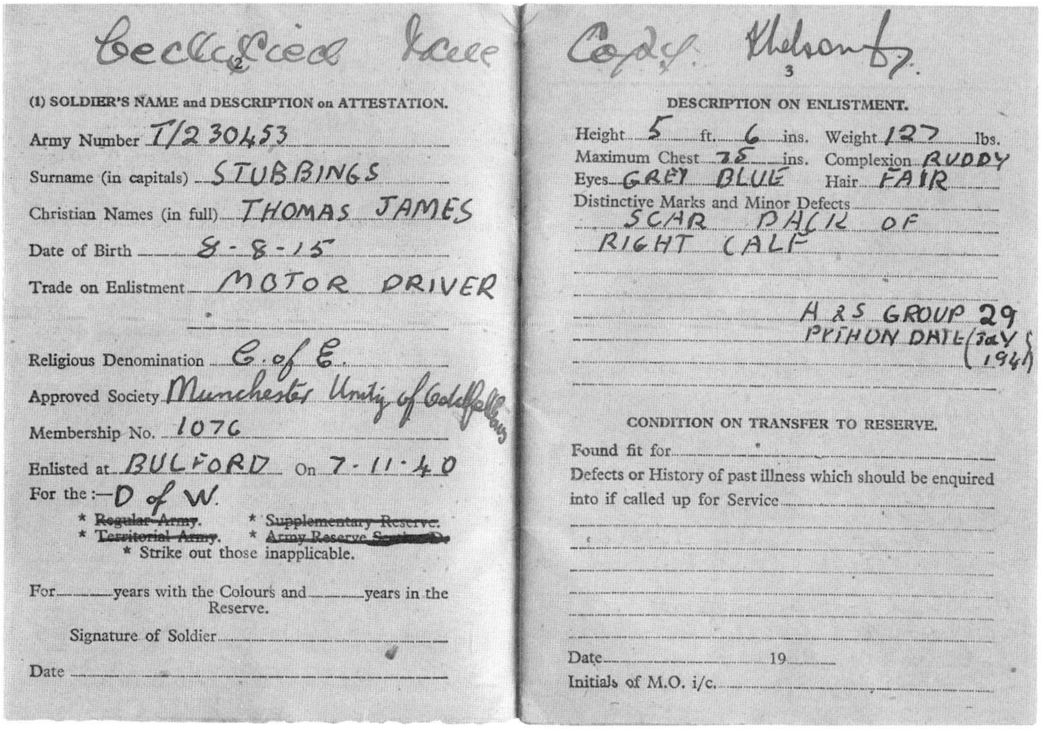

Left: Relaxing away from the front line.

The Imperial War Museum
Duxford, Cambridgeshire CB2 4QR
www.iwm.org.uk/duxford

RAF Museum
Hendon Aerodrome, London NW9 5LL
www.rafmuseum.org.uk

National Army Museum
Royal Hospital Road, London SW3 4HT
www.national-army-museum.ac.uk

National Maritime Museum
Romney Road, London SE10 9NF
www.nmm.ac.uk

Royal Naval Museum
HM Naval Base (PP66), Portsmouth,
Hampshire, PO1 3NH
www.royalnavalmuseum.org

Opposite: Part of an enlistment form for a First World War soldier, including his physical description.

Fleet Air Arm Museum
Box D6, RNAS Yeovilton, Ilchester, Somerset
BA22 8HT
www.fleetairarm.com

CASE STUDY 1 (MILITARY)

SIR RANULPH FIENNES

In 2005, Sir Ranulph Fiennes attempted yet another daring adventure, this time to climb to the summit of Mount Everest. If successful, he would have become the first person in history to have reached both poles and scale the highest point on the planet, but sadly his health did not permit the final assault on the summit. A recent venture saw him attempt to run seven marathons on seven continents in seven days – a monumental feat of endurance. However, his exploits are even more surprising given the historic background of Sir Ranulph's ancestors, though his family tree contains more than its fair share of larger than life characters.

The history of Sir Ranulph Fiennes's family IS the history of the surname, as he is in the rare position of claiming direct linear descent from ancestors who first arrived in England at the time of the Norman Conquest. Variant spellings that have appeared in nearly nine centuries of official records include Fenys, Fielnes, Fynes and Feynes and, as you may expect with such antiquity, the family are very well documented in the annals of history. The surname originated in France and, as befitted an important family, they married into an equally prominent dynasty – an early relative, Enguerrand de Fiennes, married the heiress of the Count of Boulogne, an important continental figure and a supporter of King Stephen during the anarchic civil wars of the mid-twelfth century. Through this lineage, it is technically possible for Sir Ranulph to claim descent to one of the greatest of all medieval kings, Charlemagne. However, despite inheriting all his wife's lands in England, Enguerrand did not enjoy his new fortunes for long; he was killed at Acre in 1189 having followed Richard the Lionheart on crusade into the Holy Land.

Given this rich heritage, it is perhaps no surprise to find out that Sir Ranulph is a descended from an aristocratic family –his full title is Sir Ranulph Twistleton-Wykeham-Fiennes. He had a strong military upbringing, becoming one of the youngest captains in the British Army whilst serving in the Royal Scots Greys, before eventually joining the SAS; the benefits of their rigorous training have clearly paid handsome dividends today. Sir Ranulph is descended from a long line of military figures; his father was also in the Royal Scots Greys, but tragically was killed during the Second World War just four months before Sir Ranulph was born. His uncle also died on the battlefield during the First World War in 1917.

The story of the Fiennes family is one of privilege and status. Their ancestral home was Broughton Castle, Oxford, and the title Lord of Saye and Sele had been connected with the family since 1447. Sir Ranulph's grandfather, Eustace Edward Fiennes, was formerly the Governor of the Leeward Islands in the West Indies and the family were used to travelling around the world on business – a trait that Sir Ranulph appears determined to uphold. However, the family name of Fiennes was actually lost for several generations; with the death of James Fiennes in 1673/4 the title passed through the female line, and from 1723 the lords of Saye and Sele bore the surname Twistleton. It was the decision of Sir Ranulph's great great grandfather Frederick Benjamin to add Wykeham-Fiennes to his surname of Twistleton in recognition of his long heritage, shortly after laying claim to the title and entering the House of Lords for the first time.

Yet tragedy also stalked the family; Frederick Benjamin's grandfather, Thomas Twistleton, saw his brother killed at the battle of Bruckemuhle in 1762, and eventually committed suicide in 1788. Death in battle seems to have been a common theme in the Fiennes family tree; an even earlier ancestor, William Fiennes, the second Lord Saye and Sele, was a staunch supporter of Edward IV during the Wars of the Roses, and was slain at the Battle of Barnet in 1471 fighting to secure the throne for his king. Perhaps even more unfortunate was the fate that befell his father James. He was the first Lord Saye and Sele, and fought in the Hundred Years War under Henry V. However, as a prominent member of Henry VI's regime, James became a target for popular fury and hate when the catastrophic loss of England's possession in France led to revolt in 1450. Although James was imprisoned in the Tower of London for his safety, he was delivered up to the rebels and was dragged away by the mob, and beheaded.

If you are fortunate to trace descent from, or can prove links to a prominent family, there are a number of avenues you can pursue to further your knowledge. It is highly likely that you already know a great deal about the ancestral background, but further information can be gleaned from standard historical works such as the Complete Peerage, Burke's Peerage or Dugdale's Baronage. You might also want to investigate whether you have a coat of arms or heraldic emblem. For a fee, you can commission research at the College of Arms (www.college-of-arms.gov.uk) whilst the Society of Genealogists (www.sog.org.uk) and British Library (www.bl.uk) both have large collection of pedigrees.

CASE STUDY 2

RICHARD BRANSON

Sir Richard Branson is one of the most famous businessmen in Britain, having established the Virgin empire covering the music and travel industries, despite struggling with dyslexia at school, but he is equally well known for his hair-raising adventures and record-breaking attempts. Where does his entrepreneurial spirit come from?

There are several possible origins for the Branson name. It can be translated as 'son of Brando', a personal name derived from the Germanic brand meaning sword. There is also a connection with specific places, such as Braunston or Branston in Leicestershire and Northamptonshire, derived from the old-English brand meaning somewhere that a burning had taken place, and tun meaning settlement. By the nineteenth century, the greatest concentration of Branson families lay in the east Midlands, suggesting this is the more probable explanation for the growth of the surname.

There are several colourful characters in the Branson family, including his great uncle James — renowned for 'eating grass' even when invited out for dinner, a reputation that brought him a certain amount of notoriety. However, this rather strange habit stood him in good stead, and during the Second World War he found himself advising the newly formed SAS on how to survive by eating wild plants and berries to supplement a diet of grass.

However, the traditional family profession was law. Richard's grandfather, Sir George Arthur Harwin Branson, was born in Yarmouth, Norfolk in 1871, graduated from Trinity College, Cambridge, ended up as a High Court judge and was created a Privy Councillor in 1940. He was also an author, and published a book with Walter George Salis Schwabe entitled 'A Treatise on the Laws of the Stock Exchange'. Clearly, an ability to understand the money markets is a family trait. He appears to have been quite a dominating figure; Richard's father, Edward James Branson, born in 1918, was strongly discouraged from becoming an archaeologist by George, and eventually coerced into studying law at Cambridge.

Three generations of Bransons had received legal training; George's father James Henry Arthur Branson had been born in Madras, India in 1840, and practised law in Calcutta, doubling up as a Justice of the Peace. He can be found on the 1871 census in England staying with his wife Mary and four sisters in Yarmouth, Norfolk with his in-laws Philip and Mary

Brown. George was born shortly afterwards, so it was probable that the family had travelled back for the birth. He seems to have spent some of his childhood in England; his brothers James (of grass-eating fame) and William, and sister Mary Ann, were all born in India when their parents returned after George's birth, but the children grew up in London. This was a common arrangement for well-to-do professional families with young children, as the heat and conditions in India could be dangerous and child mortality was high.

His mother's side are an equally interesting family, boasting in Richard's grandmother Dorothy Huntley-Flint (nee Jenkins) the oldest person in Britain to hit a hole in one at golf. Richard's mother Evette started work as a West End dancer (much to her father's disgust), worked with the Wrens during the Second World War as a signaller, before finding employment as an air hostess. The love of flying ran in the family – her sister Clare was a friend of the war hero Douglas Bader – and explains where Richard gets his love of transport and adventurous nature.

Richard Branson's family spent many years in India, working as lawyers and magistrates. It is possible to pursue both lines of research. Apart from the Moving Here website (www.movinghere.org.uk), which explains how to track down information in overseas archives, you can use records at the Oriental and India Office Library (OIOL), part of the British Library (www.bl.uk) to trace someone's career or life in India. The OIOL holds a biographical index and ecclesiastical records of baptisms, marriages and deaths, as well as alphabetical trade and street directories. Prominent people can feature in a range of other records as well, such as official gazettes, establishment lists and legal papers created by the British administration in India. Meanwhile, the Law Society Archives (www.lawsoc.org.uk) can be used to trace information on prominent members of the legal profession, and many of the Inns of Court hold records as well. You can also use trade and commercial directories to track the movement of professionals – a good selection exist from the mid-nineteenth century, many of which can be searched online at www.historicaldirectories.org

Case study 3

Ringo Starr

Many bands contributed to the soundtrack of the swinging Sixties, but perhaps the most famous and arguably most influential group of all was the Beatles. The famous Merseybeat guitar sound was first launched in 1962 with their debut single 'Love Me Do', but it was not until the release of their second track 'Please Please Me' in 1963 that the world sat up and took notice. Yet Ringo Starr was not in the original line up – John Lennon, Paul McCartney and George Harrison all featured but were accompanied by Stuart Sutcliffe and Pete Best, when the group regularly performed at 'The Cavern' club. Sutcliffe left in 1961 – he died shortly afterwards – and Ringo Starr was brought in to replace Pete Best before the band were to due to start their first recording session. The rest, as they say, is history, and the Beatles were propelled into the limelight to become one of the most successful chart acts of all time.

Ringo Starr was actually born as Richard Starkey in 1940, the son of a confectioner, also called Richard Starkey, and his wife Elsie Gleave. The couple had married four years previously in Toxteth and raised their family in Madryn Street. It is possible to trace both lines back in time, and each branch of the family reveals a different aspect of life in the Liverpool area over the last 150 years or so.

Starting with the Starkey line, it is clear that Richard's profession as a confectioner was totally at odds with the rest of the family background. Rather frustratingly, it has only proved possible to work as far back as Ringo's grandfather through records in the public domain, who was a rather elusive man called John Starkey. It appears that he was born around 1877, and spent most of his working life as a boilermaker based in Toxteth. Given the city's reliance on ships for its lifeblood, it is not surprising to find that John was involved in one of the major professions in the area; a boilermaker was an occupation that could have applied to any one of Liverpool's main industries, such as fitting out ships, preparing machinery for use in factories, as well as a range of other industrial activities. The exact terms of John's employment are a little sketchy, as he cannot be located with any degree of certainty from census records prior to 1901. One reason is that his name appears to change on every official document located; when his son Richard married in 1936, his name was written down as John Alfred Parkin Starkey; yet when his son was born in 1913, he was called John George Starkey; whilst when he married Annie

Bower in 1910, his name was inscribed on the certificate as John Parkin Starkey. No earlier trace of him can be found on the census records; all we know is that he was consistently referred to as a boilermaker, and lived in Toxteth.

In contrast, Elsie Gleave's father, John, followed a completely different career path. Elsie was born on 19th October 1914, a few short weeks after the outbreak of the First World War. He had married Elsie's mother Catherine Martha Johnson only six months beforehand, presumably on finding out she was pregnant, and had enlisted in the 8th Battalion Royal Lancashire Garrison Artillery to do his bit for King and country. Previously, he had worked as a tin works labourer and before him his father, William Gleave, had also plied his trade as a boilermaker. It is possible to trace the Gleave family further back in time through the census records; they reveal that the family had originated from Warrington, when John's grandfather, another William Gleave, had moved to the area in search of work in the late 1850s.

The Gleaves were not the first line of the family to have travelled to Liverpool to find employment during the city's boom period. Annie Bower married John Starkey in 1910, and was the daughter of Alfred Bower who was born in 1851. At first glance it might appear that this was yet another line of industrial workers, yet Alfred's father David was described in the 1851 and 1861 census returns as a proprietor of houses, suggesting that he ran a portfolio of properties and was wealthy enough to employ at least one house servant in 1851. By 1881, though, the business had ended and David was listed as unemployed, living in the household of his son William. Alfred had already married eight years previously to Margaret Ellen Parr, whose family originally hailed from Oswestry, Shropshire and had moved to Liverpool at some point between 1841-1845.

Therefore the stark facts surrounding Ringo's shows that there was nothing extraordinary in his background that marked him out for future greatness – indeed nothing to distinguish him from any of the thousands of fellow Liverpudlians who came from similar circumstances and whose ancestors contributed in their own way contributed to life in Liverpool during the nineteenth century. This is one of the joys of family history; sometimes the interesting aspect of our voyage of discovery is finding out that there's nothing very different about our ancestors after all.

CHAPTER 9

Moving Around

Britain has always been a melting pot of different cultures, ethnic groups and a home for refugees. Equally, as the British Empire spread across the globe, thousands of people left these shores to start a new life abroad. Even the internal structure of society was radically shaken up in the middle of the nineteenth century, as communication networks snaked across the land connecting the industrial heartlands with the ports from whence finished products were exported and raw materials were brought in. Population migration plays an important part in our families' stories, and can often explain why our ancestors mysteriously disappear. This chapter considers the various patterns of emigration, immigration and internal migration, along with the sources available to help you start exploring your roots outside these shores.

Opposite: A relaxed shot, possibly taken whilst on holiday.

EMIGRATION

One of the most frustrating parts of researching your family is when they vanish from official records. During the course of the last five hundred years, British influence spread far and wide across the globe. Wherever colonial rule was established, expatriate administrators, soldiers and settlers followed. Not all emigrants were voluntary, and many thousands more were transported from British shores to overseas penal colonies for a range of crimes and offences. Therefore it is possible that an ancestor who 'disappeared' from your family tree simply left for a life abroad. This article introduces some of the main lines of research you can pursue if you want to track them down. This could lead to some exciting discoveries, such as a hitherto unknown set of relations in another country.

SEEKING A NEW LIFE ABROAD

Just as Britain has long acted as a magnet to economic migrants and refugees from other lands, so Britons have left these shores in their thousands to seek their fortunes abroad. For at least the last five centuries, Britons travelling abroad have had to register their intentions. Until the early 1600s, this often took the form of a licence, registers of which are kept at The National Archives at Kew.

The British Empire expanded throughout the eighteenth and nineteenth century, and reached its height in the first half of the twentieth century. In addition to the countries that were part of the Empire, Britain had strong trade and diplomatic links with most other nations, and so the opportunities for foreign travel were limitless. During Britain's colonial rule, the Indian subcontinent required a huge army of civil servants as governors and administrators and to run its trade links with Britain. Many civil servants and their families sent to India for a fixed term enjoyed the quality of life so much that they stayed. This was a state of affairs that ended only when India and Pakistan gained their independence in 1947. Sources of information on the British in India include the British Association for Cemeteries in South Asia, The National Archives, which has the Indian Army list, and the British Library (www.bl.uk), which holds the records of the British Administration in India and the Far East.

Africa and the Far East attracted their fair share of traders, business owners, and civil servants seeking their fortune in these outposts of Empire. Information on Britons who lived abroad is held in the records of the Colonial and Dominions Office, and the Foreign Office Index. The Institute of Commonwealth Studies

Left: Advertising the fact that travel did not simply stop with the railways.

(www.sas.ac.uk/commonwealth studies) has information about colonial and post colonial life.

Historical records refer to emigration to North America in the 1600s and 1700s, but there is little detailed information about these movements until about the 1850s onwards. Emigrants left Britain in largest numbers in the 1800s and then again between 1900 and 1914, when emigration was curtailed by the start of World War I. During this period, the majority of migrants into the USA, around 17 million in total, passed through Ellis Island. These names are on record and can be researched at www.ellisislandrecords.org. The National Archives in Washington holds useful information including census returns and immigration records. Another source is the National Archives, which holds an index of emigrants for a few specific years, and there are published registers of passengers from Britain to North America.

The discovery of gold in Victoria in 1851, and the realisation that the country had abundant natural resources, eventually made transportation unnecessary. Soon thousands were heading to Australia in search of a better life. Emigration, particularly to Canada and Australia, remained high until the 1930s, and has continued at a lower level until the present day. Many orphans were dispatched to Australia from British children's homes such as Dr Bernardo's, regardless of whether or not they had relatives abroad. That practice continued until the 1950s. Many of those who entered Australia in this way have been recorded in lists compiled by Australian genealogical societies, set up to help trace lost relatives in the UK.

✌ RETRACING FOOTSTEPS

When seeking ancestors who moved abroad, it is important to begin with realistic expectations. Without some prior knowledge or clue, it can be very difficult to trace the route or whereabouts of emigrant ancestors; and even if you do have some information, in many cases there are simply no sources

Transportation of Convicts

From the late eighteenth century onwards, the New World – Australia, New Zealand and North America – attracted the bulk of migrants from the UK. Many of the early migrants were unwilling visitors: criminals facing capital punishment for often petty crimes committed in Britain. Their punishment was then commuted to transportation, principally to provide cheap labour. This could be for life or for a lesser fixed term, but, either way, few ever managed to make the return journey. Convicted felons were initially sent to the American colonies, but from 1787 to 1868, they went to the newly established penal colonies in New South Wales and Queensland, Australia. The National Archives has lists of convicts, and sometimes their families, if they chose to go with them, as well as other voluntary settlers. Census returns, and correspondence, including letters written by settlers in Australia, and Canada throughout most of the nineteenth century exist in a register called the Colonial Office Emigration Original Correspondence.

available, and so you may have loose ends that are never tied up. Similarly, many key resources will be located overseas, and whilst the Internet has opened access to catalogues and images, you may well need to spend some time – and money! – overseas, or in the employment of specialist researchers abroad.

One of the easiest trails to pick up is that of involuntary emigrants. Since the establishment of the North American colonies in the sixteenth century, nearly 40,000 people were sent to penal colonies as punishment for their crimes at home. Details of these cases – often very minor offences by today's standards – are likely to be found in legal records of the day, where judgements of 'transportation' were recorded. Many death sentences were commuted to 14 years in the penal colonies. After the American Revolution began in 1776, transportation to the west ceased. However, the discovery of Australia and the establishment of the New South Wales penal colony saw British criminals transported half way around the world from 1787, with this human traffic reaching its peak in the first quarter of the nineteenth century. Transportation was effectively ended in 1867, and it is estimated that over 160,000 people

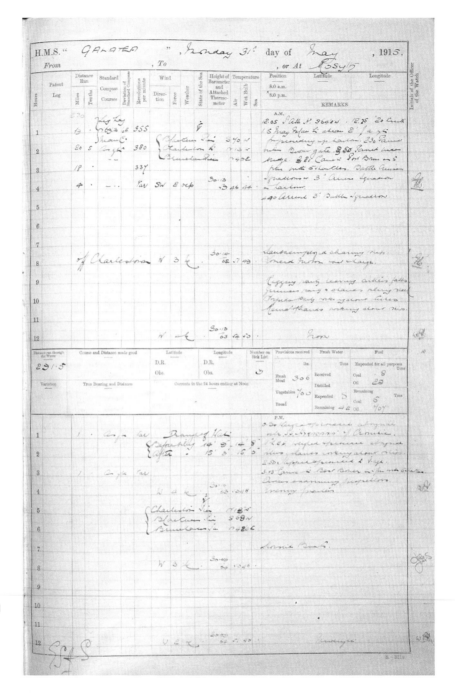

Right: A section from a ship's log, detailing voyages and places visited.

embarked on this route to a new life. There are transportation registers, census returns for the prison communities, and medical journals of the voyages. Many prisoners did not survive the long and testing conditions on board the ships, whilst those that did faced hostile conditions on arrival. Despite this harsh punishment, many families elected to join their husbands and wives in Australia, whilst the administrators were also encouraged to establish communities. Some of the relevant records are stored in Australia, but The National Archives hold many of the records of the Colonial Office relating to the administration of these lands.

One of the most important factors in establishing British rule around the globe was the power of the military. Many regiments were stationed abroad, whilst the navy was used to command the seas and transport soldiers from destination to destination. Quite often, soldiers and sailors who had reached the end of their period of service elected to stay in their last place of service. It is sometimes possible to trace where pension payments were made, whilst there was a conscious effort in the late 1840s to encourage ex-servicemen to settle in Australia and New Zealand. Likewise, during the Boer War in South Africa at the end of the nineteenth century, property of British ex-patriots was requisitioned, and compensation claims can be traced from surviving records at The National Archives.

One of the most complete archives for British military and civilian administration pertains to India, and can be found in the Oriental and India Office Library in the British Library. Records of the East India Company up to 1858, and thereafter the British Government in India, can be used to trace the careers of civil servants who worked and lived in the three main presidencies in India – Bengal, Madras and Bombay. Similarly, the European officers and men of the East India Company's army can be traced with varying levels of detail, whilst some information on native troops is available. Another excellent source is the collection of ecclesiastical registers for the Presidencies, the equivalent of British parish registers. The climate did not agree with many of the early settlers, and so the cemetery records are full of names and ages of those who succumbed to disease.

A large amount of work has been undertaken on the early settlers to North America and the Caribbean, whilst the growing Ellis Island database lists emigrants who arrived on the continent. From 1890, The National Archives holds outward-bound passenger lists. They are arranged by port of departure from the UK, though after 1906 there are registers of passenger lists that at least provide the names of ships leaving each port. Most of the early sources from the sixteenth century onwards have been exhaustively catalogued, with names of emigrants extracted. Nevertheless, a trawl of the early State Papers Colonial series of records at The National Archives is still worthwhile, if only to provide background information on the conditions the early settlers faced.

Of course, not everyone who worked abroad decided to stay. However, people continued to marry, have children and die overseas. There are lists of overseas registrations forwarded to the Registrar General available for consultation at the Family Records Centre, whilst ceremonies performed at British embassies and consulates were also recorded in separate registers. Yeo's publication is an excellent way of locating relevant registration records for Britons serving overseas, and is listed below along with other useful sources for tracing those elusive overseas ancestors.

💠 IMMIGRATION

We live in a multicultural society, and the challenges associated with integrating people from so many different backgrounds on one small island is under particular scrutiny with the events of 7/7. Yet Britain has a long tradition of welcoming people to its shores from all around the world, and the more one looks into our past, the more we need to question our conceptions of 'Britishness'. For example, the twentieth century was defined by two World Wars against Germany and her allies, but prior to the late nineteenth century, people from the German states formed the largest immigrant group in the country.

Indeed, it becomes increasingly difficult to adequately define 'British' or even 'English' the further back in time you travel. The modern gene pool contains remnants of the people who have invaded our land over the centuries, and brought their followers with them – first the Romans, then the Germanic tribes who became 'Anglo-Saxons', followed by Vikings from Scandinavia and

Normans from France. We even had a Dutch monarchy from 1689, followed by Germans ever since, starting with the Hanoverians. We have welcomed Huguenot refugees from France and the Netherlands, Jewish migrants from Eastern Europe and workers from all parts of the former British Empire. All contributed fully to making modern society what it is today, and through written records both inside and outside Britain, it is possible to trace our ancestors' overseas roots.

MIGRANT WORKERS AND REFUGEES

Most people living in the UK today would probably find that their ancestors originated somewhere else – if only they could delve back far enough in their family history. Immigration into the British Isles has occurred at a constant rate throughout recorded time. Many newcomers were economic migrants, escaping poverty in their homelands. But, from time to time, this steady influx was swelled by waves of mass immigration, usually following natural disaster, civil or military strife, or religious persecution.

Tracing immigrant ancestors is easiest if there is an unbroken religious, racial or cultural connections linking you to them. For example, Jewish people have suffered persecution throughout their history and have often been forced to seek sanctuary in Britain and elsewhere. Many Jewish immigrants chose to change their names to help them become assimilated in their new homeland, yet most still managed to maintain their religious and cultural identity. A useful source of information on Jewish residents are the records of worshippers held at all synagogues. You could start with the synagogue closest to where your ancestor lived. Records of

IMMIGRATION IN 2006

Today, immigration is a sensitive issue. However, it is easy to lose sight of the fact that at some point in your family's past, it is highly probable that a direct ancestor either formed part of a group who arrived from overseas, or married into such a community. It is therefore important to look out for clues that indicate immigrant roots, and then investigate further.

synagogues dating from the early nineteenth century and earlier are held at the United Synagogue.

Many Jewish communities living in Britain today can trace their ancestry to a particular region of the world and period of religious strife. Sephardic Jews began to arrive in Britain from the mid-seventeenth century onwards, mainly from Italy, Spain and Portugal. A second wave, this time of Ashkenazi Jews, began to arrive from Europe, and especially Russia and Poland, from the 1680s. A later and even larger influx of Ashkenazi Jews from eastern Europe occurred at the end of the nineteenth century. Sources of information include The National Archives, the London Metropolitan Archives, the Board of Deputies of British Jews, the Jewish Information department, the Anglo-Jewish Association and the Jewish Genealogical Society of Great Britain (www.jgsgb.org.uk). The Society of Genealogists contains many Jewish archives, and databases giving information on Jewish genealogy world-wide can be accessed at www.jewishgen.org.

Another important group of foreign nationals to enter the British Isles to escape religious persecution were the French Huguenots. These members of the Protestant Calvinist and Reformed Communion of France lost their right to freedom of worship in 1685, resulting in a period of intense persecution, when many Huguenots were killed. Over the following decades, more than 400,000 Huguenot refugees left France. A large proportion of these settled in England. This community brought with them important skills that were to be a major asset to their new country. The Huguenot Society is an important source of information. Alien immigrants were often heavily taxed and so surveys were conducted to keep track of them. There are three known surveys of aliens living in London, two covering the year 1571, and one in 1618. They are published by the Huguenot Society.

More émigrés were to arrive in Britain following the French revolution in 1793, especially Royalists fleeing the guillotine. Among them was the inventor and engineer Marc Brunel, who arrived in Britain – via America – in 1799. He married an English woman, Sophia Kingdom, and their son Isambard Kingdom Brunel was to become the most famous engineer of his age, famed for building the Great Western Railway, the gigantic steam-powered ships SS Great Western and Great

Britain, and the Clifton suspension bridge.

Thousands of Irish workers came to the British mainland in the eighteenth and nineteenth centuries to provide manual labour to build the country's vastly expanding transport networks – including the turnpike roads and canal system, as well as the railways. But it was natural and economic disaster that was to provide the biggest impetus for Irish immigration. The potato blight of 1845–9 was the most severe of three major famines to strike Ireland in the nineteenth century. The poverty and mass starvation this caused triggered a huge exodus that was to see the population of Ireland plummet by two million people – a quarter of its total population at the time – between 1845 and 1855. Around 75 per cent of Irish migrants headed for north America, principally New York. But many of the poorest remained in the first English ports they sailed into after leaving Ireland. By the end of 1847, there were over 100,000 destitute Irish men, women and children on the streets of Liverpool alone. And this number continued to swell over the coming years, with many of the migrants settling in the city.

Over the following 150 years, their descendants spread to other cities in Lancashire, as well as Clydeside and London, in search of work. Many eventually made the crossing to North America that their ancestors had failed to complete. But towns and cities throughout the UK, and most especially Liverpool, still boast large communities that can trace their origins to that original Irish influx in the mid-nineteenth century. The vast majority of Irish immigrants were Catholics. Sources of information on Catholic families include the Catholic Central Library, the Catholic Record Office, the Catholic Family History

COTTON FAMINE

At around the time of the Irish exodus, a different kind of famine was to strike the industrial heartland of Lancashire. During the American Civil War, the Union forces of the northern states started blockading the cotton-growing states of the Confederate south. This cut off cotton supplies to the Lancashire textile mills, bringing about an economic crisis known as the 'cotton famine', which put thousands of people out of work and into financial destitution. Many of these were forced to move to other parts of Britain in search of work, and some joined the mass migration to the United States and the colonies to found a new life abroad.

Above: **Passenger lists give details of when and where people travelled by sea.**

Society, the Catholic Archives Society (UK and Ireland), and the publication English Catholic Ancestor.

Afro-Caribbean immigration into the UK is usually regarded as starting with the docking of the MV Empire Windrush in 1948. In fact, black immigration has a very long history, dating back at least 2,000 years, to Roman times. During the 400 years that the Romans Empire occupied Britain, thousands of its troops, traders and administrators from North Africa were based here, many choosing to stay long after the empire collapsed. In the 1700s there was a sizeable population of black people living in the port towns and major cities, drawn from all corners of Empire. Some estimates suggest that at the turn of the nineteenth century there may have been as many as 20,000 black people living in London alone. Their identity is often indicated by names such as 'Pompey' and 'Scipio' listed in parish registers. The National Archives at Kew has online sources of information at www.nationalarchives.gov.uk/pathways/blackhistory. Nationals from Asia and the Far East have a long a history in the UK, too. A useful source of information on immigrants is the Inward Passenger Lists held at The National Archives, for the years 1878 to 1960. Other sources include the Institute of Commonwealth Studies (www.sas.ac.uk/commonwealthstudies), and the website www.movinghere.org.uk.

Two standard genealogical sources may give an indication of overseas origins. Marriage certificates record where the ceremony took place, and therefore the use of foreign chapels may indicate an immigrant community. For example, a large number of Eastern European Jews from Russia, Poland and states that now form part of Germany arrived in England in the late nineteenth century, and you may find marriages that took place in synagogues. Specialist research societies and libraries have been established for some of the major religious groups who sought sanctuary in Britain, such as the Huguenots from the sixteenth century onwards. As well as church records, they often have well-researched genealogies of key families. It is also worth examining local histories, as many migrant communities established themselves in particular areas. London has a particularly strong immigrant history, and the London Metropolitan Archives is a rich source of information on the social history behind many immigrant groups.

In general, aliens arriving in Britain after 1793 – when the numbers of émigrés fleeing the French Revolution reached their height – were required to register with the civil authorities. There is a range of sources at both The National Archives, and within the holdings of local and county record offices, which deal with the registration process, including certificates and passes. Some indexes to these records exist. You are likely to find information on an alien's nationality, profession, date of arrival and the last country visited. Sometimes the masters of ships carrying alien passengers forwarded lists to the Home Office; these are at The National Archives, along with inbound passenger lists after 1860. These exclude journeys begun within Europe, so will be of limited use; however the Mediterranean is included, as are any passengers picked up at a European port during the inward voyage. The records are arranged by port of arrival, so a lengthy search may be required. There are no name indexes

NATURALISATION

Places of birth are often listed in the census returns, along with an indication of 'naturalisation'. This was the process by which foreign subjects became naturalised British citizens, with full voting rights and the ability to purchase property. Application papers were submitted to the Home Officer, along with statements from credible witnesses and examinations by local police officers. The applicant frequently provided details of their age, place of birth, parentage, and residence in England. Family members are often listed as well. A successful application was awarded with a certificate of naturalisation. Duplicate certificates can be obtained from The National Archives, where many of the application papers are also housed (though for confidentiality purposes, the records are closed for 100 years). Name indexes to naturalisation papers are available, along with those who sought denization – less expensive to obtain, but with reduced citizenship rights. However, many overseas arrivals who were from British colonies did not need to apply for additional citizenship rights, as they were assumed to already have a natural loyalty to the Crown. Fewer records would therefore be available.

available, although there are some for ships' names. It may also be possible to trace official histories of celebrated events, such as the arrival in 1948 of the *MV Empire Windrush* carrying volunteers from the West Indies to help with Britain's reconstruction programme after the Second World War.

Wartime refugees were closely monitored. A large number of Belgian arrivals during the First World War (1914-1918) were recorded on personal 'history cards', now at The National Archives. There are separate records for Polish, Czech and Jewish refugees during the Second World War, some of which are at The National Archives, and many others (including the Jewish Refugees Committee) are stored at the London Metropolitan Archives. On the other hand, aliens resident in Britain, especially those of Germanic origin, were subject to internment. Some index cards survive at the National Archives, as well as files on those people monitored but not interned. Many naturalized citizens chose to change their names for fear of persecution. During the First and Second World

Wars, a change of name was required by law to be published in an official source, such as the London Gazette. Indexes for this period survive, once again at The National Archives. They also hold the indexes to changes of name by deed poll registered in the Supreme Court, cross-referenced by new and former name. This is a particularly useful source if you feel your name was 'Anglicised' at some prior date.

Naturally, these are only a few of the main sources where you could start a search for further information. Much of your knowledge is likely to be contained within your family, although extreme tact is advised if you are planning to ask detailed questions of elderly relatives; they may have experienced events that they do not wish to recall. Furthermore, if you do find you come from an immigrant community, finding your roots outside Britain is likely to involve travel to the country of origin, where online resources are limited and archives may not be as easy to access. One of the best places to find out information about tracking overseas ancestors is via the Society of Genealogists Library in London, though many Family History Centres run by

Below: Official paperwork granting British citizenship to a Russian foreign national.

the Church of the Latter Day Saints either stock or can order in relevant books. However, more resources are becoming available online, and some of the websites listed below are worth contacting for further links.

✇ INVESTIGATING BLACK AND ASIAN HISTORY

Below: After the Second World War families from the Caribbean moved to Britain to help with reconstruction work.

If you have Caribbean, African or Asian roots then there is a chance that you have ancestors who arrived relatively recently in the UK, particularly in the twentieth century, so you may already know about where they came from and whether you have relatives abroad. That said, there has been an Asian and black

presence in the UK for many centuries, and you may need to work further back in time. Either way, the best place to start your research will be online at www.movinghere.org.uk, which describes the main resources available both in the UK and abroad (with contact addresses). You might also find the Institute of Commonwealth Studies, University of London, 38 Russell Square, London www.sas.ac.uk/commonwealthstudies a useful resource, as they can provide information about the wider social background. Another good website is www.rootsweb.com, which had links to the Immigrant Ships Transcribers Guild, whilst TNA provides an online exhibition of sources at www.nationalarchives. gov.uk/ pathways/blackhistory.

There are some specialist archives in the UK. The Black Cultural Archives are at 378 Coldharbour Lane, London, whilst records of the British administration of India are housed at the Oriental and India Office Library at the British Library, 96 Euston Road, London www.bl.uk. You can also use www.ozemail.com.au/~clday for advice on how to research British, European and Anglo-Indian ancestors in India. Thereafter, you will probably need to contact the relevant archives overseas. This can be more tricky; for example, there are about 20 separate institutions in the West Indies, whilst contact with local archives in India is best routed through The National Archives of India, Janpath, New Delhi, 110001, India via their email address archives@ren02.nic.in

☙ RESOURCES FOR JEWISH HISTORY

There has been a Jewish community in Britain since at least the mid seventeenth century, though – as the famous people featured in the articles to date can testify – most people of Jewish descent arrived from Eastern Europe during the period of persecution in the 1880s. It can be difficult to work back to a place of origin, given the passage of time, but there are a surprising number of sources available to help you in your research. As well as www.movinghere.org, an excellent website for Jewish history is www.jewishgen.org. You should also consider contacting the Jewish Genealogical Society of Great Britain, whose website is www.jgsgb.ort.org.

The Society of Genealogists have a large collection of Jewish archives, plus extensive resources to help you track down places of origin world-wide, with particular emphasis on Eastern Europe. They are based at 14 Charterhouse Buildings, Goswell Road, London www.sog.org. However, much of your research will focus on local resources, usually housed at the relevant local studies centre or county record office. You should consider approaching the synagogue nearest to where your ancestors lived, in case they have records of worship and related material. The London Metropolitan Archives, 40 Northampton Road, London www.cityoflondon.gov.uk has a particularly rich collection as many Jewish migrants settled in the capital first before moving elsewhere in the UK, including material relating to the Jewish Refugees Committee.

Moving around Britain

It's also easy to forget that Britain has seen a huge amount of population movement from within, particularly after the railways arrived in the early nineteenth century and made places far more accessible for a larger number of people than ever before. For example it's possible to trace our ancestors moving from place to place, following the railway line in search of work. Other factors caused people to travel from their homes – the Irish potato famine in the 1840s saw vast numbers leave their communities to survive, either fleeing across the ocean to America or into England and Scotland. Even within England there was much social mobility – for example, traditional Cornish names crop up in the far North East, the Midlands and Kent, because our ancestors were following work, in this case mining. Whilst it become much harder to track relatives who moved around a lot, there are some basic sources to help you. Here's a quick guide to researching ancestors who might have been born or had roots in parts of the British Isles outside England and Wales.

There is a common belief that Irish ancestors are hard to trace, based on the fact that many records were lost in the burning of the Irish Public Record Office in 1922, coupled with deliberate destruction of other records – most notably census records prior to 1901, and a large number of wills. The loss of such important material is a major stumbling block, as is the fact that the records are now divided between the Republic and the North.

Right: Time for a quick photo on board ship!

Civil registration was introduced in Ireland in 1864. Records for all Ireland are at the General Register Office of Ireland, Joyce House, 8/11 Lombard Street East, Dublin www.groireland.ie whilst those for Northern Ireland after January 1922 are in the General Register Office, Oxford House, 49/55 Chichester Street, Belfast www.groni.gov.uk. Surviving census records for 1901 and 1911 have at least been made available for inspection at the National Archives of Ireland, Bishop Street, Dublin; information can be found at www.nationalarchives.ie, where other genealogical information can be found, such as surviving will indexes and parish registers. The Public Record Office of Northern Ireland is the main resource for similar material north of the border. However, it is probably best to talk to the Irish Genealogical Research Society first, who are based on 82 Eaton Square, London or at www.igrsoc.org; you might also want to try www.irishorigins.com as well.

Tracing your Scottish ancestry is often much easier than in other parts of the UK, simply because access to key material is much easier. For example, there are several archives and institutions located centrally in Edinburgh where you will find the main biographical records, the main location being the General Registrar's Office where you can access parish registers, census returns and civil

Right: Conditions aboard this vessel were very cramped!

registration material for a daily entry fee (www.gro-scotland.gov.uk). The National Archives of Scotland (www.nas.gov.uk) hold a far wider range of source material, much of which can be used to investigate the local history where your ancestors lived, but amongst its collections you can find wills and testaments. A short walk away is the National Library of Scotland (www.nls.uk) which holds secondary sources, reference works and some manuscript collections. Furthermore, images of many of the key biographical records can be viewed online for a fee at www.scotlandspeople.gov.uk making it possible to conduct your investigation from the comfort of your home. If you cannot get to Edinburgh, or you cannot find what you are looking for online, you can always hire a researcher to work on your behalf. Sticks Research Agency uses two accredited researchers in Edinburgh, Ruth Boreham and Brian Thomson.

The Scottish system of civil registration was introduced in 1855, but the delay of eighteen years allowed a more sophisticated set of records to emerge – each document contains more information than the English counterpart, with a greater degree of cross-referencing permissible from the indexes. The General Register Office of Scotland is located in New Register House, Princes Street, Edinburgh, where you can also see census records and parish registers. Most of this material is also online to view for a small fee at www.scotlandspeople.gov.uk Next door is the the National Archives of Scotland, General Register House, Edinburgh www.nas.gov.uk, where, amongst thousands of other documents, you can find testaments and wills; whilst the National Library of Scotland, George IV Bridge, Edinburgh www.nls.uk holds related material. Thereafter you should contact the relevant district record office for records relating to that area.

The best place to look for information about relatives who settled in or originated on the Isle of Man is www.isle-of-man.com/manxnotebook/. A separate civil registration system existed since 1849, whilst wills and parish registers were also administered locally. Similarly, the Channel Islands maintained their own systems of registration as well, with records kept on Jersey and Guernsey. A detailed summary of resources is at user.itl.net/~glen/, whilst useful information is provided about Guernsey at www.guernsey-society.org.uk and Jersey at www.societe-jersiaise.org.

Case study 1 (migration)

Alan Sugar

Renowned for his straight-talking no-nonsense approach to business, Sir Alan Sugar is one of Britain's most dynamic businessmen. He's the star of the BBC reality TV show *The Apprentice*, where one lucky winner is given a contract worth £100,000 and the chance to learn the ropes in the company. Yet this chance to fast track to a successful career could not be further from Sugar's own route to success, as he struggled to escape his working class background from the East End of London. Furthermore, the origins of his family lie overseas in Eastern Europe.

It is tempting to link the surname 'Sugar' with production of sugar cane, one of the most lucrative professions from the eighteenth century onwards and further associated with the slave trade. However, the use of the surname in Britain has even older origins, and along with a range of surname variants found in old English records, such as Sagar, Saggar, Sigar and Segar, stems from 'son of Sigher', a name of Germanic origin that dates from the period after the Roman withdrawal when waves of invaders and settlers from continental tribes came to Britain from the fifth century onwards.

However, there have been other periods of immigration into Britain and Sir Alan's roots lie in the movement of Jewish refugees fleeing the pogroms in Tsarist Russia during the late eighteenth century. Therefore we have to look to Eastern Europe for the origins of his line, and it is possible that the family Anglicised their name on arrival.

Alan Sugar was born in March 1947 in Hackney, in the heart London's East End, and grew up in a council house. His rise to success has been well documented; he left Brooke House school at the age of 16, though by this age he was already earning more money than his father by boiling beetroot for the local greengrocers, and selling whatever he could. Although he briefly found employment in the civil service as a statistician, he decided that working for others was not the way to earn money and set up his own company AMSTRAD – which stands for Alan Michael Sugar Trading – selling electrical equipment. His fortune was made in the 1980s with the rise of the personal computer market, and he is now estimated to be worth £760 million.

This is a meteoric rise from his family's humble origins. His parents married in 1931 at the Philpot Street Synagogue, Stepney; his mother Fanny Apple was the daughter of a car man, Aaron Apple whilst his father Nathan was a journeyman tailor at the time, later working in a garment factory in Hackney. Life was a struggle, and Alan recalls how his father used to switch lights off to save money. This reflects his own upbringing in one of the poorest parts of London. Nathan was born in 1907 in Mile End Old Town, the son of a boot maker, Simon Sugar and his wife Sarah Cohen. It is unlikely that the family had been in Britain for more than 20 years or so; six years earlier, Simon was listed in the 1901 census as still living with his parents, Solomon and Sarah Sugar, but with no defined occupation. Simon had been born in Poland, but was listed as a Russian subject. His parents were both born in Russia, suggesting that had moved around prior to their arrival in Britain. Solomon's origins are unclear from official records; he does not appear to have applied for British citizenship and consequently it is difficult to work out when he actually arrived in Britain, though his daughter Rebecca is listed as being born in Spitalfields in the 1891 census and the family do not appear in 1881.

This chronology is fairly typical. Many Jewish families from Eastern Europe were fleeing an oppressive regime in Russia; the Pogroms started in 1881 and culminated in the expulsion of Jews from Moscow, with thousands of families fleeing across the Russian Empire to the safety of Western Europe. Certainly, the area of London where the Sugar family eventually settled was heavily populated by Jewish families from Russia and Poland – in 1891 Solomon had found residence in Fashion Street – so named for the proliferation of manufacturers in the cloth and tailoring business – where his neighbours were all Polish, including Isaac Silvenberg, an upholsterer; Aaron Weinberg, a wigmaker; Abraham Abraham, a tailor; and Herman Malina, a cap maker. Communities such as these were generally poor in terms of finance, yet rich in support for one another with close-knit bonds forged from common experience.

Case study 2

Anita Roddick

As the founder of The Body Shop, Anita Roddick has established herself as one of Britain's most successful businesswomen. She was born Anita Lucia Perella in 1942, the daughter of two Italian immigrants; she acquired her familiar surname when she married Gordon Roddick in 1970. Therefore, the origins of her surname lie outside this country. Perella has many derivatives across Italy according to different pronunciation in regional dialect, but appears strongest in the Lombardy region. Meaning of the surname is varied, but in many dialects it translates as 'from Peter', suggesting the name originated from a distant yet important forebear called Peter. Anita's family hailed from Naples, though the surname can be found in cities across modern Italy. However, in the medieval and early modern period there was no 'Italy' as such, only a series of semi-autonomous city states, and so family ties within these mini-states were highly important bonds and thus surname links carried a great significance.

When looking for clues to Anita's success, one doesn't have to work much further back than her childhood growing up in Littlehampton as the daughter of a hard-working Italian immigrant family. Her parents, Gilda De Vito and Donata Perella, left the bustling Mediterranean city of Naples and came to England before the Second World War, marrying in 1936. Anita was the third of four children born to the couple, and was raised in Littlehampton. Her parents ran the first American diner in the town, and Anita grew up working at weekends, serving meals to customers curious to see a slice of Americana served up by 'exotic foreigners'.

Her mother was a major influence on her life, instilling the values of hard work, attention to detail and pursuit of quality – Anita recalls that she would be sent with her sisters and younger brother to buy the groceries each day and, on presentation to her mother for inspection, have to return them all because they were below her mother's high standards. As a member of one of only two Italian families in the area, Anita considered herself to be an outsider and she suggests that, coupled with her mother's encouragement, it gave her a fearless outlook on life and the strength and courage to succeed in business.

When Anita was only eight years old, her parents divorced. Shortly afterwards, Gilda married her former husband's cousin, Henry Pirilli – quite a scandal given the size of the Italian community of Littlehampton was originally represented by the two families. Sadly, Henry died two years later from tuberculosis and Anita was devastated, having always felt closer to her step-father than her 'real' father. The reason for this was eventually revealed eight years later, when Gilda confessed that Henry was actually Anita's biological father. She had been conceived as the result of a passionate affair that had lasted several years, yet had been brought up with her younger brother Bruno as the natural children of Donato. The lovers eventually overcame the resistance of their families, and the Catholic church – against which Gilda battled for the rest of her life – to be together.

CASE STUDY 3

MICHAEL HOWARD

Whilst he was still the leader of the Conservative party prior to the 2005 General Election, Michael Howard's ancestry was the subject of media coverage with the revelation that his grandfather, Morris Hecht, was an illegal immigrant from Romania and that Michael's father, Bernat Hecht, falsified naturalization application papers to cover up this detail. With Britain's immigration policy one of the central issues of the forthcoming election, the true story of Bernat's struggle to gain entry into Britain, and then to create an Anglicised identity for himself and his family, is one that strikes a chord with far more of our ancestors than we might first assume.

It is no secret that Michael Howard was originally born Michael Hecht in Llanelli on 7th July 1941, and that his father, Bernat Hecht, changed the family name to Howard by deed poll on 8th January 1948 – the same day that he swore his oath of allegiance to His Majesty King George the Sixth as a newly naturalized British subject. Michael Howard's origins lie in Ruscova, Romania, where his father Bernat Hecht was born on 13th November 1916. Bernat came to Britain in 1937, initially finding employment as a cantor, leading prayers in a London synagogue. In April 1940 he moved to Llanelli, where two months later he married a Russian immigrant called Hilda Kurshon and started a family.

During the 1930s, many thousands of Jews from Eastern Europe sought refuge in Britain from persecution from right-wing regimes, and it is tempting to assume that Bernat Hecht was simply one amongst their number. However, documents supporting his naturalisation application, found at The National Archives, reveal a different tale and suggest he was an economic migrant. Hecht first attempted to enter Britain in March 1937, having been offered a temporary position as First Reader at the Fairclough Street Synagogue, Commercial Road, London. However, despite travelling to Ostende via Budapest to catch a boat to Dover, he was refused entry into Britain on 21st March 1937. According to a report by the immigration authorities, Hecht did not have an official permit from the Ministry of Labour and, 'being unable to say how long he intended to stay in Britain', was forced to re-board the vessel and return to Belgium. His case caused a stir at the time, and the issue of Hecht's refusal of entry was even raised in Parliament.

After a flurry of correspondence between the Synagogue, the Home Office and the Advisory Committee for the Admission of Jewish Ecclesiastical Officers, Hecht received the green light and was allowed to enter the country on 20th July 1937 – but was only granted a four-week visa to cover his trial period of employment. For the next twelve months, his employers were forced to hand back his passport every four to eight weeks and ask for a visa extension, on each occasion providing documentary proof that his services continued to be required. Hecht therefore faced deportation on a regular basis, and on many occasions this must have seemed a real threat; for example, the Synagogue wrote to the Home Office in December 1937 asking for his paperwork to be speeded up as 'Mr Hecht informs us that his permission to stay in this country is elapsing.'

Hecht only gained a degree of breathing space in April 1938 when the Synagogue gave him a three-year contract with an annual salary of £200 – quite a sizeable sum at the time – and a 12-month visa was duly granted. A note from the Home Office accompanied a further extension until April 1940, stating that 'the Secretary of State does not desire to raise objection to the continued employment of Mr Hecht as First Reader at the Fairclough Street Synagogue during this time'. Clearly, his continued presence in Britain was dependent on his vocation – underlined by the final visa extension on file made in April 1940. Yet, according to family legend, it is at this date that he appears in Llanelli to work in a draper's store. This is a dramatic change in lifestyle, as the final correspondence on file clearly refer to the Synagogue's desire to keep employing him, and the reply from the Home Office states that 'in the event of the Rev. Hecht's desiring to change his employment he must apply to the local office of the Ministry of Labour and National Service.' Official documentation ends at this juncture.

Bernat Hecht made a formal application to become a naturalized British subject in February 1947. This was successful, with many witnesses coming forward to state what an important member of the community he had become, and a certificate was duly issued on 19th December of the same year. The struggle to remain in Britain had lasted ten long years, and as part of his desire to conform and settle in his adopted homeland, Bernat Hecht formally Anglicised his name to Bernard Howard on 8th January 1948, taking the rather unusual step of publishing the news in the London Gazette and enrolling the deed poll in the Supreme Court – an expensive process. Yet there was one detail on his naturalization form that was not accurate – he claimed that his father, Morris Hecht, had died in Ruscova in 1939 whereas in reality, Morris had been present in England illegally since at least this date, and eventually died in north London in 1952. Could this perhaps be one reason why Bernat felt the need to move to Wales so suddenly in 1940?

CASE STUDY 4

HELEN MIRREN

Helen Mirren's CV makes for impressive reading, stretching back from her first major role in Age of Consent to include hits such as *The Long Good Friday*; *Excalibur*; *The Cook, The Thief, the Wife and Her Lover*; *The Madness of King George* (which earned her an Oscar nomination); *Calendar Girls*; and of course *Prime Suspect*. In 2003 she was made a Dame Commander of the British Empire, in recognition of her work — yet her immediate family background suggests that she has nothing like a traditional British upbringing.

Clues to Helen Mirren's background can be found in some of the roles she has chosen to play on stage and screen, such as *The Passion of Ayn Rand* and *A Month in the Country*, where on each occasion she has portrayed a Russian with conviction. This is probably because she was born Ilyena Lydia Mironoff, the daughter of Basil Mironoff who was an orchestral violinist with the London Philharmonic. He claimed noble descent, but was brought to Britain when only two years old by his father Peter Mironoff who — even more remarkably — had come to buy arms to further his country's cause in the Russo-Japanese war but was unable to return home when the Bolshevik revolution broke out. With his life as a Russian nobleman at an end, Peter found work in exile driving taxis around London — a far cry from an international arms dealer — a profession that his son adopted before his musical career took off, and one that he returned to after his daughter was born so that he could support his family. Basil married after the end of the Second World War in July 1945, his bride being Kathleen Alexandrina Eva Matilda Rogers.

Kathleen came from a very large family, being the youngest of thirteen children born to Arthur Rogers and his wife Elizabeth Sarah Jones between 1886 and 1908. Arthur was by trade a butcher, and this appears to have been a family profession. His father Henry certainly had quite a claim to fame, as he can be traced through records as being one of the official suppliers of meat to the royal household of Queen Victoria. Arthur was born in 1860 and married his wife in 1886. At the time of his wedding, he was not actually working in the trade, finding work — coincidentally — as a cab driver. Indeed, his new father in law, Samuel Jones, was employed in the same line of business, and in the days before motor cars there was plenty of work to be found running people around town in the horse-drawn hackney carriages that can be seen in countless old photos of London from this time. By the time his last daughter Kathleen was born in 1908, he had taken up the family trade and was working as a journeyman butcher, eventually reaching the status of master, the same as his father.

Henry Rogers ran his business in Goswell Road, Islington. It was clearly quite substantial, as in 1871 he employed fourteen men, a butcher's boy – the rather aptly named Edward Pigg, who lived in Henry's house with his colleague Frederick Mountain – and a bookkeeper. Yet by looking at his career through census records, it becomes apparent that he had faced a great deal of sorrow and hardship alongside professional success. Although he appears to be the head of a happy and thriving family at the time of the 1861 census, with his wife Matilda and three children Nancy, Emily and Arthur, and two domestic servants, it is clear that his domestic circumstances had only recently been settled. For a start, Henry was seventeen years older than his wife – usually a sign of a second marriage – and this suspicion was confirmed when his marriage certificate was ordered. In 1852 the couple married, and his marital status was listed as widower. In the 1851 census, clues as to his former life can be found – a seventeen-year-old daughter from his first marriage called Ann was living with him, as was his sister Frances. Once more, two house servants appear in their household along with four butcher's assistants, suggesting a relative degree of affluence and therefore a thriving business. His subsequent second marriage provides further indication of his rising social status – his new father in law, William Bayley, was a tradesman as well but a gold dealer. One wonders what these enterprising Victorian gentlemen would have made of Helen Mirren's profession!

Chapter 10

Family Secrets

One of the reasons many people start looking into their past is because they've heard a story about an ancestor that requires further investigation – a scandal in the past that needs checking out, rumours of a criminal ancestor or highwayman that refuse to go away, or other salacious stories that need to be verified in official sources. Sometimes, though, you may stumble across something that you never suspected, such as illegitimacy, poverty or bigamy and this is when you need to be prepared to confront the fact that your ancestors weren't always what they seemed to be. Many people are delighted to discover a bit of colour in their past, as it makes a good story to tell to others; however, if that story affects people that you know or are still living, then it can be a different matter and your opinion of relatives may alter dramatically. Furthermore, your role as researcher doubles up as messenger, and you may want to think twice about announcing to the family that they are all illegitimate, for example. This comes from personal experience; only recently I discovered that a great uncle had worked as a spy for the Soviets in the 1920s, stealing secrets from the Foreign Office and selling them to agents on the continent. It can come

Opposite: A street urchin straight from Dickensian Britain.

Below: Many people can claim descent from an illegitimate child of Charles II.

as quite a shock to the system! I've listed some of the areas where skeletons are most likely to jump out of the closet, along with the relevant records that can help you detect or prove your suspicions.

22 ILLEGITIMACY AND ADOPTION

There has been a stigma attached to illegitimacy over the ages, mainly due to the requirement to sire children inside wedlock according to the rites of the Church. With the decline of marriage as an institution, this sense of shame has lessened amongst younger generations, but for many people who were born prior to the Second World War, it has been an issue to be avoided all of their lives. Yet illegitimacy has not always been seen in such light; after all, William the Conqueror was known as William the Bastard because he was the illegitimate offspring of the Duke of Normandy and a peasant girl, but it didn't stop him succeeding his father as Duke and conquering England in 1066. Many monarchs after him sired illegitimate children, some of the most prolific being Henry II, Charles II and William IV who all had countless mistresses and recognised several offspring, often creating titles, honours and lands for them. Bastards of aristocratic fathers and their noble-born mistresses often acquired 'Fitz' as part of their surname (meaning son of), and whilst the children of lower-born mistresses were a slightly different matter, provision was often made for sons through payments for a good education, a career in the church or the purchase of a military commission to secure a place in society, or in the case of a girl a good marriage. One way to find out about this type of illegitimacy is to check for payments made out of estate accounts, the purchase of gifts or christening presents or even the provision for or recognition of an illegitimate child in a will.

Yet lower down the social scale you go, the more likelihood that society would have frowned on illegitimate children. An obvious clue is the lack of

a father's name on a birth certificate, or an anomaly on a census record; though often a family would pull together and support the girl who had fallen pregnant. In many cases the girl's parents would informally adopt the child, listing it as their own despite a rather obvious generation gap. However, problems occurred if the family was too poor to support the daughter, and in these instances the burden of responsibility fell upon the parish. In these cases, attempts were made to find the father and make him marry the girl. If this failed, then a bastardy bond was issued forcing him to support the child and its mother, thus relieving the cost of raising the child from the parish. Many fled the parish, often joining the army to escape their responsibilities. Even amongst middle class families, the shame of illegitimacy meant that single mothers were forced to marry their partners, a fact that can be seen when civil registration shed light on the number of

Above: A group of orphans and foundling children outside their care home.

CHILD EMIGRATION SCHEMES

Yet there were other ways to deal with unwanted or abandoned children – child emigration schemes were used to move children around the world, often as indented servants to be employed in one of Britain's overseas colonies with a status little more than a slave, or to find a new life in an existing community such as Canada or Australia. From 1927 the system became regulated, and certificates of adoption were issued. It is now possible to trace natural parents through these certificates and local authority files, but it is a difficult process and not one to be embarked upon without counselling. A good place to find further advice is www.familiesintime.co.uk

marriages that happened with a few months before or after the birth of a child.

Another alternative was to put an illegitimate child up for adoption. There was no central system in place prior to the introduction of a national adoption register for England and Wales in 1927, and arrangements were often made privately or with the help of the church. Some organisations such as Dr Barnados kept records and assisted illegitimate or orphaned children a refuge and opportunity to find a new family.

Divorce and bigamy

Another major source of shame and scandal that our ancestors had to face was the breakdown of a relationship. Before 1857, there were no easy ways to secure an official separation from a partner. Although civil divorce had been introduced in the seventeenth century, it required an Act of Parliament and thus was totally impractical for all but a few individuals. There were a few grounds under which couples could separate, but none involved actual divorce and subsequently any ensuing marriage by either party was considered to be bigamous and thus illegal. In recognition of the unsustainable situation, the Matrimonial Causes Act was passed in 1857 which brought divorce within the remit of the civil courts and therefore in theory within reach of a wider section of society. Nevertheless, it still remained very difficult to prove and was a costly exercise for most people, and therefore it was only the wealthy classes of society that could afford to take this route; and in consequence bigamy was far more widespread than you might have imagined.

There are some signs you can spot, if you look carefully enough. Many people left their partners and quietly started a life with someone else in another part of the country. You can pick them up in the nineteenth century through census records. If they re-married, they often stated on the marriage certificate that they were single, or had been widowed; it's easy enough to check to see if this is the case by looking for the death of the first partner. Bigamy was an offence, and if caught the parties would face prosecution, a hefty fine or even imprisonment particularly if the original split had not been amicable or deception was involved in the process. The court records of the nineteenth and early century are full of cases of bigamy, with lurid coverage in local and national newspapers. Of course, this only represented the tip of the iceberg, and a vast number of cases went unreported, unprosecuted and unnoticed. It was only with further changes in the law in the 1930s and 1940s that introduced legal aid, and other social changes such as the Second World War that increased the need for divorce, that the incidence of divorce increased dramatically with more women filing for separation from their husbands. There is a central divorce index held by the Principal Registry of the Family Division, Decree Absolute Section, First Avenue House, Holborn, London, that covers local registries as well as those granted in the Supreme Court. Surviving case files are located at The National Archives, Kew with a union name index available for searching.

✖ POVERTY AND THE WORKHOUSE

The more you investigate your family tree, the more you start to realise how lucky we are to live in the modern world. The very real threat of poverty and starvation was commonplace for countless people throughout British history, including many of our own ancestors. Whilst it is hard today to imagine living in such grinding poverty, during a time when there was no income support, tax credits or welfare benefit, it is possible to shed some light on the circumstances our ancestors faced by examining the changing ways the state has dealt with the issue of poverty through the ages, and the records generated during this time.

Whilst this sounds an early forerunner of the welfare state, conditions facing the poor were harsh, and there was great resentment amongst the taxpayers. Stringent efforts were made to check the credentials of claimants, and in 1662 a further Act empowered the parochial authorities to move on any newcomer or stranger who was not from their jurisdiction that claimed poor relief. In 1697, even more draconian steps were taken, when an Act decreed that the poor were to be badged with a large letter P to identify them as receiving poor relief, preceded by a letter identifying the name of their parish so that they could not claim from more than one source. Twenty-five years later, the main component of the Victorian system was put in place when the first workhouses were first mooted, the idea being that the deliberately harsh regimes imposed on the unfortunate inmates would act as a deterrent for those who found it easier to live off the poor relief. Consequently, conditions varied wildly from parish to parish, and by the 1830s it was recognised that changes had to be made.

With the introduction of Poor Law Amendment Act in 1834, the system was overhauled and given a national administration and policy. Various government-sponsored schemes had been attempted in the past; as Jeremy found during his quest, initiatives had been set up in the 1820s and 1830s to move the rural poor from areas such as East Anglia to the newly industrialized north, with the aim of finding work for former agricultural labourers and redundant artisans in rural professions in the emerging factories. However, this often transferred the problem from one part of the country to another, with the mill towns quickly

CARING FOR THE POOR

The history of society's attempts to care for its poor makes rather sorry reading. Until the Poor Law Amendment Act was passed in 1834, assistance to those unable to support themselves was essentially the responsibility of the local community where they lived, and consequently there were no national standards of care. The basic administrative unit was the parish, since it was considered an ecclesiastical duty to offer alms and charity to the poor – a function traditionally embraced by the monasteries, until their dissolution in the mid-sixteenth century. To compensate for the loss of this function, an Act was passed in 1601 which created a system whereby each parish was required to offer poor relief to those in need, which was essentially levied as a local tax and administered by the overseers of poor for each parish church. As part of the scheme, the revenue collected was distributed to the needy, whilst those capable of toiling in the fields were put to work, along with abandoned children and orphans.

becoming overcrowded and areas of extreme poverty and deprivation creeping into the growing cities. Consequently, events such as the cotton famine in the 1860s – triggered by the American civil war, which disrupted the flow of raw materials to Britain's factories in the North West – created havoc, with thousands out of work and relying on charitable donations. It was during this period that co-operatives societies were established to cater for the starving poor.

Under the terms of the 1834 legislation, poor law unions were created across the country that replaced the old parochial parishes, and at a stroke secularised the business of charity. A nationwide policy was imposed on the poor, rather than the piecemeal local approach. At the centre of the policy were the workhouses, which operated on the thesis that the undeserving poor would never willingly take up a place within the workhouse because the conditions were so harsh; whilst the 'deserving' poor – those without any means of support, the elderly, the infirm – had no choice in the matter. The Poor Law Unions continued until 1930.

Above: For the poorest sections of society, life was a struggle without luxuries that we take for granted today, such as chairs.

There is a variety of ways that you can trace a relative who has fallen on hard times. The best place to start is with official records, such as birth, marriage and death certificates – the product of official registration, introduced in England and Wales in 1837, Scotland in 1855 and Ireland in 1864 – and census returns. Certificates often provide an indication of a person's social status, particularly if they list an official residence. A birth of a child might be recorded in a workhouse or pauper's hospital, indicating that the parents were unable to afford a place of their own, or were reliant on state support for their survival. The place where someone died can also reveal a great deal about their final circumstances – in the days before state pensions, the elderly and infirm had to rely on their families to support them, or work for as long as possible, and often ran into difficulties if there was no-one left to look after them. Consequently, many moved into the workhouse or almshouses, where they ended their days. You can also use the census returns from 1841-1901 to locate an ancestor, and start to make some judgements about their relative wealth. Institutions such as workhouses, pauper hospitals and charitable establishments are listed, with the name, age, place of birth and – on occasion occupation – of each inmate. These can also be used to establish whether someone spent some time inside; though it is important to bear in mind the fact that these were only snapshots taken on a single night every 10 years, so the vast majority of a person's life would be unrecorded. Since people moved in and out of such institutions, you would need to look elsewhere for clues. In particular, you should try to track down admission and discharge registers, as well as burial records for each institution. Further advice about where to find the records of workhouses is provided elsewhere in this article.

Maps can also reveal a great deal about the conditions where someone lived; for example, the maps produced by the philanthropist Charles Booth for various districts within the sprawling Victorian metropolis of London used colour to shade the poorest parts of town at given dates, and can be used today to work out whether our ancestors lived in relative luxury or poverty. Even standard Ordnance Survey maps provide a useful research resource – they can reveal in great detail the location of houses that no longer stand, providing a visual indication of the historic status of the area. Things to look out for are crowded streets, often built back to back in a fairly rapid period of time and usually linked to the construction of factories – which you can determine by examining and comparing a sequence of maps from various dates. Many urban areas were required under a series of property Acts in the late nineteenth and early twentieth centuries to demolish the sprawling slums that had grown unchecked throughout the period of industrial expansion, which through poor sanitation and low standards of living were a health risk to the residents; plans and planning papers can usually be found in local archives, which provide excellent historical context to the lost world of the Victorian poor.

It was the deliberate intention of the authorities to make workhouses as unpleasant, brutal and feared as possible, so that people would take whatever steps necessary to ensure they did not end up inside. The Dickensian impression of cruelty was often well founded; beatings were common, and in many cases sanitary conditions were poor, leading to epidemics of disease such as cholera, dysentery and tuberculosis. Many workhouses split the inmates into male and female dormitories, which meant that entire families were split up. The daily routine was hard and monotonous, and the inmates faced long days and little time to themselves. In the summer months they rose at 6am, started work an hour later and continued until midday. After a brief break, they returned to work until 6pm, when they ate dinner; two hours later they went to bed. The regime was only slightly easier during winter conditions, with an extra hour in bed and a later start at 8am. Food was of poor quality, the basics required to sustain life, and from time to time scandals emerged in the press about the appalling levels to which people stooped.

Amazingly, paupers were free to leave the institution at any time, yet the inability of so many to do so is a damning indictment of the lack of alternative support available to the more vulnerable sections of society. Many people returned to the workhouse time and time again, often becoming institutionalised, whilst these grim places were often the first port of call for orphans, foundling children, the elderly or infirm who had no families to support them. Throughout the nineteenth century, there was a growing recognition that conditions had to improve – highlighted by Charles Dickens's critique in works such as *Oliver Twist* – but change was slow to arrive. At the start of the twentieth century, a Royal Commission took four years to consider the evidence put before it by campaigners for and against the continuation of the workhouse system, and the best way to tackle poverty and the unemployed. Although it was recognised that the terms of the original 1834 Poor Law Amendment Act were out of date, no firm decision was made as to the way forward. Options ranged from creating separate institutions for the sick, mentally ill and elderly, whilst other commissioners preferred to tackle the problem head on, by urging the Government to address the causes of destitution. Consequently, neither view gained ascendancy and workhouses continued, though under a new name, the 'Poor Law Institution'. In 1929, responsibility for running the system was once again devolved locally, this time to county and borough councils. It took the creation of the National Health

Service and the welfare state after the Second World War to finally eradicate the dreaded workhouse.

The main documents relating to workhouses are the admission registers, most of which are deposited at the relevant county record office or local record office. Where they survive, you can find details of when someone entered the workhouse and when they applied to leave – if indeed they ever did. Many people also died in the workhouse, so it is worth looking out for burial registers. Other records will include minute books created by the guardians of the poor, punishment books – because the regimes usually had provision to punish inmates for misbehaviour – and correspondence. The National Archives also holds further correspondence that contains the names of thousands of people, but since there are comprehensive name indexes, you may encounter a long and frustrating search for evidence. Of course, your search may not necessarily be

Above: Many groups were forced to the edge of society through poverty, scandal or crime.

for the inmate of a workhouse – there are documents relating to staff as well, such as appointment registers contained at The National Archives that cover masters and mistresses, nurses and the people responsible for overseeing the work of the inmates. Details in the registers can be brief, but in many cases before 1900 there are additional records that can provide more personal data, such as age, details of former employment, and marital status. Applications to the various bodies responsible for poor relief should yield results, provided you know where your ancestors were living and feel confident that they had fallen upon hard times.

If you are unsure about how to track down an ancestor that has fallen upon hard time, you can find out more from Gibson and Youngs, *Poor Law Union Records: A Gazetteer of England and Wales* or go online and access www.workhouses.org.uk, a resource that lists where workhouses were and what records are available. Alternatively, you can search online for surviving records at www.a2a.org.uk whilst The National Archives has produced an information guide about the topic, which can be viewed on its website www.nationalarchives.gov.uk

✼ CRIMINAL ANCESTORS

A final area you might want to investigate with a degree of trepidation is that of criminality. Many of our ancestors fell foul of the law, often for offences that we might consider trivial by today's standards but in the past would have attracted quite draconian punishment such as transportation or even execution. The reality was that life was hard for many sections of society, and theft was often the only alternative to starvation; yet the punishments were suitably harsh to deter such offences.

Crime and punishment can be traced through a wide variety of records. Trials were often reported extensively in local newspapers, and often provide a

virtual verbatim account of the trial,
especially if it involved a salacious case.
These can be found in local study centres,
county archives and main branch libraries,
although the British Newspaper Library at
Colindale, London holds duplicate sets for
most of the country. You'd need to know
roughly when the trial took place to make
an effective search for information.
Alternatively, you can look for details of
the trial itself, either in the High Court or
assize records, held at The National
Archives, or local sessions presided over by
justices of the peace known as quarter
sessions (because they were held on
average four times a year). As a rough rule
of thumb, more serious cases were heard
before the Assize justices as they moved
around the country, but JPs were
empowered to pass sentence locally on
felonies where appropriate. The records
vary from circuit to circuit, but include

Above: Many of our ancestors had a secret criminal past.

gaol books, depositions and indictments. Where a convicted criminal was
imprisoned, you can look for calendars of prisoners that provide details of the
offence, conviction date and sentence. Transportation records also survive, at
The National Archives, and shed some light on the horrific conditions that
felons faced as they made their long journey to a penal colony in America or,
after the eighteenth century, Australia. Many died on the way over, with further
casualties in the harsh conditions faced on arrival. Yet the ultimate sanction was
capital punishment, and a public hanging often attracted large crowds and
attendant publicity in newspapers. Pamphlets were often produced to
accompany the execution, many of which now survive.

CASE STUDY I (SECRETS)

CAMILLA PARKER- BOWLES

Camilla Shand is perhaps better known by her married name, Camilla Parker-Bowles, She married the Prince of Wales on 8 April 2005 in a civil ceremony in Windsor, and previously had been his companion for many years. However, further research into the Shand family shows that she is not the first of her line to have had a controversial relationship with a member of the royal family.

According to various old books that recount the history of surnames, Shand is said to be Scottish in origin and, despite its fairly widespread appearance throughout Britain, it can be placed within a fairly small geographical region in the northeast counties of Scotland, particularly Aberdeenshire in the parishes of Turriff, Forgue, Drumblade amongst others. One of the earliest landowners in the area was Robert Schand (1539), who lived in Turriff. This is where the lands of Shand's Cross are situated – a cross often being used to mark a boundary or local jurisdiction. Therefore it is likely that this is the spiritual home of the Shand family.

As with many surnames, the exact origins lie before written records began and are therefore lost to us. Two possible theories can be put forward to explain how the family took their name. The first is based on the fact that Shand may be a derivative of De Campo, Deschamp, or Champ (originally from the Latin meaning 'field' or 'plain') which would be pronounced Shan in the local dialect, and there are many historic figures of this name in the region. However, it is equally possible that the word relates to an adjective of Teutonic origin – 'Schand' – meaning bright or elegant, and thus used to describe the particular personal attributes of the founder of the family.

If you were to scour the historic records far enough back in time – something that a number of researchers have done since the announcement of the royal wedding – it is possible to find ancestors in Camilla Shand's family tree that are shared by the pop stars Madonna and Celine Dion. However, since these common relatives were born in the early seventeenth century and represent Camilla's nine-times great grandparents, it is unlikely that they are close enough relatives to warrant an invitation to sing at the wedding celebration. Instead, they might want to invite Camilla's third cousin, Judith Keppel – the first winner of the jackpot prize in ITV's *Who Wants to be a Millionaire*.

Camilla Shand was born on 17 July 1947, the daughter of Bruce Middleton Hope Shand, a Major in the British Army. Her grandfather Philip Morton Shand was an author and architect, born and raised in Kensington. He appears to have a led a colourful life, marrying four times and pursuing an apparently remorseless love of lawsuits. This trait probably came from his father Alexander Faukner Shand, a writer as well as a barrister and Fellow of the British Academy who was the first of the line to be born outside Scotland; the two previous generations had been born north of the border, and any further back it becomes much harder to entangle the various branches of the Shand family tree. This is a common problem with family history – once you exhaust the main sources, such as birth, marriage and death certificates and census returns, it becomes much harder to track people down in the records.

Given the controversial nature of Charles and Camilla's relationship, it is perhaps no surprise that there is secret in the Shand family tree that may seem uncannily familiar. Camilla's great-grandmother, Alice Keppel, was rumoured to be the mistress of the Prince of Wales in 1898, later crowned Edward VII on the death of Queen Victoria in 1901. It is possible that Alice's daughter Sonia – Camilla's grandmother, born 24 May 1900 – was the result of this relationship, although officially Alice's husband George Keppel is listed as the father. If not though, then this would mean that Charles and Camilla are half-second cousins once removed.

Case study 2

J K Rowling

JK Rowling is the author of some of the most successful children's books of all time – the Harry Potter series – and soon she will be bringing the saga to a close. Yet her background contains some secrets of her own, though not as magical as the ones she writes about in her books!

The surname Rowling is derived from the Christian name Rollo, an ancient name that can be traced back to one of its most famous bearers, the first Duke of Normany. Rollo was originally a Viking who sailed down the Seine with his men in late ninth century to raid the land; he eventually decided to settle there, much as the Danes had done in England, and received the duchy of Normandy from the French King Charles III in return for cessation of hostilities and a Christian baptism. The name Rollo is linked to Rolf, which can be translated as 'wolf of renown', and a later version Roul was introduced to England by the Norman invaders of 1066. It is from the pet version of Roul that Rowling originated.

Joanne Rowling was born in Bristol in 1965, but was raised in Gwent and now lives in Scotland. Her parents, Anne Volant and Peter John Rowling, experienced a whirlwind romance, meeting on a train bound for Abroath (so clearly not the Hogwarts Express) when they were both only 18 years old. They married within a couple of years on 14th March 1965, and Joanne was born four months later on 31st July.

Given the imagination required to create Harry Potter's world, one might expect to find characters with creative or artistic careers throughout the family tree; it is perhaps somewhat of a disappointment to find engineers for the first couple of generations back. Anne's father, Stanley George Volant, was listed as a consultant engineer at the time of her marriage, and – rather grandly – an experimental engineer on her birth certificate. His rise into a very technical and challenging profession is perhaps all the more remarkable when one considers his background, as he was the son of a French immigrant, Louis Volant, who earned a living as a waiter. He arrived in England in the late 1890s and married Eliza Mary Anne Smith in 1900.

Peter Rowling also trained to become a production engineer, but his father Ernest became a shop owner having trained as a tool setter, whilst Peter's grandfather Frank Rowling was also a storekeeper. The exact type of store is not mentioned on official certificates, although it is safe to assume that they were not proprietors of the type of premises found in Diagon Alley or Hogsmeade. In fact, Frank started out his working life as a tobacco pipe cleaner before moving on to pipe making in the early 1900s. He was the son of William Rowling, a blacksmith by trade who grew up in the East End of London. The mid nineteenth century was a time when blacksmiths played an important role in the local community, although the diversity of jobs listed for William's children in the last two decades demonstrates that – in London at least – the work of the local smithy in fashioning iron and metalwork, and repairing broken items, was increasingly undermined by cheaper mass-produced goods.

Apart from the sudden appearance of Louis Volant in the records in 1901, another mystery surrounds this side of the family. Anne Volant's birth certificate states her mother was called Louisa Caroline Volant formerly Watts. However, in the margin a note has been added by the Superintendent Registrar on production of a declaration by the parents that Louisa's maiden name should have been written Watts otherwise Smith. This oddity becomes more interesting when her marriage certificate to Stanley Volant is examined; her father's name is left blank, whilst her own name is listed as Louisa Caroline Watts Smith. This is a strong indication of illegitimacy, further strengthened by her birth certificate, where the father's name is again blank and the mother's maiden name is listed as Smith in the registration indexes. Given the appearance of the Watts surname, it is very possible that this is the surname of her biological father, but there are no further clues in the official records.

CASE STUDY 3

MICHAEL PARKINSON

When you think of chat shows, you think of Michael Parkinson. His name has become a byword for the genre, and the list of guests who have appeared opposite the genial host is stellar. From Hollywood movers and shakers to Prime Ministers, everyone who's anyone queues up to talk shop. His shows have brought us many golden memories, such as his interview with Mohammed Ali where he barely managed to get a word in, or the unforgettable assault by the late Rod Hull and his sidekick Emu. Yet who's there to ask the questions of the host himself? *The Family Detective* has taken a look at his roots, and reveals some interesting talking points concerning his background.

Michael Parkinson was born in 1935 in Cudworth near Barnsley, in the West Riding of Yorkshire, the son of a coal hewer John William Parkinson and his wife Freda. Coal mining was a profession that was in the Parkinson blood; at least three generations of Parkinson worked in the pits, all living in Brierly, a village in the district of Hemsworth. John's father Samuel was born in 1876, and found employment as a colliery lampman, ensuring that fellow workers had sufficient light by which to hack away at the coalface. In 1899 he married Florence Kate Sawyer, the 19-year-old daughter of a soldier who appears never to have known his daughter; Richard Sawyer served as a private in the Royal Horse Guards, and married Florence's mother Anne Batterham in London near to his barracks in Knightsbridge. Only seven months later Florence was born, suggesting a shotgun wedding (no pun intended) but by this date Anne had moved back to her parents home in Lincolnshire, and Richard was later listed as having died. It was left to Florence's grandparents Abraham and Frances Batterham to raise her from the age of only a few months old until the time she met and married Samuel Parkinson. The Batterhams were clearly quite a strong couple, as they also provided a home for another young grandchild William, only a few months older than his cousin Florence.

Samuel's father William Parkinson was a labourer down the pit in Brierly, and his story is no less remarkable. He was born in 1830 in Brierly, the son of Thomas and Hannah. The couple ran a very small farm of only 5 acres, where William first started his working life, and - like the Batterhams - the family also supported an unattached grandchild. By 1861 William had left home and was living with his sister Emma whilst working as a labourer; however, it appears that he harboured a secret. Although unmarried he was living with his eight-month old son and this probably explains his sister's presence in the household. Fast forward ten years, and by 1871 he was head of an enlarged household, a widower supporting his mother (now 84), unmarried sister and her four children. There is no sign of his own son, and he has risen to the status of a farmer of 80 acres. These mysteries are perhaps strange enough, without the revelation of his second marriage in 1873 where he lies about his age, claiming that he was only 40. There is a very good reason for this deception; his bride, Frances Anne Langley, is stated to be only 15 years old whilst her bride was thirty years her senior. Both parties signed with their mark, suggesting illiteracy, and two years after he was listed as a farmer of 80 acres, William was described as a colliery sinker, a huge chance in circumstances. His son, Samuel Parkinson, was born in 1876, a year after his older sister Emma; but by 1881, their mother was no longer part of the household and William's siblings Jane and Joseph were now resident. One possible explanation was that Frances had died young, but William is clearly listed as 'married' rather than 'widower' in successive census records, suggesting that she left - or her family forced her to leave.

Written record only takes us back so far and leaves tantalizing clues as to the internal dynamics of a family, but in circumstances such as those revealed here it is tempting to speculate about what William's life must have been like. One wonders what questions Michael would have asked his great-grandfather if he had been sitting opposite him - what were the circumstances behind the appearance and disappearance of his first son Samuel; why did he decide to leave the farm and go down the mines; and what on earth did his family think of his marriage to a teenager one third his age? Perhaps it is just as well that history has cloaked the answers.

CASE STUDY 4

MICK JAGGER

Mick Jagger is one of the most recognisable faces on the planet, having fronted the Sixties rock band the Rolling Stones for over four decades. He is currently touring again, much to the delight of his fans, and at 62 years old none of the raw energy of his past performances is missing. However, the transition from notoriety in the 1960s, linked to drug-taking and other excesses of the rock and roll lifestyle, to establishment figure, has been a long journey – but one that seems rather ordinary in comparison with the struggles faced by one of his Jagger ancestors.

Michael Philip Jagger was born in 1943 in Dartford, the son of Basil Fanshawe Jagger and his wife, Eva Ensley Mary Scutts. They married in 1940, when Basil was working as a schoolteacher and Eva plied her trade as a hairdresser. Her father, Alfred Charles Scutts, was listed as a boat builder, a common profession in the Dartford area where so much history was linked to the sea and the docks. Rather curiously, the name of Basil's father was left blank on the marriage certificate – which can be taken as a sign of illegitimacy – although the profession of the elusive Mr Jagger was also recorded as schoolteacher. Luckily, it is easy enough to solve this slight mystery; Basil's birth certificate reveals the name of his father, David Ernest Jagger, confirms that he was a teacher, and reveals the origins of his rather exotic middle name, as his mother was called Harriet Fanshawe before she married in 1908. Teaching was – and still is, of course – a very respectable position and one that required a good education. It is somewhat of a surprise to learn that the background of David's family was not at all what you would expect, and on closer examination a tragedy started to unfold that explained a great deal about the dynamics of the family.

David Ernest Jagger was born in Whitehaven in 1880, and at the time of the 1901 census he was living with his parents, David Jagger and the rather gloriously named Sidwell Elizabeth Jagger, at their home in Eckington, near Chesterfield. David Ernest – recorded as 'Ernest D' on the census return – was already working as an assistant schoolmaster at the time, and had two colleagues living in the house with him, namely George Baker and William Appleby. Yet the census revealed some rather unusual pieces of information, not least the fact that David Ernest had a step-sister, Mary Hodge; that his mother was born in Cornwall; and that David Ernest had been born in Whitehaven, Cumberland. This suggested that some family upheaval had taken place, which was confirmed by a closer examination of David senior's life.

David Jagger – Mick's great-grandfather – was born in Morley, Yorkshire, in 1845. He married Sidwell Elizabeth Hodge in June 1879, and the certificate confirms that both parties had lost previous partners, which helped to explain the appearance of Mary Hodge in 1901, as well as David Ernest's half-brother called John Edwin Jagger who was listed in the 1881 census aged 9. John Edwin was born on 18th November 1871; nine days later, his mother Margaret Jagger was dead following complications connected to her labour. She was only 22 years old, and for the next eight years David brought his son up on his own. The couple had only been together a year; their marriage took place on 12th November 1870. Yet – unbelievably – David was listed on this document as a widower, which meant that this was the second time that he had faced the agony of losing a wife. Sure enough, further investigation revealed that David had previously married Emma Dobson, aged 22, in 1867 at the Whitehaven Register Office, and just over a year later she had died of phthisis – the medical term for tuberculosis; its symptoms were a wasting away of the body, and so David would have endured witnessing his wife's long, lingering death.

Yet his story does not end there. Further evidence suggests that his childhood was, if anything, even tougher; his father John was a grocer in Morley, and it appears that his mother Abigail helped out in the shop, leaving little time to look after their children. Both were aged mid-forties at the time of the 1851 census, and had their last two children relatively late in life – David was only 5 at the time – and it seems as if they died shortly afterwards. When the 1861 census was taken, David and his brother Edwin were living as boarders with the Drake family in Bradford, with Edwin learning the trade of a printing compositor and David earning a living in a warehouse. Their parents were not listed anywhere, and further evidence for their demise is supported by the fact that the rest of the family were split up; the youngest son Joseph, who was only 11 years old in 1861, was living in the household of his married sister Ruth in Bradford, along with another brother John.

Quite how David Jagger survived these trials and tribulations is cause of amazement, even in an age when death and disease claimed wives and mothers at a young age, especially during the dangers of childbirth. Not only did he bring up his son, find the courage to move on not once but twice, raise another son and take on the responsibility of a step-daughter, but he also changed professions from a printer's compositor to the better paid position of assurance agent. It is through his struggles to raise his family through adversity that David Ernest was provided with a platform to become a schoolteacher, and eventually move the family to Dartford. Mick Jagger penned the song 'Can't Get No Satisfaction' – the title would apply rather aptly to the early life of his great-grandfather.

CASE STUDY 5

SEAN CONNERY

When people mention the character James Bond, you tend to imagine the face of the actor you saw play the role when you were growing up. Yet for most people, the James Bond is Sean Connery, who defined the role between 1962 and 1971, and reprised the role one last time in 1983 in the aptly titled *Never Say Never Again*. With his lilting Scottish accent he brought style and sophistication to the role, as well as a large dash of charm. To date, his film career spans nearly half a century, from his acting debut in *Lilacs in the Spring* in 1955, for which he was uncredited. Yet closer examination of his background makes his rise to the top of the film industry even more remarkable given his somewhat humble origins. And, as one of Scotland's greatest sons, there's a surprise lurking deep within the family tree.

Sean Connery was actually born Thomas Sean Connery in August 1930 at the Royal Maternity Hospital, Edinburgh, the son of rubber worker Joseph Connery and his wife Euphemia. They married two years previously in 1928, three days after Christmas, in Edinburgh, where she earned a living as a laundry worker. Her background is fairly easy to trace. Born Euphemia McBain McLean in 1908, she was the daughter of a railway worker called Neil McLean and his wife Helen Forbes Ross. The McLean line goes back to Pittenweem, the site of a brutal witchcraft trial in the early eighteenth century, on several sides. Neil's parents were John McLean and Euphemia McBain, whose father William was a local fisherman who fell on hard times and died in Pitenweem a pauper in 1875. His wife was Mary Gourlay, born in 1793 and daughter of Thomas Gourlay. With all these names and the strong geographical link to Pittenweem, it would not be that surprising if they had ancestors who were present during the terrible events that unfolded in the village in 1705, when a group of locals were accused of witchcraft by Thomas Morton. The local clergyman, Patrick Cowper, whipped local feelings into a frenzy by preaching against the work of the devil in his sermons. A mob gathered, and one of the accused, Janet Cornfoot, was pursued and imprisoned. Although she escaped, the mob caught up with her, dragged to the seafront, swung her from a rope tied between ships masts, then stoned, beat and crushed her to death under a door piled with rocks. To make sure she was dead, a man drove his horse and cart over her body.

Yet the real revelations in the Connery family tree concern Joseph's parentage, as his birth certificate issued in Glasgow in 1902 reveals that he was technically illegitimate, the son of Thomas Connary, a pedlar, and Jeannie McNab. Furthermore Thomas was illiterate as well, signing the document with his mark, and there are even questions about where he was based at this time, the question about his usual place of residence receiving the enigmatic answer 'inmate'. His failure to write probably led to the his surname being spelled Connary, and Joseph's birth certificate was eventually corrected to Connery in 1967. Certainly he appears to have had a hard life as a general labourer, scrapping a living as best he could. By the time he died 1947, he was described at the widower of Jean Lawson McNab having made an honest woman of her in 1938 at St Patricks Roman Catholic Church. He was 59 and she was 51. Yet the marriage was to last only two years, as she died of cancer in 1940.

The marriage certificate begins to fill in some of the blanks about Thomas's life, as there is no sign of his birth certificate, or indeed any credible appearances on census records. Yet it is possible to establish his parentage from the information it contains; Thomas's father is revealed as James Connery, a general labourer who had previously married Elizabeth McPhillips. James died of bronchitis in 1914 on 16th July, just a few weeks before the outbreak of the First World War, his wife having pre-deceased him seven years earlier. Yet James Connery holds a secret, namely that he was an Irish tinker from Wexford, who had come to Scotland to find work. It may seem a fairly tenuous link, given the other branches of Sean Connery's family tree that are firmly rooted in Scottish soil, but nevertheless there is no doubt that the surname originates from across the water in Ireland. Yet for those concerned that Scotland's finest is about to be claimed as an exile from the Emerald Isle, it is clear that the Irish influence is very remote indeed. If you needed any evidence, it is comforting to note that Sean Connery's performance as Jim Malone in the 1987 film *The Untouchables* alongside Kevin Costner was rated the 'worst ever' attempt at an Irish accent in 2003 by Empire Magazine, who described it as the least credible in film history.

CHAPTER 11

Conclusion

By now, you've probably realised that there is no end to number of ways you can explore your past. The case studies featured in this book illustrate that everybody has an interesting story lurking in their background, as long as you know where to look and how to interpret what you find. Yet its easy to think that family history stops and starts with the people that you encounter and research on the family tree that you're building – but actually, you can use your research to open up a number of related lines of work, each of which will reveal more about your ancestors, and the way they used to live. The message is that there needn't be an end to your research, even if you have hit a brick wall and can't go any further back in time. On the one hand, there are other branches of your family to uncover; whilst on the other hand, you can spend some time looking at the historical context surrounding the community where they grew up, the places in which they worked, the house in which they lived, or the major events that took place and shaped the world around them. Family history offers an amazing opportunity to view our history through the eyes of our ancestors, and is a world away from the old-fashioned name collecting and tree building that has been the traditional image of genealogy.

Opposite: **We can tell from her dress that this was a woman of some status.**

🙰 FINDING THE ANCESTRAL HOME

One of the most important associated areas that you can research is the history of the ancestral home. There is something very exciting about finding out where your ancestors came from, and most of the basic sources that you use – in particular civil registration certificates and census returns – provide an address. This means you can work out exactly where your immediate ancestors considered home to be, and with some careful research even discover if the house still stands.

Tracing the history of a house relies upon a range of related research skills, although fewer are online and most documents will be based at the relevant county record office. The first step is to plot out on a timeline the addresses where your ancestors lived, compiled from all the certificates, census returns and other sources. As with family history, it's worth starting with the most recent properties, particularly if they have a postcode. However, the further back in time you work, the harder it can be to find the whereabouts of the house. Many addresses have changed over time – streets were often re-named, houses assigned names or new numbers – and in many places outside towns and cities before the twentieth century, house numbers weren't even consistently used at all. This means you will have to rely on other sources to find out whether your ancestor's house still stands.

One of the best sources for twentieth century housing are the electoral lists, which show voting eligibility for each property. They are traditionally arranged by street and then house number, so you can quickly work out how long your family spent at each address listed on the certificates you've found. Electoral lists can be found at county record offices, local study centres and main libraries, and are particularly good for the second half of the twentieth century, although with some patient searching you should be able to locate your ancestors even earlier. If your relatives lived in towns and cities, the chances are that earlier rate books survive. Rates were local taxes raised to pay for the upkeep of the community, and are usually arranged by property. So once again, if you know where your ancestors lived, you should be able to locate them fairly

Opposite: Official records of property transfer shed light on the history of your ancestral home.

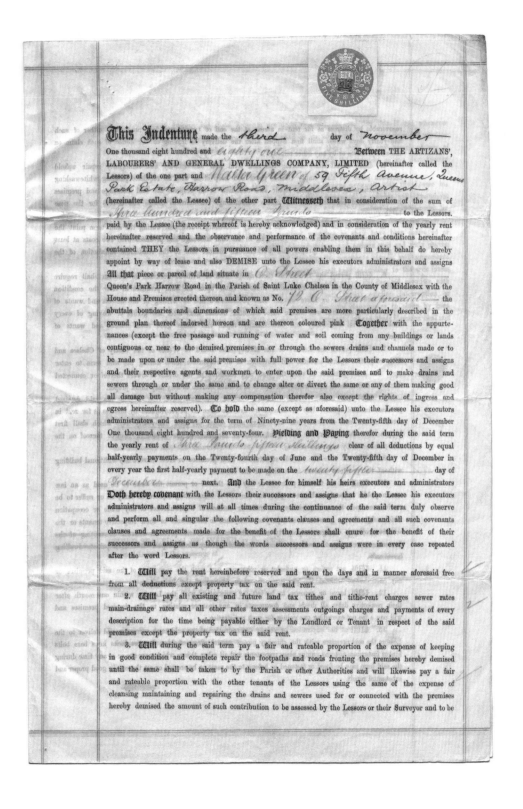

This Indenture made the *third* day of *November* One thousand eight hundred and *eighty one* **Between** THE ARTIZANS', LABOURERS' AND GENERAL DWELLINGS COMPANY, LIMITED (hereinafter called the Lessors) of the one part and *Walter Green* of 59 *Fifth Avenue, Queens Park Estate, Harrow Road, Middlesex, Artist* (hereinafter called the Lessee) of the other part **Witnesseth** that in consideration of the sum of *Three hundred and fifteen Pounds* to the Lessors, paid by the Lessee (the receipt whereof is hereby acknowledged) and in consideration of the yearly rent hereinafter reserved and the observance and performance of the covenants and conditions hereinafter contained THEY the Lessors in pursuance of all powers enabling them in this behalf do hereby appoint by way of lease and also DEMISE unto the Lessee his executors administrators and assigns **All that** piece or parcel of land situate in *O Street* Queen's Park Harrow Road in the Parish of Saint Luke Chelsea in the County of Middlesex with the House and Premises erected thereon and known as No. *19 O Street aforesaid* the abuttals boundaries and dimensions of which said premises are more particularly described in the ground plan thereof indorsed hereon and are thereon coloured pink **Together** with the appurtenances (except the free passage and running of water and soil coming from any buildings or lands contiguous or near to the demised premises in or through the sewers drains and channels made or to be made upon or under the said premises with full power for the Lessors their successors and assigns and their respective agents and workmen to enter upon the said premises and to make drains and sewers through or under the same and to change alter or divert the same or any of them making good all damage but without making any compensation therefor also except the rights of ingress and egress hereinafter reserved). **To hold** the same (except as aforesaid) unto the Lessee his executors administrators and assigns for the term of Ninety-nine years from the Twenty-fifth day of December One thousand eight hundred and seventy-four. **Yielding and Paying** therefor during the said term the yearly rent of *Three Pounds fifteen Shillings* clear of all deductions by equal half-yearly payments on the Twenty-fourth day of June and the Twenty-fifth day of December in every year the first half-yearly payment to be made on the *twenty fifth* day of *December* next. **And** the Lessee for himself his heirs executors and administrators **Doth hereby covenant** with the Lessors their successors and assigns that he the Lessee his executors administrators and assigns will at all times during the continuance of the said term duly observe and perform all and singular the following covenants clauses and agreements and all such covenants clauses and agreements made for the benefit of the Lessors shall enure for the benefit of their successors and assigns as though the words successors and assigns were in every case repeated after the word Lessors.

1. **Will** pay the rent hereinbefore reserved and upon the days and in manner aforesaid free from all deductions except property tax on the said rent.

2. **Will** pay all existing and future land tax tithes and tithe-rent charges sewer rates main-drainage rates and all other rates taxes assessments outgoings charges and payments of every description for the time being payable either by the Landlord or Tenant in respect of the said premises except the property tax on the said rent.

3. **Will** during the said term pay a fair and rateable proportion of the expense of keeping in good condition and complete repair the footpaths and roads fronting the premises hereby demised until the same shall be taken to by the Parish or other Authorities and will likewise pay a fair and rateable proportion with the other tenants of the Lessors using the same of the expense of cleansing maintaining and repairing the drains and sewers used for or connected with the premises hereby demised the amount of such contribution to be assessed by the Lessors or their Surveyor and to be

Right: A snap from a family album can bring a face to the name on the official documents.

quickly. Since they exist in the nineteenth century, they can be a great source when used alongside census returns. Another vital source for pinpointing the location of ancestral homes are street, post office and trade directories, which start in the late eighteenth century but really become useful from the mid nineteenth century onwards. Several companies compiled them – Pigots and Kellys being two of the most prominent – but the Post Office also created a long sequence, and the emergence of telephones saw new titles emerge in the twentieth century, such as the Yellow Pages. Directories were originally intended to provide information about where companies and traders were located, but quickly expanded to include residential addresses as well. Once again, there is usually a street index, but by the late nineteenth century some versions also had name indexes as well. You should be able to find surviving versions at most county archives or local study centres, whilst a project has started to compile a database of searchable directories at www.historicaldirectories.org.

So finding out how long various members of your family stayed in a house can be solved in part by your original research, combined with these additional sources. But clearly, that is only part of the problem; the next stage is to identify where the house stood, and indeed if it still stands. Maps are the key to solving this particular problem, and there are several areas you can investigate. As with all lines of research, it's best to start with the modern period. If you have the postcodes of the houses in question, you can use the Internet to find their location via websites such as Multimap that show you the site of the house on a map, or you can even find a satellite image via Google Earth. However, postcodes in their modern form are a fairly recent invention, and so you will have to rely on other sources to find out where the house once stood. Thankfully, there are some very detailed maps and land surveys available to help with this process.

The Ordnance Survey started its life as a branch of the War Office, but from 1841 it became a separate institution with a remit to create a survey of Britain. Although the earliest maps date from 1801, detailed maps at a scale of 6 inch to the mile appeared from the 1850s onwards, with regular revisions and updates. They include street names, and when used in sequence can show quite clearly how an area changed over time. There are even more detailed maps for built up areas in towns and cities, so it is perfectly possible to pinpoint individual houses on them. Many of the most detailed maps include house numbers or names, as well as street names, so it should be possible to locate your ancestral homes quite quickly. Most county archives and local study centres will have a strong collection of OS maps for the relevant area, whilst the British Library holds a complete set.

In addition to OS maps, there have been a number of surveys conducted by the government. One of the most thorough was established under the terms of the 1910 Finance Act, often referred to as the Lloyd George Domesday or the Valuation Office Survey. Essentially, it was a survey of all property in the UK for tax purposes, though the progress of the research was interrupted by the 1st World War and it was never fully completed. However, sufficient records survive to give most people a change of locating their ancestors' homes. There are two stages to the process – first, to locate the property on a series of maps, compiled from OS sheets; and second, to link the property on the map to an entry in a 'field book', where details of the ownership and occupancy of the house were noted. This is an amazing source, as it will confirm that your ancestor was in the property around the period 1910-1915, as well as giving you a description of the exterior and interior of the house. The records are at The National Archives, Kew, along with another important survey, the Tithe Apportionments of the 1840s.

These were created through pressure to shift the burden of clerical tax – a tithe being a tenth of all produce grown in a parish. As with the 1910 survey, maps were drawn up for every parish where tithes still existed, linked to schedules detailing the ownership and occupancy of the land. Many houses were listed as part of this process, and when used carefully with the 1841 and 1851 census returns, you should be able to pinpoint exactly where your ancestors used to live.

GOING DEEPER

Of course, many of these ancestral homes will no longer be standing, so you will not always be able to visit in person. However, you can use these maps to get a sense of the social conditions through which they lived, which should be an equally important part of your research. Without fully appreciating the community in which your relatives lived, you view them in isolation and therefore it is vitally important to investigate the wider social background behind the lives of your relatives. I've outlined elsewhere how to research occupations listed on census records and certificates, and explained how you can go further back in time if you so wish. However, it is also worth considering how you can investigate some of the important changes that affected our relatives at a local and national level.

Once you have located a particular area or community in which your ancestors lived – and bear in mind the fact that people really didn't move around that much, even once the railways had transformed the transport network in the mid-nineteenth century – you can focus on how that area changed over time, and ponder the implications that those changes would have had on your ancestors' lives. Take the railways, for example; the rapid expansion of a new transport network meant that communities were joined to one another, in many cases for the first time, which meant that new goods and services would appear within a very short period of time. The alterations to society in the mid-nineteenth century cannot be overstated, and makes our recent transition into the IT era seem rather sedate. New technology, as showcased by the Great Exhibition in 1851, started to make an appearance in homes up and down the country, helping large proportions of the rapidly expanding population to better their standard of living. As I've shown elsewhere, though, the flipside of the coin was that more people started to fall below the poverty line, with all the associated horror of the workhouse. Yet the advances outweighed the disadvantages of industrialisation – more people were able to find work in the booming factories, foundries, mines and shipyards; public works improved the way cities and towns were run, as sewer networks started to eradicate the threat of waterborne diseases such as cholera and typhoid; the introduction of gas lighting meant that streets were lit and, in general, were safer; railways and canals transported people and goods across the country, whilst improvements to the roads made travel faster and safer.

You can research all of these aspects of nineteenth century change, along with earlier trends, later developments, the impact of the two world wars, and specific lines of work to the local area, at the relevant local studies centre or county archive. Many historic research groups have investigated some of these topics, and you will find plenty of books on local history at libraries. Indeed, you should also pencil in some time at the relevant local or specialist museum, many of which will hold information from prehistoric times through archaeological discovery through to the present day. These are all valid lines of enquiry when attempting to place our ancestors in their historical context.

Nor should you forget the impact of national events on local communities. It might be worth compiling a timeline against which you can plot your ancestors' lives, so that you get a sense of what was happening in the world at large. It is an excellent way of re-discovering the joy of history – many people have said that they found the subject dull or boring whilst at school, but have found it to be a fascinating subject when given relevance in the context of their distant relatives. Many big-picture history books are still heavily biased towards the great and the good, the movers and shakers, but there has been a recent shift back to the people who lived through great events. In particular, many archives and educators have embraced this newly found love of history and linked their collections to important events, but with the family historian in mind. Indeed, the national curriculum incorporates elements of family and local history, and represents a great opportunity to bring the subject to a new generation of potential enthusiasts. There really is no end to where your research may take you!

✦ SUMMARY

Finally, I thought it might be useful to sum up very briefly all the initial steps you should undertake if you are planning to undertake research into your family history – a top ten tips, if you like.

At a glance research summary

1. Write down what you know about yourself and your family.

2. Talk to your family, focusing on names, dates and places.

3. Look for clues in heirlooms, photographs and personal papers.

4. Draw up a family tree, showing how people are related to one another.

5. Work out a research strategy, focusing on verification of your initial tree.

6. Use certificates and census records to extend your family tree to the nineteenth century.

7. Consolidate and update your family tree, and refine your research strategy to focus on individuals

8. Gain a deeper knowledge of some of the characters on your family tree with more detailed research eg military career, place of work.

9. Start to widen your research to locate ancestral homes.

10. Undertake some top level research into the historical period, both locally and nationally, in which your ancestors lived.

Congratulations – you are now well on the way to becoming a family detective!

Resources

ANCESTRY
Website: www.ancestry.co.uk

BLACK CULTURAL ARCHIVES
1 Othello Close, Kennington, London SE11 4RE

BORTHWICK INSTITUTE
University of York, Heslington, York YO10 5DD

THE BRITISH LIBRARY
96 Euston Road, London NW1 2DB

BRITISH LIBRARY NEWSPAPERS
Website: www.bl.uk/collections/newspapers.html

CHURCH OF THE LATTER DAY SAINTS
Website: http://www.familysearch.org

THE COLLEGE OF ARMS
Queen Victoria Street, London EC4V 4BT

COMMONWEALTH WAR GRAVES COMMISSION
Website: www.cwgc.org

FAMILY RECORDS CENTRE
1 Myddelton Street, Islington, London EC1R 1UW
Tel: 020 8392 5300
Website: www.familyrecords.gov.uk/frc
Opening hours: Mon, Wed, Fri 9 am–5 pm; Tues 10 am–7
pm; Thurs 9 am–7 pm; Sat 9.30 am–5 pm. Closed
Sundays, public and bank holidays.

*The FRC is located just outside Exmouth Market in Islington, London,
a short walk from either Farringdon or Angel tube stations, and served
by plenty of good bus routes. Nearby are several other important family
history resources — for example, the headquarters of the Society of
Genealogists is only a short walk away.*

FEDERATION OF FAMILY HISTORY SOCIETIES (FFHS)
Website: http://www.ffhs.org.uk

FLEET AIR ARM MUSEUM
Box D6, RNAS Yeovilton, Ilchester, Somerset BA22 8HT
Website: www.fleetairarm.com

GENERAL REGISTER OFFICE (GRO)
New Register House, Prince's Street, Edinburgh, Scotland
Website: www.gro.gov.uk

*A search fee is charged for looking at the central registers and indexes, but the
process is much quicker than in England or Wales as the certificate data is
instantly available on microfiche. Access to the indexes is also available online at
www.scotlandspeople.gov.uk, another subscription–based website that also incorporates images and indexes to civil registration certificates and old parish registers.*

GENERAL REGISTER OFFICE OF IRELAND
8/11 Lombard Street East, Dublin
Website: www.groireland.ie

GENERAL REGISTER OFFICE OF NORTHERN IRELAND
Oxford House, 49/55 Chichester Street, Belfast BT1 4HL
Website: www.groni.gov.uk

GUILD OF ONE NAME STUDIES
Website: www.one-name.org

HARLEIAN SOCIETY
c/o College of Arms, Queen Victoria Street,
London EC4V 4BT
Website: http://harleian.co.uk

THE IMPERIAL WAR MUSEUM
Lambeth Road, London SE1 6HZ
Website: www.iwm.org.uk

THE IMPERIAL WAR MUSEUM
Duxford, Cambridgeshire CB2 4QR
Website: www.iwm.

INSTITUTE OF COMMONWEALTH STUDIES
University of London, 28 Russell SquaWC1B 5DS
Website: www.sas.ac.uk/commonwealthstudies

INSTITUTE OF HERALDIC AND GENEALOGICAL STUDIES
Website: www.ihgs.ac.uk

IRISH GENEALOGICAL RESEARCH SOCIETY
Society Library, Church of St. Magnus the Matyr
Lower Thames Street, London EC3 6DN
Website: www.igrsoc.org

JEWISH GENEALOGICAL SOCIETY OF GREAT BRITAIN
Website: www.jgsgb.ort.org
LAW SOCIETY ARCHIVES
Website: www.lawsoc.org.uk

LONDON METROPOLITAN ARCHIVES
40 Northampton Road, London EC1R 0HB
Website: www.cityoflondon.gov.uk/lma

MARITIME HISTORY ARCHIVE
Newfoundland, Canada

MINISTRY OF DEFENCE
Website: www.mod.uk

THE MODERN RECORDS CENTRE
University of Warwick, University Library, Coventry CV4 7AL
Website: www.warwick.ac.uk/go/modernrecordscentre

THE NATIONAL ARCHIVES
Ruskin Avenue, Kew, Richmond, Surrey TW9 4DU
Tel: 020 8876 3444
Websites: www.nationalarchives.gov.uk
www.nationalarchives.gov.uk/pathways/blackhistory
Email: enquiry@nationalarchives.gov.uk
Opening hours: Mon, Wed, Fri 9 am–5 pm (document ordering 9.30 am–4.30 pm); Tues 10 am–7 pm (document ordering 10 am–4.45 pm); Thurs 9 am–7 pm (document ordering 9.30 am–4.45 pm); Sat 9.30 am–5.00 pm (document ordering 9.30 am–3.30 pm). Closed Sundays, public and bank holidays, and usually the first week in December for stocktaking.
Admission and access:
ID required (passport, driving licence, credit card, national ID card). No advance booking required. Onsite car park
Onsite disabled parking available with wheelchair access to main building and lifts to all floors

The National Archives is located in southwest London, just down the road from the Royal Botanical Gardens, Kew. There are good transport links, including parking facilities onsite. The nearest tube station is Kew Gardens, about a ten-minute walk from the archives, whilst overground trains stop at Kew Bridge. You can also catch one of several buses that serve the area.

NATIONAL ARCHIVES OF INDIA
Janpath, New Delhi, 110001, India
Email: archives@ren02.nic.in

NATIONAL ARCHIVES OF IRELAND
Bishop Street, Dublin 8
Website: www.nationalarchives.ie

NATIONAL ARCHIVES OF SCOTLAND
General Register House, 2 Princes Street, Edinburgh EH1 3YY
Website: www.nas.gov.uk

NATIONAL ARMY MUSEUM
Royal Hospital Road, London SW3 4HT
Website: www.national-army-museum.ac.uk

NATIONAL COAL MUSEUM
Caphouse Colliery, New Road, Overton, Wakefield WF4 4RH
Website: www.ncm.org.uk

NATIONAL LIBRARY OF SCOTLAND
George IV Bridge, Edinburgh EH1 1EW
Website: www.nls.uk

NATIONAL MARITIME MUSEUM
Romney Road, London SE10 9NF
Website: www.nmm.ac.uk

NATIONAL RAIL MUSEUM
Leeman Road, York YO26 4XJ
Website: www.nrm.org.uk

NATIONAL SOUND ARCHIVE
British Library,
Websites: www.bl.uk
www.bbc.co.uk

ORIENTAL AND INDIA OFFICE LIBRARY
The British Library, 96 Euston Road, London NW1 2DB
Website: www.bl.uk

PEOPLE'S HISTORY MUSEUM
103 Princess Street, Manchester M1 6DD
Website: www.peopleshistorymuseum.org.uk

PRINCIPAL PROBATE REGISTRY OF THE FAMILY DIVISION
First Avenue House, 42–49 High Holborn
London WC1V 6NP

PUBLIC RECORD OFFICE OF NORTHERN IRELAND
66 Balmoral Avenue, Belfast BT9 6NY

ROYAL AIR FORCE MUSEUM
Hendon Aerodrome, London NW9 5LL
Website: www.rafmuseum.org.uk

ROYAL NAVAL MUSEUM
HM Naval Base (PP66), Portsmouth, Hampshire PO1 3NH
Website: www.royalnavalmuseum.org

RURAL HISTORY CENTRE AND MUSEUM OF ENGLISH RURAL LIFE
University of Reading, Redlands Road, Reading RG1 5EX
Website: www.rdg.ac.uk/rhc

SOCIETY OF GENEALOGISTS
14 Charterhouse Buildings, Goswell Road, London EC1M 7BA
Website: www.sog.org.uk

STICKS RESEARCH AGENCY
Website: www.stick.org.uk

TRADES UNION CONGRESS
Congress House, Great Russell Street, London WC1B 3LS
Website: www.tuc.org.uk

Index

Note: page numbers in **bold** refer to illustrations.

AUTHOR'S ACKNOWLEDGEMENTS
The author would like to thank The National Archives Image Library for the use of various images.

PUBLISHERS' ACKNOWLEDGEMENTS
The Publishers would like to thank the following for their help:

For design: David Fordham and Lisa Pettibone; for additional research: Richard Emerson; for picture research: Sarah Newbery and Victoria Hall; for lending illlustrations for use in the book: Natalie Hunt, Julia Kellaway, Anne Newman, Mike Prior, Gail Smith, Christopher Warwick.

PICTURE ACKNOWLEDGEMENTS
The Publishers have made every effort to trace the copyright holder of all illustrations used in this book, with thanks due to the following for permission to reproduce pictures:

p2 David Fordham; p8-9 The National Archives Image Library; p10 Mary Evans Picture Library; p12 David Fordham; p13 David Fordham; p15 Natalie Hunt; p17 Natalie Hunt; p18 Natalie Hunt; p21 Natalie Hunt; p22 Natalie Hunt; p25 Natalie Hunt; p26 David Fordham; p27 David Fordham; p28-29 Gail Smith/Mike Prior; p30 David Fordham; p31 Natalie Hunt; p32 Top Foto Picture Agency; p35 Top Foto Picture Agency; p36 Top Foto Picture Agency; p38 David Fordham; p39 The National Archives Image Library; p40 Mary Evans Picture Library; p41 Top Photo Picture Agency; p43 Mary Evans Picture Library; p47 David Fordham; p48 David Fordham; p49 David Fordham; p52 Top Foto Picture Agency; p54 David Fordham; p57 David Fordham; p65 David Fordham; p66 David Fordham; p69 David Fordham; p71 Natalie Hunt. p72 Gail Smith/Mike Prior; p73 Gail Smith/Mike Prior; p74 Gail Smith/Mike Prior; p75 Gail Smith/Mike Prior; p76 Gail Smith/Mike Prior; p80 The National Archives Image Library; p82 Julia Kellaway; p83 David Fordham; p85 The National Archives Image Library; p88 The National Archives Image Library; p93 The National Archives Image Library; p94 The National Archives Image Library; p95 The National Archives Image Library; p96 David Fordham; p99 The National Archives Image Library; p104 The National Archives Image Library; p107 David Fordham; p112 David Fordham; p114 David Fordham; p120 The National Archives Image Library. p123 David Fordham; p124 The National Archives Image Library; p127 David Fordham; p131 The National Archives Image Library; p137 Carey Smith; p138 Top Foto Picture Agency; p146 The National Archives Image Library; p148 The National Archives Image Library; p149 The National Archives Image Library; p154 The National Archives Image Library; p155 The National Archives Image Library; p157 The National Archives Image Library; p158 David Fordham; p160 The National Archives Image Library; p163 David Fordham; p165 David Fordham; p166 David Fordham; p180 David Fordham; p182 The National Archives Image Library; p183 The National Archives Image Library; p184 Natalie Hunt; p185 David Fordham; p186 David Fordham; p187 Gail Smith/Mike Prior; p188 David Fordham; p189 'Pip, Squeak and Wilfred' medals, Imperial War Museum; p194 The National Archives Image Library; p195 The National Archives Image Library; p196 Gail Smith/Mike Prior; p197 The National Archives Image Library; p204 David Fordham; p207 The National Archives Image Library; p210 The National Archives Image Library; p216 The National Archives Image Library; p219 The National Archives Image Library; p220 Top Foto Picture Agency; p223 David Fordham; p224 David Fordham; p234 The National Archives Image Library; p235 The National Archives Image Library; p237 The National Archives Image Library; p242 The National Archives Image Library; p245 The National Archives Image Library; p247 David Fordham; p258 David Fordham; p261 Carey Smith; p262 David Fordham.